PROFESSIONS FOR THE PEOPLE

PROFESSIONS FOR THE PEOPLE
PEOPLE
The Politics of Skill

edited by

Joel Gerstl
and
Glenn Jacobs

SCHENKMAN PUBLISHING COMPANY

Halsted Press Division
John Wiley and Sons
New York   London   Sydney   Toronto

Copyright © 1976
Schenkman Publishing Company
3 Mount Auburn Place
Cambridge, Mass. 02138

Distributed solely by Halsted Press.
  a Division of John Wiley & Sons, INC., New York

Library of Congress Cataloging in Publication Data

Gerstl, Joel Emery.
  Professions for the people.

  1. Professions--United States. I. Jacobs, Glenn,
joint author. II. Title.
HT690.U6G47   301.44'46'0973   75-2092
ISBN 0-470-29702-6
ISBN 0-470-29703-4 pbk.

TABLE OF CONTENTS

INTRODUCTION*

From the standpoint of history it appears that the processes of professionalization, de-professionalization and re-professionalization are cyclical. At the present time we are at the point of advanced elitist professionalization, and, should history repeat itself, on the verge of deprofessionalization. Jethro K. Lieberman (1970, p. 3) warns: "Professionals are dividing the world into spheres of influence and erecting large signs saying 'experts at work here, do not proceed further.' " He shows that via such mechanisms as licensing, self-regulation, and political pressure the professions are augmenting the erosion of democracy. Professional turf is now ratified by the rule of law. If this is the case, it represents a significant development: the division of labor in society is again moving toward the legalization of social status qua occupational roles. To put it another way, the constitutional arrangements of our society may have elements in common with the estates system of medieval times. As E.C. Hughes (1971, p. 291) put it:

> . . . constitutions are the relations between the effective estates which *constitute* the body politic. In our society, some occupations are among the groups which most closely resemble what were once known as estates. While there has been a good deal of study of the political activities of occupational groups, the subject has been somewhat misunderstood as a result of the strong fiction of political neutrality of professions in our society.

An estates system is one in which: "Law establishes and maintains unequal strata. . . . Changes in rank and status depend on legal acts by a superior and not the achievements of the individual" (Bergel, 1962, p. 68). The present situation is neither a purely feudal estates system nor the ideal typical open class society. Lieberman suggests that the professions have travelled full circle, commencing with their passage from medieval feudalism (the guilds), through the development of trade, industry, science, specialization, the breakdown of the old estates and the crumbling of the guild system, to the contemporary situation

---

*Co-authorship and editorship is by necessity a collaborative effort, and so this introductory essay represents the outcome of the amalgamation of our thought: the conceptual outlining of deprofessionalization and current sociological thinking on the professions is Gerstl's; the professions' historical development and Durkheim's sociology (corporatism) were outlined by Jacobs.

wherein a professional estate again covets the privileges of status (1970, pp. 37-52).

The following analysis of history and sociological theory attempts to glean an understanding of the socio-political ramifications of the growth of the professions as they bear on the issue of the corporate state as the modern counterpart of the estates system.

PROFESSIONS: HISTORICAL RETROSPECT

During the feudal period, the craft and merchant guilds were precursors of professionalization. They were well articulated in a social context of the society of "The Five Alls": "I rule all. I judge all. I fight for all. I pray for all. I work for all" (Heaton, 1948, p. 72). The feudal system of orders or estates was one in which there was a blurring of private rights and public duties: men did not simply 'own,' they had 'rights' (Gilb, 1966, p. 6). Within this framework the guilds defined, defended and exercised the guildsmen's rights and their monopoly of skill. This was legitimized by the church as fitting into the cosmological order — work was a calling. While the so-called learned professions (medicine, law and theology) were themselves a monopoly of the church (and later the aristocracy), the guilds became the primary *organizing* bodies of the medieval town and were self-governing. They restricted competition, set prices, defined the quality of raw materials and craftsmanship, controlled entrance and training, and generally developed ordinances touching on the guildsman's relations with fellow members, non-members, members of other guilds, future members, dependent workers, and consumers (Heaton, 1949, p. 203).

As the Middle Ages drew to a close the gap widened between the *petite bourgeoise* craft guilds and the *haute bourgeoise* merchant guilds. The former were bound to an inelastic local market; the latter served larger domestic or foreign markets. As the merchant guilds grew with the emergence of capitalism

> Wage earners organized journeymen's guilds, struck to gain higher wages when prices rose or labor was scarce, and resisted wage cuts when times were bad. Merchants might seek, or be forced by depressed conditions to lower the price . . . and masters found themselves between the upper millstone of these reduced payments and the nether one of journeymen's refusal to share in the loss (Heaton, 1949, p. 210).

The ascendancy of capitalism on the heels of feudalism thus saw the crushing of the power of the craft guilds by the upper guilds or guild merchants. The monetary power of the upper guilds challenged the feudal aristocracy, and trading associations spearheaded international trade and colonization. Consequently, the craft guilds, originally conservative, began to act analogously to the modern labor unions (Krause, 1971, p. 20). Newly developed industries were relatively free from guild control so that by the eighteenth century they had virtually disappeared.

ENGLAND

The English professions in the eighteenth century were an acceptable successor to the feudal ideal of landed property as a means of earning a living. Like landed property, a professional "competence" conveniently "broke the direct connection between work and income . . ." (Reader, 1966, p. 3) for the gentryman. A professional career provided effete, aristocratic, protective coloration, and at the same time enabled one to make a considerable sum of money without sullying his hands with a "job" or "trade." One could carry on commerce by sleight of hand while donning the vestments of professional altruism. To boot, one could also work without appearing to derive income directly from it. As Reader explains:

> The whole subject of payment . . . seems to have caused professional men acute embarrassment, making them take refuge in elaborate concealment, fiction, and artifice. The root of the matter appears to lie in the feeling that it was not fitting for one gentleman to pay another for services rendered, particularly if the money passed directly. Hence, the device of paying a barrister's fee to the attorney, not to the barrister himself. Hence, also the convention that in many professional dealings the matter of the fee was never openly talked about, which could be very convenient, since it precluded the client or patient from arguing about whatever sum his advisor might eventually indicate as a fitting honorarium (1966, p. 37).

The established professions — the law, medicine, and the clergy — held (or continued to hold) *estate-like* positions:

> The three 'liberal professions' of the eighteenth century were the nucleus about which the professional class of the nineteenth century was to form. We have seen that they were united by the bond of classical education: that their broad and ill-defined functions covered much that later would crystallize out

into new, specialized, occupations: that each, ultimately, derived much of its standing with the established order in the State. . . . (1966, p. 23).

The barrister's claim to social standing was derived from the importance of the law, hence, the Bar, to the English constitution. This was augmented by the Inns of Court, "four ancient unincorporated private clubs, responsible to no outside authority and of an indefinite but privileged legal standing." They determined "absolutely who should be allowed to practice as a barrister in England" (Reader, 1966, p. 21). These clubs were supposed to function as places of legal education though in reality the barrister was left to himself to learn the law. The Inns of Court could thus serve as finishing schools for men who had no devotion to the law.

The situation was similar in medicine where the College of Physicians exercised a hegemony. As Reader (1966, p. 16) states: "It habitually, and as many people held, illegally, refused to admit anyone who was not a graduate of Oxford or Cambridge, although neither university, for many years, gave any medical education at all." It also excluded anyone who was not a member of the Church of England, "an exclusion bitterly resented by Dissenters."

The clergyman was considered a gentleman and an official of the establishment, that is, if he represented the Church of England. However, this "could not be said of any dissenting minister. He gained no social prestige at all, but rather the reverse . . . because the Dissenters . . . had only a precarious legal existence" (Reader, 1966, p. 15).

To the extent that the professions' rights and privileges are established by law — codified or customary, and in its praxis — it may be said that economic and political life are integrated; and to that extent it is worth repeating that the learned professions constituted *estates*.

The estatism of the English professions was challenged by the mobilization of their "lower branches." As might be expected, up to that point knowledge, skills and techniques remained stagnant under conditions where professional schooling consisted merely of the traditional classical education at universities, and where a professional career sufficed to perpetuate an aristocratic life style. It was assumed that a gentlemen merely needed a liberal education and "could learn the rest fairly easily when the need arose" (Reader, 1966, p. 11). The lower branches, so-called, were not part of the learned professions proper. In medicine they consituted the surgeons (an evolutionary step up from the barbers) and apothecaries; in law, the attorneys. The men who inhabited these branches came from lower strata than did the physicians and barristers. Yet, particularly in medicine, it was among these socially inferior occuaptions that most of the advances in knowledge were being made. And while they were considered merely craftsmen and shopkeepers (or clerks), they "were not hampered by veneration of the classics" (Reader, 1966, p. 32). At least the surgeons cut people up to see what really went on inside!

Concomitant with the mobilization of these occupational segments came the development of professional associations, competitive standard examinations, the rise of professional schools, and the opening (though by no means equal access) of the professions — especially medicine — to women (Reader, 1966, *passim.* and pp. 167-182). In short, in the British context, reform and mobility proceeded side by side. By the last quarter of the nineteenth century "the professional classes . . . had moved a long way from the radicalism of forty or fifty years before. It was only natural, since they had achieved so much of what they had been campaigning for" (Reader, 1966, p. 146).

It appears that with the rise of the professions and their consolidation in Europe (and in the United States) their constituted position as estates was only temporarily challenged, for as Carr-Saunders stipulates, the professions associationally and organizationally tend toward monopoly. Purportedly this assures the maintenance of standards of professional performance and competence. However, from the standpoint of societal organization it is occasioned by the complicity of the State (Carr-Saunders and Wilson, 1933, pp. 352-365).

UNITED STATES

In the United States the ideology of professionalism was a response to the unorganized character of the professions and science from the Revolutionary period through the Jacksonian era (Hindle, 1956; Daniels, 1968). It is inappropriate to separate science from the professions in this context since professions historically are closely connected with academies, and science is as much an establishment of technicians as it is of disinterested knowledge-producers (Lee, 1966, pp. 209-299; Lee, 1973, pp. 122-138). Put another way, neither are the sciences so pure nor the professions so applied as we could prematurely believe. This observation is even more accurate in describing professional life in eighteenth and nineteenth century United States where the rough and ready quality of American and Jacksonian utilitarianism forced

> the emergent profession . . . to justify its work in terms of its social value. It is incumbent upon the profession to demonstrate that it is in the interest of society at large to support a special group in the cultivation of esoteric knowledge. One obvious method open to the scientist is to appeal to practicality, and in the nineteenth century this was widely used. But in America it took a unique form appropriate to the Jacksonian context in which the appeal was made. The strategy here was to link appeals both to patriotism and the Democratic assumptions of Jacksonian America . . . Science was recommended to all who would hear as the highest example of useful knowledge. It was widely proclaimed that it would not only enrich and elevate the individual, but would make the nation great in both peace and war and advance mankind in general on the road to that happiness for which it was destined (Daniels, 1968, pp. 41-42).

Thus professionalism could hitch its calling to the star of manifest destiny. Scientists found themselves appealing to the national conscience — or helping to form it — by chiding the government and the populace for its lack of support for research, and by comparing the backwardness (vis-a-vis specialization) of the United States with the more congenial situation in England and on the Continent. Lest we mistake this lack of professional organization for general social anarchy, we are reminded that the learned professions were the hobbies of gentleman dilettantes. The professions were as likely "competencies" for the Americans as they were for the British. The professionals rounded out the upper class (Aronson, 1964, pp. 38-55); moreover, though they constituted a numerical minority, the gentry, merchants, and professionals monopolized most local, provincial and continental offices in American society between 1750 and 1830.

Earlier there had been a proliferation of, and frequent quarreling between and within, sects or segments. This became "particularly acute with the flourishing of the sectarian medical movements beginning in the late 1820's" (Daniels, 1968, pp. 15-16). The situation was complicated by the circumstances of professional and scientific communications: the supporters and backers of the journals for example, often used them as vehicles for their disputes. This plus the precariousness of the printing industry resulted in a condition where more periodicals ceased publication in a year than the number of new ones to be founded.

Still, the professions, such as they were, were in the hands of the upper class. No wonder that students slighting this fact fail to note that the onset of the Jacksonian period represents a discontinuity in the history of the professions. Instead of recognizing the period as one offering the professions rejuvenation through their replenishment and growth by the instrusion of the lower classes, one student of their social history (Gilb, 1966, p. 11) blithely remarks: "No dedication to craftsmanship characterized the America of the 1830's and 1840's. As late as 1869, Harvard Medical School had no entrance requirements, and awarded medical degrees upon oral examination after a brief period of residence."

Gilb fails to mention, however, that schools such as Harvard, like their English counterparts who also held a monopoly over the learned professions, were finishing schools for the aristocracy. In this light, professional quackery was the monopoly of the upper class who dosed and bled their clientele. It was true that apprenticeship was, at best, uneven, and admission standards in medicine and law, perfunctory. However, the Jacksonian spoils system and the resentment of debtors against lawyers as creditors' advocates created a situation where "non-experts" filled government posts, and where it was impossible for bar associations any longer to enforce guild-like standards for admission. It was a period in which it was believed "anybody could do anything and ought to be allowed to try. . . . Regulation was unnecessary . . . whether by government or by guilds" (Gilb, 1966, pp. 12, 11, 13). Calhoun (1965) correctly observes that this aspect of professional life in the Jacksonian period defied classification of its anti-professionalism (such as the attacks on its licensing laws) into clear conservative or radical political camps. Nonetheless, it was political. For populism is, at its best, radically democratic. While the currents of deprofessionalization would appear, from an establishment view, to be philistine, in actual fact (see Tabachnik herein) they could just as well be interpreted as forces producing a more open society. Thus Jacksonian Populism provided public criticism which made the "content of professional knowledge . . . neither stable nor securely progressive," although it also afforded a way station "dampening . . . both intellectual arrogance and intellectual individualism . . . on the way to a bureaucratic resolution of earlier problems" (Calhoun, 1965, pp. 191-192, 192-193). The period was socially fluid, and represented one in which upwardly mobile groups

> including men who wanted access to professional standing in terms less stringent than had developed in the latter part of the eighteenth century, used this rhetoric [populism] as a weapon to open opportunities for themselves (Calhoun, 1965, p. 188).

In this respect the United States was repeating English history, owing to the mobility of occupational and class segments.[1] By the middle of the nineteenth century the pendulum was being forced back toward professionalization by the forces of urbanization and industrialization, and, hence, the rational organization of labor and centralized control. This "not only made a more complex division of labor possible but also led city dwellers and employers to expect more of the professional men who served them, in turn making mandatory larger and more vigorous professional training" (Gilb, 1966, p. 17). In other words, the economy and society demanded "warrenties of competence" or certified credentials: the professions formed organizations, and the trend reached its plateau by the end of the century.

Whereas the last half of the nineteenth century witnessed a major wave or organization of national and state associations, the turn of the century was a period of consolidation in which professional associations sought more inclusive membership and greater associational "integration" on national, state, and local levels: the associations lost their parochialism and became more inclusive. As such, they lost the character of honor or social societies and began to turn toward government to secure public confidence and the monopolization of skill. This resulted chiefly in the creation of licensing boards, state bars, payroll deduction plans for associational dues, the enactment of interest group legislation (e.g. teacher tenure laws), etc. The maturing professional associations emerged as quasi-private/quasi-public organizations (Gilb, 1966, pp. 27-52). As Gilb stresses early in her study:

> One of the chief characteristics of American statutory and case law today is a gradual moving of the line between public and private to include more and

---

[1] It had earlier repeated British history in another light: throughout the colonial period scientists and professionals in the United States emulated their British counterparts.

more organizations . . . in the halfway zone called quasi-public. Government is an arm of the organized groups, but so are organized groups the arms of the government . . . (p. 21).

Indeed, the above features and their reflection in professional ethical codes of noncompetition (especially the guild survival of the injunction against advertising), and the development of specialized training programs represent a movement "neatly full circle from American individualistic egalitarianism back again to a socioeconomic order bearing some resemblance to medieval corporate society" (Gilb, 1966, p. 16). The establishment of public licensing board manned by professionals "serves as a symbol to the legislature of the profession's legitimacy, and it works . . . to present the profession's point on subsequent legislative proposals." This helps create a social order "in which rights adhere to functional status." Such an order renders "the American socio-economic-political system . . . closer to its medieval ancestor than it is to the preindustrial system of the early nineteenth century," i.e., it represents a drift away from contract and toward status (pp. 151, 224, 227). This is the main thrust of Gilb's thesis. Professional associations are guilds in modern dress.

Modern professional associations are *organizational* counterparts of the guilds. They are occupational self-interest organizations. In as much as the professions still perform custom work and exercise a monopoly of training and skill, the guild analogy is plausible. However, aspects of economic history lead to a different conclusion. There has been a shift of emphasis on the part of professionals from control over the quality of the product or service, to control of price. This has recently manifested itself in the rationalization of billing and collection systems, but the process has been a long time in the making. Despite the fact that the guilds attempted "to preserve a rough equality among 'the good men of the mistery,' " there remained the admonition of whether "these things [brotherhood, economic altruism, standards of training and craftsmanship, etc.] outweighed the evils of conservative methods and corporate exclusiveness" (Tawney, 1926, pp. 31-32). Apparently "the doctrine which silences scruples and closes all accounts with the final plea of economic expediency" won out, for: "It was not great capitalists but enterprising guildsmen, who began to make control of the fraternity the basis of a system of plutocratic exploitation" (Tawney, 1926, pp. 32, 64).

The guilds thus bore the seeds of their own destruction as they soon favored the *cash* over the *craft* nexus, all the time bleating *"beruf . . . beruf."*[2] The modern professional association is thus in keeping with modern pultocracy.[3]

PROFESSIONAL SOLIDARITY AND THE CORPORATE STATE

In the *Division of Labor in Society* Durkheim noted the passage of society from the stage of mechanical solidarity to that of organic solidarity. In the preface to the second edition he envisioned the withering away of the territorially represented state. It would be replaced by bodies such as corporations, syndicates and guilds. (Parenthetically, "corporation" is the French word for guild). While the territorial state was characteristic of some advanced societies, the state itself is a constituted authority vested in an organization of officials within a structurally differentiated society (Durkheim, 1957; Giddens, 1971, p. 100). Thus territory is not generic to Durkheim's conception of the state.

The state grows in importance as social differentiation progresses and individualism expands (Durkheim, 1933; Richter, 1960; Coser, 1960). In this manner Durkheim attempted to dispense with the Marxian argument that the economic basis of the state acts as a repressive agent for the ruling class. In his eyes "the state must play a moral as well as

[2] John R. Commons' economic history of the shoemakers' guilds and trade unions in the United States (1909) makes a similar point: in the guild stage of their development the functions of merchant, master, and journeyman were joined. The market was a personal one and all work was custom or "bespoke" work: the customer placed his order before the product was made. The guild merchant-master's bargaining power was threatened by the customer's inability to judge the quality of the goods versus their capacity to gauge price. It was sufficient, therefore, for the purpose of the guild as protective association to focus on the *quality* of the product rather than the price in order to meet the threat of marginal nonguild producers (e.g. convict labor). However, as markets expanded, competitive threats changed and three functions were eventually split into three interest groups and protective associations, with the major division being the employer-employee one; here competition constituted a menace primarily to *prices* and *wages,* and secondarily to quality, as first, the journeyman's, and later the master's economic survival were threatned by speculative retailing and wholesaling. The expanding markets widened the emergent system of contract labor, hence, supplanting the craft by the cash nexus. See also Morris (1946).

[3] If the analogy applies at all, the guild is a prototype of the modern labor union, i.e., the craft guild: it is the *merchant* guild which represents a more plausible prototype of the professional association, although it is not its historical ancestor.

economic role" in giving a "firm moral unity to society" (Durkheim, 1933, p. 30; Giddens, 1971, p. 99). While he conceded that the state could tyrannize as well as safeguard the individual, such a development only occurred if secondary groups intervening between the state and the individual are not strongly developed (Durkheim, 1957; Giddens, 1971, p. 101).

These secondary groups are pivotal in his analysis. For underlying his contention that the division of labor is as "moral" a fact as an economic one (1933, pp. 40, 61), is the prediction that occupational associations would act as buffers between the individual and the state. The associations are called corporations, and to the extent "of the increasingly important position the occupation takes in life as work becomes more specialized . . . the corporation has been . . . the heir of the family" in maintaining social solidarity (Durkheim, 1933, pp. 16-17). These groups are the "only groups which have a certain permanence" (1933, p. 6). Indeed, they eternally recur. Durkheim traces their occurrence in Rome, the Middle Ages, and their reappearance in modern times (1933, pp. 6-10). In other words:

> The fact that after having disappeared the first time they came into being themselves, and in a new form especially, removes all value from the argument . . . that they are no longer in harmony with the new conditions of collective existence (Durkheim, 1933, p. 9).

The corporations would be the nuclei of social solidarity — lynchpins of society.

> Around their proper occupational functions, others which come from the communes or private societies will be grouping themselves. The functions of assistance are such that, to be well filled, they demand feelings of solidarity between assistants and assisted, a certain moral homogeneity such as the same occupation produces . . . Society, instead of remaining what it is today, an aggregate of juxtaposed territorial districts, would become a vast system of national corporations. From various quarters it is asked that elective assemblies be formed by occupations, and not by territorial divisions; and certainly, in this way, political assemblies would more exactly express the diversity of social interests and their relations (1933, pp. 26-27).

Durkheim envisioned broad-based occupational structures or "cross-occupational complexes" as mediators or buffers between the state and other levels of society (Durkheim, 1933, p. 28). They would represent *all* interests, not merely partisan ones. While the state expressed the interests of the masses, it would lead for their own good. The inevitability of the national corporation was sufficient reason for Durkheim to herald it as the coming good. In fact, he envisioned the absence of the corporative institution as a "malady *totius substantae,* affecting all the organism": "we must put ourselves to work establishing the moral forces which can determine its realization!" (Durkheim, 1933, pp. 29, 31).

There was little new in Durkheim's analysis and polemic. Hegel's political philosophy contained similar sentiments. The mission of the corporation, in Hegel's view, was to succeed the family in its role of moral integration. The corporation as a guild-like body "introduces objective morality into civil society by means of the sentiments of professional honor" (Strauss and Cropsey, 1963, p. 639). Both Hegel and Durkheim failed to consider the implications of a scheme of society based on cooperative organizations of businessmen and workers — the corporate state as fascism.

Durkheim "unofficially skirted the edges of a movement called *solidarism* which had been started by 'radical socialists' " (Lukes, 1972, pp. 350-354; Schwendinger and Schwendinger, 1974, p. 256). It proposed a fuzzy doctrine stressing the unanimous need for solidarity in the republic. Such rhetoric articulated well with Durkheim's emphasis on cooperation inspired by external constraint; this constraint was always counterpoised by an assumptive competitive struggle for scarce values. In effect, it was Durkheim's view that "without social discipline there can be no individual freedom, since 'self-mastery' is learned at the 'school of duty' " (Neyer, 1960, p. 42).

Furthermore, Durkheim's writing evinces a coyness regarding socialism. Attempts to discern his predilections towards it more resemble fishing expeditions than clearly enunciated positions (Richter, 1960; Neyer, 1960). It is this coy ambiguity that partially explains his blindness to the implications of the occupational or corporate state. Perhaps, too, Durkheim's inability to frame the totalitarian implications of his sociology within the technocratic tradition of St. Simon and Comte inured him to his own prediction of the total state (Salomon, 1955). He was sure that socialism was inevitable, but it would stem from the extreme individualism he took to be the quintessence of the occupational state. Solidarity was the *deus ex machina* rendering specious the dichotomy of individualism and collectivism: with it he could stretch the definition of socialism to include "every doctrine which demands the connection of all economic functions . . . to the directing and conscious centers of society [i.e., the state]" (Durkheim, 1958, pp. 54-55).

It is no mere coincidence that Fascism in Italy, and National Socialism in Germany used socialist rhetoric in their propaganda and ideologies (Friederich and Brzezinski, 1956, pp. 73-76; Weber, 1971, pp. 95-110; Carsten, 1967, pp. 45-55, 137-139; Lee and Lee, 1937, pp. 10-13; Kele, 1972; Hamilton, 1971). Moreover, most fascist regimes adopted a model wherein "each of the nation's principal industries and occupational groups was constituted, by government fiat, as a 'corporation,' as an 'estate' [*stand*], or as a 'front' " (Bowen, 1947, p. 2). While these doctrines remained vague projects "to be realized in some distant future" they were nonetheless used as levers to repress labor-management conflict (Bowen, 1947, p. 3; see also Brady, 1937; Villari, 1932; Neumann, 1942, pp. 228-234; von Beckerath, 1931, pp. 134-137; Einaudi, 1968, pp. 335-338, 341). Furthermore, as Bowen suggests in his study of corporatist doctrines in Germany, the most lively discussions of these doctrines occurred during periods of profound political crisis in German history (1947, pp. 210-211).

Durkheim had "experienced social and political chaos during his most impressionable formative years," years of disorder for the Third Republic (Coser, 1971, pp. 157-158); and given his position in a sociological tradition reactionary to the French Revolution (Salomon, 1955), it is certainly no accident that he shared with the stream of German corporatists their exaltation of the "old corporative order," the *Ständestaat*. This constituted an organic theory of the state which stressed, on the one hand, *opposition* to extreme liberal individualism (cf. Durkheim's criticism of Spencer), Marxian materialitist socialism (class conflict), and the egalitarianism of the French Revolution; on the other hand, it proposed "a truly 'social' outlook" replacing individual rights with the "binding ties of the community" (Bowen, 1947, pp. 15-16). This was to be realized in "the statutory establishment of a univseral scheme of vocational or professional organizations in which each 'corporation' would be endowed with a more or less extensive body of legal rights and duties . . . Every vocational group would be organized, and every occupationally active person would be a member of the appropriate professional organization" (Bowen, 1947, pp. 16-17). Finally, all of these schemes aimed at the elimination of industrial strife and the formation of a council embracing employers and workers associated with a single enterprise. A pyramidal structure would be shaped out of combinations of these bodies at regional and national levels with a corporate chamber or national economic council at its apex "subsidiary to . . . co-equal with, or . . . superseding the territorial parliament" (Bowen, 1947, p. 17). Here, as in Durkheim's case, the new society was inspired by the historical persistance of guildlike associations and their romantic association with the past (Bowen, 1947, pp. 7, 211).

Corporatist thinking was put into practice in Germany by the founder of "cartel corporatism," Walther Rathenau. In 1914-15, as the creator of the Raw Materials Department in the War Office, he devised the "first comprehensive modern attempt to plan a nation's entire economic activity" (Bowen, 1947, pp. 164-165). Armed with ideas such as "consciousness of organic necessity" and "unitary will," the war offered this dreamer a blessing in disguise; war industrial companies were set up for key industries to dispose of earmarked resources and commodities, and to distribute them at controlled prices to manufacturers according to the priorities of the central administration. While the war cartels appeared to be a step toward state socialism, they actually stood midway " 'between the capitalist form of private enterprise and a bureaucratic scheme' " (p. 171). Rathenau envisioned a peacetime application of his ideas as the "New Economy," or, a "community of production" — not a confederation but an "organism" (p. 177).

This case provides a chilling forecast of what was to come in Germany. Professionalization is pivotal to strategies such as Durkheim's and Rathenau's, since the desire for an elitism based on expertise is often central to visionary schemes whose plausibility is enhanced by social crisis — indeed, wasn't technocracy the dream of Comte!

Our historical sketch of the consolidation of the professions into estates juxtaposed with Durkheim's prophesy gives an ominous picture of the present and near-future. Modern sociology's position vis-a-vis the professions and society affords little by way of resolution of ambiguities and implications.

THE MAN WHO CRIED BERUF: THE SOCIOLOGIST AS APOLOGIST

As indicated earlier, emulation of the aristocratic life style included the posture of noblesse oblige, which, in its bourgeoise context took the form of "altruism." This vaunted altruism persisted until current reassessments unmasked professionalism as an ideological cloak. These reassessments have come from within and without the professions. Movements within the professions have run the gamut from occupational self-interest and unionization, through radical reoganization of delivery of services (e.g. regional medical delivery), to broad critiques (Dumont, 1970). External pressures have included the revolt of the client (Haug and Sussman, 1969), attempts at community control, and litigation (e.g. growth of malpractice suits and antitrust actions against professional organizations), not to mention incisive social criticism (Lieberman, 1970). Sociological work, however, has not adequately accounted for these recent developments. Symptomatic of this is the extraordinary fact that while the increasing importance of professions in postindustrial society — numerically and functionally — is undisputed, the very term "profession" remains elusive. Apart from the confusion resulting from the loose usage of the term in everyday speech, its continued ambiguity is also due to the changes that have altered the traditional professions, the diverse characteristics of occupations claiming professional status, and the special interests of many who have attempted to grapple with the concept.

Whether the professional claims of aspiring occupational groups are accepted is one aspect of trying to relate the various species — the "semi-para-would-be-new professions." Despite the growth of these variants, the genus from which they derive continues to evade specification.

Many students of the professions have, during the past four decades since the pioneer work of Carr-Saunders and Wilson (1933), attempted to specify the formal criteria unique to professions. None have entirely succeeded in separating necessary from sufficient conditions. The very search for attributes has been maligned (Roth, 1974), but to abandon a problem is not to resolve it. Yet, even specialized qualifications, the core element in the traditional model of "learned" professions, have been shown to be ambiguous. Neither content nor duration of professional training stands apart from that of the nonprofessional (Friedson, 1970).[4]

[4] Not to mention sociologists' abandonment of the commonplace fact that all occupational task roles, from the standpoints of participation and socialization, require long informal, if not formal, apprenticeships and/or peer learning periods.

The knowledge base of the established professions derives primarily from the realm of the sacred, most obviously in the case of the clergy, but also in the moral concerns of law, medicine, and academia. Increasingly, as secular and rational values have become more and more technologically and commercially entrenched in our society, the legitimation of professional work has come to rely upon scientific foundations — even theology uses empirical archeological evidence. The third area that underlies professional work is that of aesthetics — skill at its best is built upon a foundation of talent or flair.

These are, however, broad parameters. No profession relies exclusively upon only one of the three realms, although there are considerable differences in emphasis. For example, medicine is, of course, strongly based on science, but it continues to have a major aura of mystery, frequently expressed as the art of healing. The sciences, in spite of frequently narrow positivistic ideologies, obviously deal with the mysterious, and, in the act of creation, have much in common with the arts. Although the mystery can be penetrated only by the use of esoteric skills, they do not intrinsically make the professions a class apart. At best, the knowledge base can be defined as neither too broad nor too narrow (Wilensky, 1964), hardly an operational definition.

It is very difficult to resist the commonsense notion that there *ought to be* some qualitative difference between professions and other occupations. Few writers have allowed themselves to admit that perhaps the emperor is naked. For example, Habenstein's basic "Critique of 'Profession' as a Sociological Category" (1963) has not succeeded in changing traditional perspectives. Krause (1971) makes the crucial point: "We will be considering professions as occupations which are like all other occupations, only 'more so'. All occupations have central skills, an occupational code of ethics, a group culture, some occupational authority, and some permission to practice on the part of the community" (p. 78; see also Haug, 1974).

The crucial consideration is that of the consequences of being "more so": professions have power and prestige. It is for this reason that, "Professionalism far exceeds professions, and it becomes a model for occupational aspirations for most workers in commercial and industrial jobs" (Taylor, 1968, p. 115). In other words, since the professionals have it so good, the mystique of professionalism is expected to be useful in other contexts. Seldom is it recognized that professionalism may be detrimental for particular purposes, even if prestigious. Because the professionals have succeeded in their claims for societal prestige, the assumption tends to be that professionalism can in no circumstance be a liability.

Having exhausted more plausible distinguishing features, some writers conjure "altruism" as the necessary ingredient. Here, at least, Marxians and Weberians would agree that pecuniary valuation has pervasively streamlined professional praxis. And here, at its last outpost, the defense of definitional viability disintegrates. Even those professional precursors, the feudal guilds, soon favored the cash over the craft nexus.

How often today must patients smart at being denied treatment for failure or inability to display health insurance cards? What client does not chafe at the dissolution of altruism when his/her funds run out? Finally, here we see in bold relief the necessary blurring of "profession" and professional*ism*; the first an intellectual smokescreen for the other. In short, if professionalism is a mundane ideology, then "profession" and "professional" are sociological contributions to the pile. Being such, they are prone to be turned into propaganda, "ideology on the march!" (Lee, 1973, p. 118). The ideology such usage is congenial to is a corporatist one.

In recent years, however, there have been some attempts made, if not to shoot down, at least to dimple the blimps of professionalism. Never has it been argued that the functions fulfilled by most professional groups are not vital, though rank order of functional importance is impossible to prove. More significant is the extent to which present professional structure provides efficient and humane solutions to basic societal needs — health, welfare, etc. In other words, the question comes down to: is bigger and better professional growth the only alternative?

Clearly, in the context of postindustrial society, human services will be of ever-increasing importance. But what forms will the delivery system likely take? Many aspects of the current organization of professional work indicate that the traditional model survives only in remote circumstances, despite frequent ideological statements to the contrary. Of paramount significance is the bureaucratic context of professional work. Despite evidence that professional and organizational goals *need* not invariably differ (Perrucci & Gerstl, 1969), they frequently do. Many current trends suggest even greater divergence of goals in the future.

The issue of inconsistent current trends has been interpreted as a possible *de-professionalization* by Marie Haug (1973). She points to the erosion of professional expertise (knowledge monopoly) and autonomy by cybernation, to the potential recognition of experience over credentialism, and to the revolt of the client over the issue of the service ethic.

It may well be just as much of an oversimplification to talk of the professionalizing society as to posit the alternative hypothesis of de-professionalization. To the extent that, as Haug indicates, "Professionals hold administrative positions in service organizations, they can monitor the tug of war over the new divisions of labor which are emerging" (1973, p. 207). Given the present strength of professional power, threats to established patterns of entrenchment appear minimal.

Another alternative is discernable when it is recognized that professions not only perform specific functions, but at the same time generate social responses. The heterogeneous segments and movements within the professions (Bucher and Strauss (1961)) are augmented by explicitly anti-establishmentarian movements, which took a variety of forms in the past decade.

These aberrancies, heresies, self-criticisms, and visions practical and utopian are the subject of this volume. In addition to noting the professions' place in the division of labor as "hidden hierarchies" (Gilb, 1966), our aim is to reveal aspects of their hidden dialectics.

We begin with a historical case study of de-professionalism in the Age of Jackson in law and medicine by Tabachnik. Contrary to established views the de-professionalism of that period was not an atavism. Rather, it marked a precedent for current demands for professional accountability. Moreover, such demands, then as now, came from within the professions as well as from laymen. Likewise, the essays that follow limn out the nature of social conflicts within professional contexts.

Sanders and Lyon's essay on the arts breaks out of the mold which stresses the conventional professions. They draw upon writings by and about artists, and their own research with theater companies, comic artists, and art market personnel to develop a presentation of the "new humanistic artist." The new artist stresses 1) collective artistic production, 2) public participation in the "art work," 3) the political impact and context of art, 4) independence from traditional elite art institutions and 5) experimentation with a wide variety of artistic genres. The humanistic artist emphasizes the *demystification* of artistic production.

Another nontraditional profession is sports. Juliani delineates how in the 20th century, sport has emerged as an enormously popular form of recreation and leisure for Americans. In particular, professional sport has become well established as a social institution and as a legitimate career within our society. Recently, however, numerous criticisms of ex-athletes turned writers, point to an imminent crisis. The current wave of dissent and protest emerging among professional athletes is shown to be inherent in the social and economic relationships which make up organized sport. The same structural features which make the organization of sport unique render a genuinely radical and militant movement among professional athletes an unlikely event in the forseeable future.

Turning toward the traditional professions, Wenger's analysis of academia places emphasis upon professionalism as an ideology and a mythology which has been subject to erosion in recent years. His account deals with both public education and colleges and universities. Professionalism as an ideology is shown to support an occupation's control over client relations. Erosion has involved unionization on the one hand, and the revolt of the client on the other — both in pressures toward community control and student participation in decision-making. The issue of tenure frames distinctive aspects of academic work with regard to autonomy.

Kidder shows that those who seek to use their professional positions in law to produce social change are confronted with a number of common dilemmas. Conventional expectations about both the profession and the institutions of law provide both leverage and threat for the activist. The law's attention to individual cases may help the individual client while perpetuating the conditions of inequality which created the client's problem. Both radical and liberal-activist lawyers face these dilemmas. A comparison with lawyers in India reveals how advocacy is generally characterized by tension and distrust between professional and client. That such tensions affect "lawyers for the people" reveals threats to even those lawyers with "good intentions."

Resnick describes developments in medicine. He discusses segments and their ideologies. He traces a progression from political activism by the Student Health Organization to vanguard professional activity by young physicians. The ideology of the original movement becomes simultaneously a model for young physicians and a threat to conventional physicians. National health insurance would incorporate and legitimate parts of this ideology.

Perrucci provides a coda. He examines the patterns of movement professionals in the 1960s in terms of themes cutting across occupational groups. Attention is given to issues of emergent conditions in the past decade, membership trends, goals, and prospects for continuity. Perrucci's major consideration is the waste of talent: as professions grow in number and power, the gap between their potential and their performance becomes greater. Major dilemmas limit the likely success of radical factions. These include the discrepancy between broad societal critiques and action programs that are very local and limited. Yet this may be the only viable alternative given a commitment to *doing* professional work without being co-opted. It is carried out most successfully by that new professional organization, the law commune. That this might be a prototype for other professions suggests interesting possibilities. The extent to which nonmovement professionals have become involved with aspects of change may be seen as an aspect of the success of radical groups, even if they themselves fade or change form in the present decade.

In short, while the movements reported here have been radical in intent, they have been reformist — at best — in effect. Reformation is not to be belittled. The excursus into the Jacksonian period substantiates this. Nonetheless, reform, despite its stridency and its rhetoric, still represents commitment to professional mores and morals.

Professional work, reformist or reactionary, is wedded to its social contexts. The contemporary scene includes: the multinational corporate state, the depletion of resources and the questioning of technology and growth, the Malthusian crunch — famine, pestilence and war, economic crisis and the emergence of naked political cynicism. Will professionals in this age of increasing organizational scale and power be able to shift their emphasis from the traditional issue of autonomy from clients to the more crucial autonomy from taskmasters? Our hope is that this volume will aid in keeping questions such as these in focus as opposed to the usual sociological contributions to the liturgy of professionalism.

REFERENCES

Aronson, Sidney H. 1964 *Status and Kinship in the Higher Civil Service.* Cambridge: Harvard University Press.

Bergel, Egon E. 1962. *Social Stratification.* New York: McGraw-Hill.
Bowen, Ralph H. 1947. *German Theories of the Corporative State.* New York: McGraw-Hill.
Brady, Robert A. 1937. *The Spirit and Structure of German Fascism.* London: Victor Gollancz.
Bucher, Rue, and Anselm Strauss. 1961. "Professions in Process." *American Journal of Sociology* 66 (Jan.): 325-334.
Calhoun, Daniel H. 1965. *Professional Lives in America.* Cambridge: Harvard University Press.
Carr-Saunders, A.M., and P.A. Wilson. 1933. *The Professions.* Oxford: Clarendon Press.
Carsten, F.L. 1967. *The Rise of Fascism.* Berkeley: University of California Press.
Commons, John R. 1909. "American Shoemakers, 1648-1895: A Sketch of Industrial Evolution." *Quarterly Journal of Economics* XXIV: 39-81.
Coser, Lewis A. 1960. "Durkheim's Conservatism and Its Implications for his Sociological Theory." *In Essays on Sociology and Philosophy,* edited by Kurt H. Wolff. New York: Harper and Row.
Coser, Lewis A. 1971. *Masters of Sociological Thought.* New York: Harcourt Brace Jovanovich.
Dumont, Matthew P. 1970. "The Changing Face of Professionalism." *Social Policy* I (May-June): 26-31.
Durkheim, Emile. 1933. *The Division of Labor in Society,* translated by George Simpson. Glencoe, Ill.: The Free Press.
Durkheim, Emile. 1957. *Professional Ethics and Civic Morals,* translated by C. Brookfield. London: Routledge and Kegan Paul.
Durkheim, Emile. 1958. *Socialism,* translated by Charlotte Sattler. New York: Collier Books.
Daniels, George H. 1968. *American Science in the Age of Jackson.* New York: Columbia University Press.
Einaudi, Mario. 1968. "Fascism." In *International Encyclopedia of the Social Sciences* V. 5: 334-341. New York: Macmillan.
Friedrich, Carl J., and Zbigniew K. Brzezinski. 1956. *Totalitarian Dictatorship and Autocracy.* New York: Frederick A. Praeger.
Friedson, Eliot. 1970. *Profession of Medicine.* New York: Dodd Mead.
Giddens, Anthony. 1971. *Capitalism and Modern Social Theory.* London: Cambridge University Press.
Gilb, Corinne Lathrop. 1966. *Hidden Hierarchies: the Professions and Government.* New York: Harper and Row.
Habenstein, Robert W. 1963. "Critique of 'Profession' as a Sociological Category." *Sociological Quarterly* (Nov.).
Hamilton, Alistair. 1971. *The Appeal of Fascism: A Study of Intellectuals and Fascism.* New York: Avon.
Haug, Marie R. 1973. "Deprofessionalization: an Alternate Hypothesis for the Future." *Sociological Review* Monograph No. 20 (Dec.).
Haug, Marie R. 1974. "The Erosion of Professional Autonomy." Paper presented at the annual meetings of the American Sociological Assn., Montreal.

Haug, Marie R., and Marvin B. Sussman. 1969. "Professional Autonomy and the Revolt of the Client." *Social Problems* 17 (Fall): 153-160..

Heaton, Herbert. 1948. *Economic History of Europe.* New York: Harper and Row.

Hindle, Brooke. 1956. *The Pursuit of Science in Revolutionary America 1735-1789.* Chapel Hill: The University of North Carolina Press.

Hughes, Everett C. 1971. *The Sociological Eye: Selected Papers on Work, Self, and the Study of Society.* Chicago: Aldine.

Kele, Max H. 1972. *Nazis and Workers.* Chapel Hill: Univ. of North Carolina Press.

Krause, Elliot A. 1971. *The Sociology of Occupations.* Boston: Little, Brown.

Lee, Alfred McClung. 1966. *Multivalent Man.* New York: George Braziller.

Lee, Alfred McClung. 1973. *Toward Humanist Sociology.* Englewood Cliffs, New Jersey: Printice-Hall.

Lee, Alfred McClung. 1973. *Toward Humanist Sociology.* Englewood Cliffs, New Jersey: Prentice-Hall.

Lee, Alfred McClung, and Elizabeth Briant Lee. 1932, 1974. *The Fine Art of Propaganda.* New York: Octagon Books.

Lukes, Steven. 1972. *Emile Durkheim: his Life and his Work.* New York: Harper and Row.

Morris, Richard B. 1946. *Government and Labor in Early America.* New York: Columbia Univ. Press.

Neumann, Franz. 1942. *Behemoth.* New York: Oxford Univ. Press.

Neyer, Joseph. 1960. "Individualism and Socialism in Durkheim." In *Essays on Sociology and Philosophy,* edited by Kurt H. Wolff. New York: Harper and Row.

Perrucci, Robert, and Joel E. Gerstl. 1969. *Profession Without Community: Engineers in American Society.* New York: Random House.

Reader, W. J. 1966. *Professional Men: the Rise of the Professional Class in Nineteenth Century England.* London: Weidenfield and Nicolson.

Richter, Melvin. 1960. "Durkheim's Politics and Political Theory." In *Essays on Sociology and Philosophy,* edited by Kurt H. Wolff. New York: Harper and Row.

Roth, Julius. 1974. "Professionalism: the Sociologist's Decoy." *Sociology of Work and Occupations* I (Feb.): 6-23.

Salomon, Albert. 1955. *The Tyranny of Progress.* New York: Noonday.

Schwendinger, Herman, and Julia Schwendinger. 1974. *The Sociologists of the Chair.* New York: Basic Books.

Strauss, Leo, and Joseph Cropsey. 1963. *History of Political Philosophy.* Chicago: Rand McNally.

Tawney, R. H. 1926, 1947. *Religion and the Rise of Capitalism.* New York: Pelican (Penguin) Books.

Taylor, Lee. 1968. *Occupational Sociology.* 1968. New York: Oxford Univ. Press.

Villari, Luigi. 1932. "The Economics of Fascism." In George S. Counts, et. al. *Bolshevism, Fascism, and Capitalism.* New Haven: Yale Univ. Press.

von Beckerath, Erwin. 1931. "Fascism." In *Encyclopedia of the Social Sciences.* v. 6: 133-138. New York: Macmillan.

Weber, Eugen. 1971. "Fascism as the Conjunction of Right and Left." In *The Place of Fascism in European History,* edited by Gilbert Allardyce. Englewood Cliffs, N.J.: Prentice-Hall.

Wilensky, Harold L. 1964. "The Professionalization of Everyone?" *American Journal of Sociology* LXX (Sept.): 137-158.

Wolff, Kurt H. (ed.). 1960. *Essays on Sociology and Philosophy: by Emile Durkheim et. al.* New York: Harper and Row.

LICENSING IN THE LEGAL AND MEDICAL PROFESSIONS, 1820-1860: A HISTORICAL CASE STUDY

Leonard Tabachnik

There has been in the twentieth century a marked tendency, by raising standards, to change a particular occupation from craft status to a professional status. The process of professionalization has been largely accomplished by the direct intervention of the state through the creation of professional degrees and by the passage of laws for licensing and certification. This recent sanction of professionalism by politicians and the public is due largely, if not entirely, to a number of basic beliefs. First is the general belief that professionalism protects the public from irresponsible and incompetent practitioners, and therefore contributes to the virtual elimination of quackery; a related belief is that by raising the level of competency, political corruption will also disappear. Second is the belief that professionalism, through specialization, adds to a growing body of knowledge, resulting in the long term advancement for science. Finally, there is the belief that through services rendered, whether in the field of science or social engineering, professionalism contributes toward a better society. These basic beliefs are still embraced despite the increasing numbers no longer so optimistic about professionalism as society's panacea for its ills.*

However this may be, the belief that professionalism advances science and protects the public from quackery was completely rejected by state legislators during the Age of Jackson. In regard to the only two professions then licensed, that of law and medicine, many state legislators came to the belief that licensing laws, by giving special interest groups monopolistic powers, actually hindered the development of the professions, and provided no guarantee of protection for the public. In

---

* See Theodore J. Lowi's discussion of this in his introduction to Harold F. Gosnell, *Machine Politics: Chicago Model* (Chicago, 1968 ed.).

many instances they found that the term "quack" had been used as an epithet for political purposes to brand a qualified opponent as incompetent. Because of the abuses, many state legislatures repealed their licensing laws. By 1840 only 11 of 30 states maintained regulations for admission to the bar; and by 1845 only eight of 30 states had effective medical legislation. This movement for the repeal of licensing laws is generally referred to by historians as "de-professionalization."

The Jackson period provides us with a unique opportunity to introduce historical evidence into the current debate on licensing in the professions. This backward view, however, is not to advocate a return to the past. Institutions, evolving as they do in a cultural setting, have a history, and the professions as they exist today must be seen in the perspective of the entire period of American history, not just the last 50 or 70 years. Experience with the past may help us better gauge when we are either overly subscribing to or rejecting a policy which may be in need of some critical re-evaluation. Addressing a symposium on the subject of professions, Kenneth Lynn recently sounded the call for such a re-evaluation when he said: "For more than anything else, our professionals need to liberate themselves — just as their colonial predecessors did — from the monopolistic notions of who should do what job and narrow-minded conceptions of their obligations to the community at large." (*Daedalus* [1963], p. 653)*

*   *   *   *   *

The modern notion of associating competence with licensing originated in the 1870's and was promoted primarily by the American Bar Association and the American Medical Association. The impression one gets from reading the reports issued by the dominant leadership of the two professional associations at that time is that the battle for the professions in the late nineteenth and early twentieth centuries was between the Children of Light and the Children of Darkness. The argument appears to be that those competent in their fields favored higher standards and strict licensing in order to eliminate quackery, while the incompetent wished no regulation so that they could peddle their wares without interference. According to these official accounts, under the

* Full citations for references in the text appear in the bibliography.

enlightened leadership of the A.B.A. and A.M.A., after a long struggle standards were slowly restored. The turning point in this struggle came when state legislatures agreed to support licensing as a means of imposing standards.

This picture, however, is far from complete. There is abundant evidence that many respectable leaders in the two professions opposed state regulation through licensing on ideological grounds. Their main arguments were that regulation was an infringement of personal rights, and that it was monopolistic because it legislated for a special class. (Fitz, *Legislative Control* [1894], p. 582)

In the debate over the need for licensing, each side appealed to history for support of its point of view. Those who opposed licensing did not accept the idea that the repeal of such laws during the Jackson period had really harmed the professions. They, therefore, saw no reason for breaking the continuity begun in the Jackson era. Those who favored licensing, on the other hand, depicted the Jackson period in the worst possible terms, describing it as the beginning of the downfall of professionalism. A report issued by the American Bar Association after its first meeting in 1877 stated that:

> The general standard of professional learning and obligation began to decline in the greatest American cities about the year 1840, and preserved a downward tendency until 1870, when it reached its lowest ebb. It is sufficient to note that this is ascribed to the changes in laws regulating admissions to the bar, and by means which ignorant, and it is said, the unprincipled, were launched on professional experience and temtations in extraordinary numbers, without preparation of any suitable kind. *(Proceedings,* V.I. [1877], p. 212).

In succeeding years the A.B.A. continued to publish reports from various state bar associations attesting to these conditions. A letter from the Maine Bar Association stated the following: "From the organization of the association until 1843 standards were high. But in 1843, under the impulse of a class of demagogues, the legislature swept away all existing rules . . ." (ibid., p. 241). A report from the New Hampshire Association came to a similar conclusion. "From 1800 to 1840 the bar was able," the report stated. Then it noted that "[b]y 1842 a great outcry had been raised against the profession. It was said that they were exclusive; that they did not represent the people; that the judges were lawyers, and that the court and bar conspired together to shut out the most deserving people in the state. The new class was known as 'moral Character' lawyers. Many loafed and received a degree'' (ibid. [1881], p. 242).

The American Medical Association launched its own crusade for higher standards, complaining that the lack of regulation in the profession had led to charlantism on the grandest scale. "The most ingorant and depraved men,'' reported a committee to the A.M.A., "assume the title of doctor, and men of little or no training in study or observation assume to practice medicine. In most sections of our country no proof of knowledge or skill is required, the thoroughly trained practitioner very often finds himself on the same plane in the public estimation with the shameless charlatan'' (*Transactions* [1877], p. 50).

Historians, for the most part, have presented in their discussions of the state of the professions during the Jackson period a point of view similar to that of the A.B.A. and A.M.A. A historian of the medical profession writing about the pre-Civil War period states that "The Jacksonian period has been viewed as a Dark Age of the profession — dashing the expectations of an earlier generation, long frustrating attempts at reconstruction by a later generation, and jeopardizing the lives of thousands'' (Kett [1968], p. 1). A similar view is found among those writing the history of the legal profession. One writer describes the period as "The Demoralization of the Legal Profession in the Nineteenth Century'' (Blackard (1940), p. 317). Anton-Herman Chroust in his two volume history of the legal profession in America also makes a harsh indictment of the Jackson period. "This era,'' he writes, "and its popular ideals in a great measure retarded and, in many instances, even hindered the development of a strong legal profession, as a profession, by fostering a suspicious opposition to, and distrust of, an educated bar and, for that matter, any 'elite' based on special training, high achievement, and impeccable deportment'' (Chroust [1965], p. 171).

Such a negative attitude about the professions in the Jackson period has invariably led historians to focus on what they believe to be those elements of continuity with the present. Thus, in the historical literature one reads much more about the nascent roots of modern medicine and law than about the actual state of the professions during that period. The establishment of the American Medical Association in 1847, for example, is viewed as a heroic battle of a dedicated minority confronting ignorance and superstition. This approach to history, which implicitly affirms a belief in progressive development has two major weaknesses. First, by identifying with that position which has become the dominant point of view it either distorts or ignores other historical points of view. Second, it assumes that institutional development in the professions, or the lack of it, was archaic during the Jackson period, and, therefore, has no lesson for modern times. It is only recently when there is a search for new approaches regarding the direction of the professions that the Jackson period has received a more sympathetic examination; as, for instance, in a recent study of the medical profession by Rosemary Stevens. While Stevens does not advocate a return to the de-professionalism of the Jackson period, she does see some redeeming qualities in that movement. For example, with the weakening of legal and professional controls, medical education expanded on an unprecedented rate. In 1800 there were only four medical schools in the country. Between 1810 and 1840, twenty-six were founded; and between 1840 and 1876, forty-seven were added (Stevens [1971], p. 24). This expansion of medical education provided for a substantial increase in the number of doctors available in the country. At the same time, she does not view with alarm the fact that many of these doctors were less scientific oriented than their counterparts today. In fact, she argues a case for a level of medical education which is more clinical oriented and whose practitioners could provide satisfactory performance within the rigorous training that goes into the education of the scientific doctor. This interpretation is a third approach, a synthesis, of two historical experiences: the de-professionalism of the Jackson period and the rigorous professional standards that are operating in more recent times (ibid., p. 531).

TRADITIONS OF "DE-PROFESSIONAL" THEORY IN AMERICA

The Jackson attack on the professions drew upon four traditions: Puritanism; democratic thought; the frontier experience; and laissez-faire doctrine. There is, of course, a degree of overlapping of categories, but each source is distinct and deserving of a separate discussion.

a) Puritanism

There are two aspects of Puritanism which have a bearing on the professions. First is the idea of consociation — that men are to be with one another and not over one another — and this attitude prejudiced any attempt by a professional class, whether they be clergymen, lawyers or doctors, to create a separate elite class of citizens which may be turned into a new priesthood. More important, though, in terms of the discussion at hand, is the idea of an educated laity. Although this concept had a religious basis for the Puritans, it was readily transferred to other areas as well. If it was fundamental to the Puritans that every individual be literate enough to approach God on his own through the Bible and without an intermediary, it was also their belief that the citizen should be acquainted with the basic laws of his physiology as well as the laws of his society. These beliefs did not preclude the recognition that some may be more knowledgeable than others in the various fields, but it did lessen the need for a separate professional class where distinctions between laity and expert were hard and fast. The classical statement in support of such a principle was made by President Ezra Stiles when he established a Professorship of Law at Yale in 1777:

> The professorship of Law is equally important with that of Medicine; not indeed towards educating Lawyers or Barristers, but for forming Civilians [citizens]. Fewer than a quarter perhaps of the young gentlemen educated at College, enter into either of the learned professions of Divinity, Law or Physic: The greater part of them after finishing the academic Course return home, mix in with the body of the public, and enter upon Commerce or the cultivation of their Estates. And yet perhaps the most of them in the Course of their Lifes are called forth by their country into some or other of the various Branches of civil Improvement & the public offices in the State. Most certainly it is worthy of great attention, the Dicipline and Education of these in that knowledge which shall qualify them to become useful Members of Society, as Selectmen, Justices of Peace, Members of the Legislature, Judges of Courts, & Delegates in Congress. How Happy for a community to abound with men well instituted in the knowledge of their Rights & Liberties? . . . (in Boorstin [1958], p. 204).

b) Democratic thought

In the Jackson period when the theoretical framework for equality was formulated at many state conventions, the doctrines first elaborated in the political arena were later applied to the professions. The argument for political equality can be found in the New York State Constitutional Convention of 1821 where the principal was accepted that every citizen, whether or not he owns property, has a stake in society and is, therefore, entitled to representation. Later during the 1830's and 1840's this same argument was applied to the professions — that every citizen has the right to enter and practice a profession.

The democratic faith in man's ability to carry out any function was first exercised by the Jacksonian practice of "rotation in office." In his first message to Congress, President Jackson pointed out that "the duties of all public offices are, or at least admit of being made so plain and simple, that men of intelligence may readily qualify themselves for performance" (in Aronson [1964], p. 17). A consequence of this rule is that any applicant with sufficient intelligence could aspire to office. At the Pennsylvania Constitutional Convention in 1837 when John Sergeant, the Whig president of the convention, made a distinction between "political" and "civil" offices as a means of keeping selected positions such as judgeships from the elective process, he was in the minority. In an answer to Sergeant, another member of the convention declared that "to say that the people are incompetent would be to establish the monarchical principle that the people are unfit to govern, and we ought to reform the Constitution by establishing a monarchy" (in Hartz, p. 30). What was being questioned here was that an appointments system did not necessarily guarantee merit. At this time the public believed that the appointive system had been abused, often corruptly, and that better qualified and honest office-holders would be selected if more of the offices were made elective. Under the impact of this thinking, in fact, a political revolution took place in most American states during this period. Whereas, before the 1830's, very few public offices were elective, by the 1850's many such offices, including local school boards, became elective. This same distrust of a selection procedure based on appointments also affected the public's attitude toward the professions.

c) The frontier experience

The farther a person travelled from the large cities the greater the chances that he would find self-made lawyers and doctors who possessed little or no professional education. He would find, for example, that the western-frontier lawyer relied more on natural reasoning and experience than on "book-learning" or precedents. Frontier culture also discouraged specialization. As Roscoe Pound has said: "The pioneer feels himself equal to anything and would leave everyone free to change his occupation as and when he likes and to take up freely such occupations as he chooses. To him specialization and differentiation in the profession were unnecessary hinderances to the spontaneous activities of free men. Any distinction of one calling from another was prima facie wrong. Any distinction between those who were trained and those who were not was invidious and smacked of the old world aristocratic polity . . .'' (in Blackard, p. 322).

d) Laissez-faire doctrine

A fourth tradition which contributed to the de-professionalism of the Jackson period was that movement for the abolition of monopolies. This movement, and the accompanying ideology, took root in an expanding economy. From about 1820 to 1860 American society underwent a dramatic transformation from a handicraft to an industrial society, a period Walter Rostow has referred to as America's ''take-off'' stage. This economic expansion in turn created an entrepreneurial class which favored an open society and attacked the monopolistic practices of the previous generation. Representative of this new entrepreneurial power was President Jackson's veto of the Second Bank of the United States which effectively destroyed an institution centralized in the hands of a relatively few men. When he established his so-called ''pet'' banks it diffused power to the local level and a whole new class of Jacksonian bankers emerged.

It was at this time, too, that labor unions and professional associations were considered hinderances to a free market.

DE-PROFESSIONALIZATION OF LAW AND MEDICINE

Prior to the Jackson period fairly difficult qualifications were required for admission to the legal and medical professions, and these standards were usually controlled by the professional associations. First, most states required lengthy prescribed periods of preparation. Second, a classical college education was encouraged, usually through a system of incentives. Third, in a number of states the profession was graded in at least two levels. Fourth, most of the power for maintaining standards and control of the profession was left by the legislatures to the professional associations themselves. Under these conditions the legal profession seemed to have so thrived that one historian has referred to this early period as its ''golden age'' (Chroust, p. 211). During the same period the medical profession also gained control over licensing. By

1830 there were medical societies in nearly all the states of the Union, and many had succeeded in convincing state legislators to delegate to them powers for establishing standards and the control of licensing in the profession (Stevens, p. 23).

Despite these impressive gains, by the mid-1830's the credibility of the professional associations had been so undermined that many state legislatures withdrew the licensing powers once so liberally accorded to the associations. The reason the public and state legislators denied professional associations the right to set standards and the power to award licenses is a matter that is often overlooked in a discussion of this important subject. Even the leaders of the A.M.A. in the 1870's admitted they were unable to explain why this withdrawal occurred. A report on the subject submitted to the A.M.A. in 1877 stated: "About 1840, every state in the Union, except North Carolina, Pennsylvania and Virginia, had, or had had the now much desired medical examining boards, appointed in some cases by the Governor, but in many cases by the regular medical societies. These boards did not prove satisfactory to the profession, and were so unsatisfactory to the sovereign people that their representatives did, from about 1840 to 1852, repeal or annul, in nearly, if not quite all the states, the laws establishing such boards" (*Transactions* [1877], p. 304).

a) The legal profession

Attacks against the legal profession came at a time when, as we have seen, the professional associations had made substantial gains in establishing themselves as the undisputed body to screen new entrants. Screening restricted the number of lawyers admitted to the bar and succeeded in raising professional salaries. The resultant elevated position of lawyers became a source of concern in many quarters. Many who wanted to enter the profession for the profit it would bring resented the barriers put up by the legal associations. Others simply resented their monopolistic powers. Though relatively few in number, lawyers as politicians, judges and government officials were beginning to play a dominant role in the civic affairs of the state.

One of the most vigorous attacks against the profession took place in Massachusetts where, in fact, the bar associations were strongest. Massachusetts was the first state to pass a law withdrawing the power of licensing from the bar associations, and the arguments presented became the model for the rest of the nation. The movement which began in the early 1830's culminated in 1835. A law was passed stating that any candidate who studied law for three years in the office of an attorney was automatically admitted to the bar upon application to the Supreme Court or the Court of Common Pleas. A college degree was no longer required, and the idea of a graded profession, the distinction between a counsellor and attorney, was completely abolished.

This law, though it virtually opened the gates to any aspiring lawyer, was actually the result of a compromise between two contending proposals. An original committee submitted a report which favored the status quo. However, a highly radical plan, submitted by Frederick Robinson, had, for all practical purposes, attempted to establish the principle of a lay legal profession. As a result, a committee of three was appointed in 1835, one of whom was Robert Rantoul, Jr., the radical Jacksonian Democrat, to work out a compromise between these two positions (Gawalt, p. 125). Though Robinson's ideas were not adopted in their entirety, his influence, through his writing, was great. His major ideas on the subject can be found in a pamphlet entitled *Letter to the Hon. Rufus Choate, Containing A Brief Exposure of Law Craft* (1832).

In his essay Robinson outlines three major points in favor of abolishing the bar:

1. That every citizen, as the Massachusetts Constitution provides, has the natural right to argue before the courts of the state. Yet the bar, by following its own selfish interests, has established a web of technical procedures which serve as impediments to discourage laymen from appearing before the courts. This it does in several ways. Lawyers and judges, he said, being part of a "holy alliance" intimidate any layman presumptuous or fool enough to appear before the court. They make all sorts of outlandish demands of him so as to embarrass and demoralize him. He further accused the bar of purposely creating meaningless rules toward this end, and encumbering the law with obscure language that would serve to confound the layman. Under these circumstances the layman has little choice but to approach the professional lawyer for help. Robinson's solution was to simplify the procedure of the courts and codify the laws so that an intelligent layman could be his own lawyer.

2. That the bar is a monopoly and should be treated as such. "It seems," he writes, "to have been the whole study of your brotherhood in this way to involve the laws, and the practice of the law, in such a dark

maze of uncertainty as to render it impossible for anyone to practice law without the previous understanding with every other practitioner.'' In the end, he noted that the legal profession is a trade and that it should be denied the right to combine in restraint of trade.

Related to his argument of restraint of trade is the idea that the bar had made access to the profession so difficult that under the present rules, men like Benjamin Franklin and Patrick Henry would not qualify as lawyers.

3. Finally, Robinson advanced the argument that the bar association is not compatible with a republican form of government because it creates a system of subordination. "What can be more anti-republican," he wrote, "than associations of this kind? The tendency and object of them are to settle society down into casts and render the barriers between them impossible." He then proceeded to accuse the wealthy classes of hoarding positions in the professions for themselves by requiring long periods of education and apprenticeship, thereby making certain that few from the lower and middle classes will enter the profession. "You look upon yourselves," he wrote, "as a 'superior order,' as the future lawyers, doctors, priests, judges and governors of mankind, and you look upon the rest of the world as inferior, plebians, laborers, educated only for manual employment."

Massachusetts was not unique in this matter of deprofes-sionalization. Similar movements in a number of other states during the following decade led to the virtual elimination of admission require-ments to practice law. Laws or constitutional amendments to that effect were passed in New Hampshire in 1842; Maine in 1843; New York in 1846; Georgia in 1847; and Indiana in 1851. The Indiana Constitution had by far the most generous provisions. It provided that, "Every person of good moral character, being a voter, shall be entitled to admission to practice law in all courts of justice."

Nor are the arguments presented by Frederick Robinson to be taken as the product of one disappointed man. He was articulating a position held by wide segments of the population. A New Yorker, writing in 1871 about the popular ferment in his state during the 1840's, explained how the change came about:

The declaration (in the New York Constitution of 1846) that 'any male citizen of the age of twenty-one years, of good moral character, and who possesses the requisite qualifications of learning and ability, shall be entitled to practice in all the courts of this State,' theoretically permitted all intelligent men to enter the profession. It was intended to do even more than this, that is, to allow every man who wished to set up a law office. The popular impression of that day was that the lawyers were a priviledged class. And there were some grounds for this impression. Almost all the public offices were filled by members of the bar. They were exempt from jury duty, and, practically, from service in the militia and from civil arrest. They seemed to do little labor for large pay, and their business was secure from the dangers of a commercial crises. It is not surprising that those who followed their callings believed that a position at the bar was an open sesame of honor and wealth, and that they regarded with jealousy, the existence of certain rules and customs which rendered the attainment of that position difficult. The most obnoxious rule, under the old system, was the one which made a long apprenticeship essential for admission to the bar. This rule, in effect, excluded the great body of the people as the time required was greater than could be afforded by one compelled to earn his own livlihood. . . . (in Blackard, p. 324).

b) The medical profession

The first successful attacks against medical licensing did not come from ignorant laymen, but from physicians within the profession. The attack was sparked by the passage in 1827 of a licensing law by the New York State Legislature forbidding out-of-state colleges to sponsor a medical faculty in the city of New York; refusing to recognize degrees from out-of-state colleges as licenses; and, forcing licentiates to become members of the local medical society or their licences would be considered null and void by the state's Board of Regents. The passage of the law brought a great deal of protest from physicians who resented the fact that it gave the one medical school in the city, the College of Physicians and Surgeons, a monopoly over medical education. It was clear that the law prevented the charter of a recently created rival medical school established in the city under the auspices of Rutgers University. It was also clear that the law gave to the medical society enormous power by endowing it with the power to license and to prohibit anyone from practicing medicine who was not a member of the society. As a result of these grievances a *Circular Letter,* signed by 154 physicians, was issued. An analysis of the names attached to the letter show the following: that 46 were members of the New York County Medical Society; a larger number were associated with the effort to open the Rutgers Medical School; and the remainder were young physicians who viewed licensing as a hinderance to their success.

Like most licensing laws, the purported aim of the 1827 law was to protect the public from quackery. However, in their *Letter* the dissenting physicians maintained that the legislation would not eliminate quackery, and that by giving the medical society monopolistic powers the development of the medical profession would be retarded. In a list of grievances they accused the medical society of hindering the development and dissemination of scientific knowledge; checking aspiring talent; preventing the best physicians from teaching; and, creating jealousies in the profession. A free market, they concluded, was the best guarantee for promoting high standards in the medical profession.

In contrast to our own age which places so much faith on examinations to determine those qualified for the medical profession, in the Jackson period many physicians came to believe that the examination process had been corrupted and was often used for political ends. In a public statement a group of physicians noted that:

> The present mode of examination . . . does not afford the people any good voucher that justice has been done to them, in the recommendation of men to whom they are to entrust their health and lives, nor does it afford any check on favoritism, the influences of consanguity and pupilage, the recommendations of powerful men . . . and personal animosities, these examinations being conducted in private, and often by interested individuals, whose word alone must be taken as evidence of the qualifications of the candidates (in Hugins, [1960], p. 168).

During the 1870's criticism of the medical profession increased, much of it coming from doctors themselves, creating a climate in which it became more difficult to convince the public of the integrity of experts. One respected physician, for example, wrote: "To such an extent are the feelings of hostility carried in the practice of medicine that one physician will not even use the remedies recommended by one who he dislikes, when his own reason and conscience, . . . tell, and demonstrate to him that they are the best adopted in a given case" (Calhoun [1965], p. 51). He also pointed out that often a testimonial or a devastating criticism, rather than having anything to do with the value of a doctor's work, was the result of personal relationships. At the same time, the public was becoming distrustful of the dominant approach to medical treatment. American doctors still relied heavily on bleeding their patients and using chemicals such as calomel in large quantities. One New York State senator summed up the situation well when he said: "The people of this state have been bled long enough in their bodies and pockets, and it was [sic] time they should do as the men of the Revolution did: resolve to set down [sic] and enjoy the freedom for which they bled'' (in Shafer [1936], p. 210).

It is not surprising that the public was ready to give hearing to those with different approaches to medical treatment. The most persuasive group was, by far, the Thomsonians, whose main principle was the objection to the use of chemicals, either for palliation or cure. Instead they preferred to use vegetable compounds and herbs. The Thomsonians, like many of their counterparts in the legal profession, advocated the simplification of medical language so that through the use of medical handbooks every citizen would become his own doctor. "May the time come," stated a Thomsonian journal, "when men and women will become their own priests, physicians and lawyers — when self-government, equal rights, and moral philosophy will take place of all popular crafts of every description" (in Rosenberg [1962], p. 71).

In the end the arguments presented by the various dissenting groups prevailed with the state legislature. In 1843 and 1844 the New York State Legislature reported out of committee reports favoring the repeal of legislation which had formerly placed penalities on "irregular" physicians. The arguments used by the committee are interesting because they turn the case for state regulation on its head and present a case for laissez-faire.

The committee's report began by reaffirming the purpose of legislation as being for the public good, and when such legislation becomes destructive of these ends, or when they advance the interests of a special class at the expense of other portions of the community, it is a duty to repeal such laws. It was the committee's belief that the existing laws were in fact serving special interests and it proceeded to recommend the repeal of these laws. Three major arguments were presented:

1) Discrimination

That experience had shown numerous instances in which unlicensed physicians are called upon by licensed physicians to provide medical aid, but because of the statutes, they do not receive the proper remuneration for the same services performed by a licensed physician.

2) Credentials

With the diffusion of mass education the average literate citizen can now determine for himself the capabilities of a physician. He no longer has to rely on "a sheep-skin, with the broad seal of a medical institution and M.D. attached to it." That the people, left to act upon their own reason and judgment, would be no more willing to entrust their health and lives to ignorant quacks than to deal with a crook in business. Competition (it said) would in the end prove beneficial to the profession itself. "And your committee has yet to learn that science, and a long established profession, have anything to *lose* from open and fair competition — or to fear from error and quackery, when free to combat them with the power of light and truth."

3) Scientific progress

On the issue of the need to advance scientific research the committee held that the existing laws actually "operate to *restrain* rather than *incite* research." Experience has shown, they noted, that the laws serve to protect one school of thought which uses the power given to it by the state to coerce others. In a key passage the committee warned that the term *quack* was often used to smear the opposition. Those under the protection of the law "apply the epithets of *quack* and *empiric* with great force and effect to those (perhaps equally scientific as themselves), who in their investigations venture to overstep the prescribed limits of the legalized profession . . . " (State of New York, *Documents*, 1844).

By 1845, under the impact of these arguments, ten states completely repealed their medical licensing laws and four states merely repealed penalities against unlicensed practitioners. The states that repealed their licensing laws were: Maine, Vermont, Massachusetts, Connecticut, Maryland, South Carolina, Alabama, Mississippi, Indiana, and Ohio. New York, New Jersey, Georgia, and Louisiana repealed the laws against unlicensed practitioners (Coventry [1845], p. 1591).

CONCLUSION

There are two basic questions raised in this discussion of de-professionalization in the Jackson period. The first is whether or not there is a connection between professionalism — licensing and degrees — and competency; and the second, whether the professional associations, the guardians of professional standards, had, in fact, abused their powers. The two questions are connected because, as we have seen, the demand for repeal of the licensing laws originated among those who believed that the professional associations were abusing their powers.

As for the first question it is still not clear what lasting effects de-professionalization had on professional competency during the Jackson period. There is a great need for empirical studies which can tell us more about medical and legal practices during the period. The evidence available to us about the decline of the professions comes mainly from two interested parties, the A.B.A. and A.M.A., and their sources are questionable. It is interesting to note that at the same time that the leaders of the professional associations were lamenting the decline of the professions they were admitting, at times, that even without licensing conditions were not as bad as one would have expected. On this point one bar association official stated: "Such abolition of requirement for professional duty operated less injuriously than might have been anticipated" (*Proceedings* [1881], p. 241). In the case of medicine, one recent authority on the subject has observed that the rise of the proprietary or private medical schools during this period probably "raised instead of lowered the average standards" (Stevens, p. 28).

An answer to the question is further complicated by the fact that some authoritative agencies continued, even after the repeal of the licensing laws, to pass on the qualifications of those candidates wishing to enter the professions. In law, the courts became the most important agency for passing judgment on a candidate's qualifications, and in medicine it was the schools. Since very little is known how these agencies operated it is impossible to draw conclusions.

What is clear is that the crusade against the two professions during the Jackson period was really an attack against the aggrandizement of enormous powers by the professional associations. Since the licensing laws had provided these associations with power it was these laws which became the target for attack. Some critics questioned whether the high standards demanded by the professional associations were not artificially high. Others doubted the relevance of certain educational requirements, such as Greek and Latin, for the practice of law and medicine. This criticism went to the heart of what, in fact, makes a competent lawyer or doctor, a question that is still largely debatable. Most critics agreed that those who controlled the professional associations were using their power for political purposes to brand their opponents, who may have been equally competent, as quacks. The abuses had become so widespread that state legislators agreed to open the professions to a free market by repealing the licensing laws.

In a situation such as that of the Jackson period, where politicians and the public are convinced that the licensing laws were being abused, two solutions are available. One solution is that taken by the Jacksonians when they chose to abolish licensing in the professions. Another solution is to maintain licensing and deal effectively with the abuses. Although the state has ultimate authority over the professions it has, in the name of preserving standards, granted to them a large amount of autonomy. Yet as the political scientist, Oliver Garceau, has written: "Professionalism is a concept freely used to seal off the group from critical inquiry. It spreads an order of sanctity" (Garceau [1961], p. 5). The demands for de-professionalism today may be an indication that some form of examination of the problem may be in order. If the past is to be a guide, the demand for the repeal of licensing laws is merely a barometer indicating that enormous power has been accumulated in the hands of a few which many claim is being abused.

BIBLIOGRAPHY

Aronson, Sidney H., *Status and Kinship in the Higher Civil Service* (Cambridge, 1964).

Blackard, W. Raymond, "The Demoralization of the Legal Profession in nineteenth century America," in *Tennessee Law Review* (Vol. 16, 1940).

Boorstin, Daniel J., *The Americans: The Colonial Experience* (New York, 1958 ed.).

Calhoun, Daniel H., *Professional Lives in America: Structure and Aspiration, 1750-1850* (Cambridge, Mass., 1965).

Circular Letter (A) to the Practitioners of Physic and Surgery in the State of New-York from the Practitioners of Physic and Surgery in the County and City of New-York . . . with a Memorial intended to be submitted to the Legislature of the State of New-York (New York, 1829).

Chroust, Anton-Herman, *The Rise of the Legal Profession in America* (Norman, Okla., 1965), Vol. 2.

Coventry, Charles B., "The history of medical legislation in the State of New York," in *The New York Journal of Medicine,* Vol. 4 (March, 1845).

Daedalus, "The Professions," Fall, 1963.

Davis, Nathan S., *Contributions to the history of medical education* (Washington, 1877).

Fitz, Reginald H., "Legislative Control (The) of Medical Practice," *Boston Medical and Surgical Journal,* Vol. 130 (1894).

Flexner, Abraham, "Medical Education in the United States and Canada," *A Report to the Carnegie Foundation for the Advancement of Teaching,* Bulletin No. 4 (New York, 1910).

Garceau, Oliver, *The Political Life of the American Medical Association* (Hamden, Conn., 1961).

Gawalt, G.W., "Massachusetts Lawyers: A Historical Analysis of the process." Doctoral dissertation, Clark University, 1969(University Microfilm).

Hartz, Louis, *Economic Policy and Democratic Thought: Pennsylvania, 1776-1860* (Cambridge, 1948).

Hugins, Walter, *Jacksonian Democracy and the Working Class: A Study of the New York Workingmen's Movement, 1829-1837* (Stanford, 1960).

Kett, Joseph F., *The Formation of the American Medical Profession: The Role of Institutions, 1780-1860* (New Haven, 1968).

Proceedings of the American Bar Association, 1877-1890.

Reed, Alfred Z., *Training for the public profession of the law* (New York, 1921).

Robinson, Frederick, *Letter to the Hon. Rufus Choate, Containing A Brief Exposure of Law Craft* (Boston, 1832).

Rosenberg, Charles E., *The Cholera Years* (Chicago, 1962).

Shafer, Henry B., *The American Medical Profession* (New York, 1936).

State of New York, *Assembly Documents,* Number 62, February 11, 1843.
    Assembly Documents, Number 68, February 1, 1844.

Shryock, Richard, *Medical Licensing in America, 1650-1965* (Baltimore, 1967).
    Medicine and Society in America, 1660-1860 (New York, 1960).
    Medicine in America: Historical Essays (Baltimore, 1966).

Stevens, Rosemary, *American Medicine and the Public Interest* (New Haven, 1971).

Transactions of the American Medical Association, 1870-1885.

THE HUMANISTIC PROFESSIONAL:
THE REORIENTATION
OF ARTISTIC PRODUCTION

Clinton R. Sanders
and
Eleanor Lyon

INTRODUCTION

Professionalism involves the creation and maintenance of an exclusionary mystique. Protected by definitional and organizational boundaries, the professional enjoys the security afforded by the possession of knowledge or skills which are perceived by the client public as necessary and valuable. The lay public accepts the mystique promulgated by the professional group, thereby participating in the maintenance of professional power. As Hobbes succinctly stated, "Reputation of power is power."

Even the most cursory review of the sociological literature on professions (e.g., Greenwood, 1957; Gross, 1958; Perrucci and Gerstl, 1969) reveals the difficulty of agreeing upon a list of characteristics which distinguish a profession from other occupational groups. As Roth (1974) persuasively maintains, this search for a definitional list has drawn attention away from more critical problems of professionalization, among which are lack of accountability to clientele, monopolization of skills, accrual of political power, and manipulation of access to training in order to insure service scarcity.

All institutions, organizations, and occupational groups develop stories which are designed to present themselves and their activities in the best possible light (Becker, 1974). In order to maintain this often tenuous facade, the members interact to develop perspectives and ideologies which justify their status and exclusionary position. This organizational boundary-setting is most apparent in those highly educated occupational groups — lawyers, physicians, clergy, and university professors — which have traditionally been labelled professions.

43

A common thread running through most discussions of professional attributes is that, at base, professionalization is a process of self-labelling. Professions are those occupational groups that can successfully convince the public of the societal necessity of their skills and the "rightness" of their authority. The maintenance of this authority rests upon control of access to and utilization of the "essential" skills and upon codes of conduct which emphasize public service.

As a group, artists have historically asserted that their particular skills are as essential to social health as those of the accepted professions (Kaelin, 1972: 380). Their claim to exclusivity has at its core the quasi-mystical concept of artistic creativity. To the artistic professional:

> Art is the home of individuality and creativity, the arena of human activity in which people of great genius create extraordinary works of great beauty and originality expressing a unique ability in such a way as to provoke in an audience memorable emotional experiences (Becker, 1974).

Armed with this potent talisman of "innate creativity," professional artists, like their counterparts in the established professions, have successfully insulated themselves from a broadly based public.

The artistic professions have not escaped the scrutiny which an increasingly aware public has been focusing on professional groups since the mid-1960's, when the legitimacy of power and exclusionary practices in many settings began to be increasingly questioned (see, for example, Simmons and Winograd, 1966: 12-14; Reeves, 1974). Consequently, we are seeing the emergence of a new artistic perspective which challenges the traditional artistic ideology and the dominance of established artistic institutions. The emerging perspective stresses participation over exclusion, relevance over "art-for-art's-sake" mystification and creative participation over isolated production.

In the following discussion we present the developing attitudes, perceptions and activities of the new, humanistic, artistic professional.[1] We

[1] We have employed the label "humanistic" to encapsulate the new artist's emphasis upon his/her relationship with the public and the demystifying view that all human beings have artistic potential. While not completely "new" historically, these concerns reflect a departure from conventional patterns in the artistic professions and are more pervasive and widespread than in previous manifestations. The relationship between this perspective and the "avant-garde" will be discussed later in the paper.

While it may not be immediately observable in all artistic enterprises, especially those adhering to traditional expressive forms (e.g., symphony orchestras or classical ballet companies), we maintain that this new artistic perspective is having significant impact on the art world in general.

have chosen to draw our examples primarily from painting and theater. Not only is the new artistic perspective most observable and well-documented in these two areas, but they are activities with which we are most familiar. In addition to material culled from a wide variety of writings by and about artists, data for this discussion are taken from studies of artistic production conducted by the authors during the past four years. These studies have focused on traditional and avant-garde theater groups (Lyon, 1974), comic artists (Sanders, forthcoming) and urban outreach efforts of art museums. Further information was provided by numerous interview conversations conducted with working artists, gallery directors and art teachers over the past year. Our purpose is to present a coherent picture of an emerging perspective on artistic production and dissemination which is having significant and, in our view, valuable impact upon the traditionally elitist and insulated art world.

THE TRADITIONAL ARTISTIC PROFESSIONAL

The label "artist" is variously and broadly applied, ranging from those individuals whose occupational time is entirely devoted to primary artistic production through those "Sunday painters" for whom artistic activity is an enjoyable means of filling leisure time (Foster, 1974a). The "professional artist" presented here defines him/herself as professional (i.e., seriously engaged in the production of art), creates art works for monetary renumeration as an occupational activity and is aware of a colleague group which evaluates her/his work and defines the producer as professional.[2] This definition covers both the "serious" artist for whom art is a calling and the "commercial" artist who views art more instrumentally — i.e., primarily as a tool to achieve monetary and status rewards (Foster, 1974a; Griff, 1968; Griff, 1964; Strauss, 1970).

A major aspect of the traditional artistic role is its social isolation. The artist commonly presents her/himself and is seen by the public as being set apart from the social mainstream. A variety of studies of artistic occupations (e.g., Rosenberg and Fliegel, 1970; Griff, 1968) have noted this disjunction. Herbert Read (1966:71) maintains that the artist is "the individual endowed with exceptional sensibilities and exceptional

---

[2] This definition of the artistic professional is commonly employed; see, for example, Merriam, 1964: 124-125.

facilities of apprehension (who) stands in psychological opposition . . . to the people . . .'' This point of view is commonly referred to as the ''cult of creativity.''

Artists' experience with specialized art educational institutions plays an important part in encouraging their sense of uniqueness and separation from their ''non-artistic'' peers. In his outstanding study of art students, Griff (1968) emphasizes that those who later choose to participate in formal art education learn early in their educational careers that being identified as possessing artistic talent has distinct and satisfying rewards:

> The public-school art teachers begin to exert their influence quite early in the career of the artist, generally in grammar school. Impoverished or misguided though their teaching may be, they may introduce the youngster to the satisfactions and delights of drawing and painting. These teachers serve to keep interest in art alive throughout the school years by bestowing approval upon the child, singling him out for special honors, placing his work in public view, or assigning him honorific tasks . . . (Griff, 1968: 148)

Within the specialized milieu of the art school the student learns more than the knowledge and techniques of her/his chosen career. He/she is also socialized into the perspective of the traditional artist, learning what artists are and do. Individualism is stressed both explicitly and implicitly, leading the student to become committed to the value of the artist's unique vision.

This sense of specialness is further reinforced by the practical difficulties of pursuing the ''ideal'' art career. For many young artists, formal art training promotes serious anxiety. The educational process builds rather unrealistic occupational expectations and goals. The art initiate comes to value serious, non-commercial art production as her/his ideal calling, while the structure of the serious art market system drastically limits the availability of positions to which the young artist aspires.

Griff focuses on the difficult career decisions which face the young artist at the conclusion of his/her sojourn in art school. Basically, three art alternatives are conventionally available: a career in art education, artistic production for overtly commercial purposes, or the creation of ''serious'' art products which are distributed to collectors and investors through the tightly controlled and highly selective channels of the art market system. This last alternative is the most valued as the ''true'' calling of the professional artist. Yet, the traditional art market has room for only a small percentage of those who desire this route to artistic success. Most aspirants accept non-art jobs which allow them sufficient time to continue to engage in isolated creation until they either "break into" the world of "serious" artists or they are sufficiently disheartened to accept "secondary" art occupations in educational or commercial settings. Because of the difficulties of pursuing the ideal career, those few individuals who do successfully enter the serious art market view themselves as belonging to the artistic elect.

While it may not provide significant economic rewards for the not-yet-established artist, the artistic role does provide other advantages. The "unique" character of the role carries over into the area of behavioral expectations. "Outlandish" or eccentric behavior on the part of artists is accepted and even implicitly encouraged, both by the public and the art community, as the natural expression of their special sensibilities. One highly experienced actor interviewed spoke for many of her fellows in describing their special license:

> Theater people are less inhibited, they care less about what the neighbors think. And they enjoy the freedom that that allows. They're *consciously* different from their neighbors, maybe. But it's seen as OK, because they're actors.

In sum, the traditional artistic professional sees her/himself and is seen by others as set apart from the rest of society. The mystique of creativity surrounds and is accepted by the artist, fostered through early special treatment, a special arts education where he/she is socialized into techniques, sensibilities and behavior appropriate to the particular art world, and the practical difficulties involved in sustaining a commitment to professional artistic activity.

With the technologically impelled rise of industrial society and the associated consumer culture, art, as another product to be consumed, has been increasingly tied to a market system. The artist has come to depend upon established economic interests to whom art represents a worthwhile investment (Pellegrini, 1966: 299-301; Elkoff, 1960; Lahr, 1969). Wealthy backers.[3] foundations, businesses, and industries pro-

---

[3] Even in fund-raising drives for the local symphony, ballet, opera, or resident theater company, where broad-based public support is solicited, the bulk of the funds are obtained from relatively few large donors (Baumel and Bowen, 1966: 319).

vide support for the larger, more established artistic institutions primarily out of a desire for economic gain (direct and as a tax write-off) and the social status which accrues to the "patron of the arts" (Reiss, 1968: 89; Chagy, 1970: 61). This direct economic dependence of art upon the business and financial community has an irresistible conservatizing influence upon the form and content of contemporary mainstream art (Herman, 1965: 126-128; Poggi, 1968: *passim*.). In fact some business-originated grants and donations are explicitly impelled by awareness of the potential contribution of the arts to the maintenance of "social order." [4]

The artist's valued creative independence is further limited by the control exerted by the intellectual elite upon whom the artist depends for appreciation and encouragement.[5] Literature on the arts frequently distinguishes those among the public who "understand" art from those who do not (Ortega, 1948: 5-6; Rosenberg and Fliegel, 1970; Rosenberg, 1969: 200). Some artistic activities (e.g., painting and sculpture) are increasingly focused on esoteric technical and formal aesthetic concerns. The knowledgeable critic/expert interprets and evaluates art works for those who seek secure investment or who maintain a status-based interest in the art world.

Whereas the more esoteric arts rely primarily upon individual support through grants or investments, the performing arts depend as well on continuing support from larger numbers of the public. Here the critic is very powerful, acting as a cultural "opinion leader" (Katz and Lazarsfeld, 1955). In this role, the critic informs the interested public about which productions represent the most efficient use of entertainment time and identifies formulae which are most marketable (Hersch, 1972). The critic's power is most apparent in the primary market centers. A few critics in New York, for example, have the power to determine whether

---

[4] This is clearly seen with regard to theater in the following excerpts from a speech delivered in 1969 to a meeting of the Rand Corporation (quoted more fully in Baxandall, 1969: 53, 56):

> Traditionally . . . social dramaticism . . . has been a key and vital bulwark of government.

> . . . Our supremacy on the terrain of social dramaticism . . . constitutes the holding corporation through which our otherwise scanty personal powers secure the property order of society generally.

[5] In that the university often acts as an employer of successful artists, the relationship with the intellectual community may be economic as well as evaluational (Kaelin, 1972: 371).

or not performances of a given play on Broadway will continue (Goldman, 1969: 84; Little and Cantor, 1971: 235). Critics' power has a conservatizing influence on the determination of which plays will be selected for production, as seen in the following actor's complaint:

> If just a handful of men can sit out there . . . and totally wipe out a million dollars in one night, people are going to quit taking a chance. And they *have* quit taking chances. They're now doing revivals of revivals and things they feel pretty sure of.

The relationship between the traditional artist and the economic and critical elite is potentially conflictive. While the traditional artist recognizes the interpretive importance of the elite, he/she — as would any other professional — resents the control exerted by the public. However she/he seems to accept this control as a (frequently repugnant) fact of artistic life, and continues to seek success within the system. Many, like the following actor, do not seem to perceive any realistic choice: "We aren't any of us here . . . able to pick and choose . . . You work to pay the rent, you know, and you do whatever comes along."

For the traditional artist, success is rooted in the product-oriented competitive system, which is similar to other consumer markets. Success is found in the positive evaluation of critics and other evaluators and in representation in the traditional art temples, such as major museums, influential galleries, and Broadway theaters. These temples are supported by and designed to serve the elite. As a consequence, they present major barriers to the development of a broad-based public. Public expectations of appearance and demeanor appropriate to temples, as well as the price of admission, also act as barriers.

We have seen, then, that traditional artists accept and perpetuate the exclusionary mystique surrounding artistic activity, reinforced by formal arts training and public perceptions of artists. With their individualistic orientation and their dependence upon the financial and critical elite, their art works are most often directed toward the market, a select group of peers, or their own satisfaction (art for art's sake), rather than being motivated by broader social concerns. Traditional professional artists, finally, have adopted elite-based criteria for success and are resigned to working within the existing market structure. We now move to consideration of the emerging new, humanistic, artistic professional whose values, perceptions, and activities differ significantly from those outlined above.

THE NEW ARTISTIC PROFESSIONAL

In contrast to the traditional artistic professionals, those we are calling "new artists" seek to demystify public perceptions of artists and their activities. To this end they are often involved in collective production, express a desire for public participation, actively seek independence from elite arts institutions and engage in experimentation with a variety of genres with a broadly defined political context (Tax, 1972: 26-27; Chalupecky, 1969: 89).[6]

The new artists do not view themselves as essentially different from other members of the community. Instead, they emphasize art as an activity and skill rather than as a product which flows from the mystical fountain of innate creativity. Although the organization of theatrical endeavors and a history of union battles would seem to encourage actors' demystification of their activities, the following actor's view is at odds with the "exceptional" self-conceptions of her more traditionally-oriented fellows and well represents the emerging perspective:

> You can go on about being artists forever, but the management is making money off our talents and we have to have a union. . . . Without actors the theater does not exist and it is your labor with your body that makes the profit possible. And so it's the same as steel workers or anything else.

As we saw in the previous section, specialized training is central to the socialization process whereby the traditional artist acquires the attitudes and values which are characteristic of her/his professional perspective. In addition, formal art education introduces the artist to the various conventions which are traditionally utilized.

Many new artists feel this formal training process neglects other necessary aspects of artistic knowledge. Artists who are formally

---

[6] This broad range of divergence from the traditional artistic perspective differentiates the contemporary humanistic from "avant-garde" artists who have historically existed on the margins of the art world. While the French avant-garde at the turn of the century, for example, evidenced collaboration and experimentation in a variety of genres and created a temporary counter-establishment mechanism for exhibiting their work, they perpetuated the cult of creativity and did not define their work within a context of social change (see Shattuck, 1968). Further, the new artistic perspective presented in this discussion is manifested today in urban areas throughout the Western world rather than being confined to a few specific cultural centers such as Paris, London or New York.

Our conceptualization of the new humanistic artist is informed by Bucher and Strauss's (1961) discussion of "segments" within professions. They maintain that "segments" are identifiable collegial groups, similar to social movements, which espouse particular objectives, priorities, and modes of organization.

trained are commonly seen as rigidly traditional, employing technical skills to the exclusion of feeling, as in the following quote from an interview:

> I've met a number of [local drama school]-trained actors and they're crippled . . . personally and emotionally, too . . . What they do to you . . . is teach you to be a text-book; they don't teach you to be human out there on stage.

Another actor clearly outlined in an interview the resulting conflict, as he saw it, between those who value discipline and technique and the new artists' emphasis on energy, enthusiasm, and experimentation:

> People who work most of the time in very traditional, sort of establishment type theaters, have a concept of people who are doing other things, what is called experimental theater . . . as a bunch of . . . well, one term that's used a lot is "sweat and grunt experimental theater." "They just go out there and play around and they don't really know what they're doing . . . and they're not good craftsmen and they shouldn't be in the business" type of thing. People in experimental theater . . . very often have this concept of "those plastic assholes up there on a traditional stage. They're all technique and tricks and skill and they have no real spontaneity or warmth in their performances. They're just skilled craftsmen who punch in and go out there and read their lines."

The new artists are further attempting to lower barriers which separate the public from the artist and his/her product by employing themes and artistic approaches which are familiar and speak to the everyday, human concerns of the public. One author calls this reorientation "liberation" in speaking of a theater company:

> Part of this liberation is in their use of images from the collective conscious and subconscious of ordinary people . . . where other groups and movements . . . have taken their images from art and literature so that their presentations have often been accessible only to intellectuals and critics (Fox, 1972: 3).

A new mode of artistic production is commonly employed by new artists. Rather than stressing the individuated and specialized creative act, they favor cooperative and collective activity, valuing the creative process as much as the final product.

A common social activity of underground comic artists, for example, is the "jam session" in which collaborative comic strips are produced as each artist embellishes or takes off from the work of the previous artist (see Estren, 1974: 222-225). While this pattern is encountered in a variety of other art forms, it is perhaps most often seen in the performing arts (Shank, 1972: 3).

Most of the alternative or experimental theather companies studied by one of the authors worked collectively. This involved a departure from the traditional theatrical division of labor, meaning that actors participated in technical aspects of preparation for performances (building sets, finding or constructing props and constumes, etc) as well as their on-stage activities.[7] Decisions ranging from play selection to determing the approach to a particular play were often made collectively, as well. Although this frequently led to conflict-laden rehearsal seesions, most of those involved valued the collective process enough to continue. Some experimental companies have also tried eliminating the role of director, but found that someone usually assumed the position informally (Shank, 1972: passim.; Rea, 1972). Collectivity in these companies extends to financial matters, too, in that income from the box office is shared equally among members after production costs are met, and priority expenditures are determined democratically — a stark contrast to the powerlessness often felt in these matters by actor in the traditional situation.

Emphasis on the artistic process rather than the final product is also found in action painting, "enviornmental" art works (Rosenberg, 1972:36 and passim.), multi-media "happenings" (Kirby, 1965), conceptual art (Bongarts, 1974) and improvisational theather, which enjoyed a recurrence of popularity in the mid-1960's.

At the same time as it emphasizes the "de-elition" of the artist's self-perceptions and the themes she/he employs, the new artistic perspective stressed the inherent intelligence and capability of the public. This concern is demonstrated by the current emphasis upon audience involvement in artistic creation and presentation (Shank, 197:7; Tax, 1972:26; Shank, 1974:111; Suvin, 1969:30). In this light the approved role of the artist is tearing down the barriers which have traditionally (and artifically) separated the artistic producer from the consuming public. The central message of the new art is that all people are potential artists and possess the resources to create and appreciate art. As Halprin (1968:164) states: "(The artist) is no longer a solitary hero figure, but rather a guide who works to evoke the art within us all."

[7] This departure from the conventional division of labor may also be found in small experimental dance companies.

Success, as defined by the traditional art professional, entails positive public evaluation of her/his products by critics and other "legitimate" experts, in volvement in established artistic insitutuions, and substantial monetary gain. The new artist, on the other hand, employs different criteria of success, emphasizing control over the nature and focus of the creative process rather than the financial and reputational rewards which may accrue to the final product. It is recognized that there is commonly a direct relationship between the extent of the financial reward the the control which those who support the arts (agents, patrons, granting agencies, etc.) exert over the artistic product and the creative process. When asked to give a personal definition of success, one interviewed actor spoke for many when he succinctly replied ". . . doing what I want to do and making a living at it."

The disjunction between market-generated and personal criteria of success is particularly evident in underground comic art. Underground artists are predominantly anti-establishmentarian and distrustful of the standard market-based criteria of artistic success. These artists, like new artists in other media, feel that success in the traditional sense requires the abdication of artistic control. This relationship between success and external control is viewed with some amusement by Harvey Kurtzman, an established overground comic artis (Estren, 1974:256);

> You've got this paradox — yes, you do your best work when you don't have conditions, but when you become part of the 'establishmen' of sucess, you unavoidably inherit the conditions of that establishment, i.e., the easy life, formula work, material possession.

Most new artistic professionals realize that art opportunities are so limited at present that considerations of economic survival commonly lead to involvement with distasteful commercial endeavors. The often emotional conflict induced by the choice between two repellent alternatives is clearly seen in an excert from one of the authors' field notes. A number of actors had just attended a shoddy commercial production and left the theater devastated. After screaming for a time out of fear and frustration, they tried to talk about their reactions to the performance:

A. I think I'd rather drive a cab. What about you, B?
B. Don't make me choose, I'd rather be on unemployment. I couldn't take it.
C. Oh you'll be in shows like that.
B. Nooo!!
C. I'm sure you will.

Success, as defined by the new, humanistic, artistic professional requires independence from the elite art institutions and evaluators who are commonly courted by traditional artists. It is felt that the majority of the contemporary established art temples are unnecessary and even moribund. A member of an experimental theater company rejected the traditional standard of talent and success (appearance on Broadway — Theater's "art temple") when he asserted, "All you're judging is your commercial viability; you're not judging your talent by going to the fucking New York market . . . New York theater is moribund . . ." Another actor expressed his dissatisfaction with the character of major theatrical center in anti-professional terms:

> I think this is the age of the amateur again. Like professionalism is at a low. That's What's wrong with Broadway — it's just professional now. The professional actors and the professional writers and professional directors, and it's not exciting. You need to get people who don't know the rules.

In order to obtain independence, new artists are increasingly engaged in developing new artistic institutions which reflect the concerns of the new art. One clear example of the development of alternative institutions is seen in the newly established Radical Theater Repertory, which handles bookings and publicity for a variety of counter-cultural theather groups across the country. The purpose of RTR is expressed by co-founder Oda Jurges:

> Some parallel institution was needed to help these groups evade commercial pressures and to give some kind of organizational background to the radical theater movement.[8]

Other examples of this phenomenon are seen in the growth of production and distribution cooperatives in the area of underground art (Estren, 1974: 247-253), union-like organizations of painters and the rise of journals such as The Cultural Activist (New York) which are devoted to new art values.

In addition to developing new institutions designed to counterbalance the power of traditional artistic organizations and associations, a number of artists are committed to the significant alteration of policies in existing institutions to better serve the needs and interests of the community. The art museum, for example, has been a major target.

[8] From an interview with Saul Gottlieb and Oda Jurges printed in *The Drama Review,* 13 (Summer, 1969), p. 80.

Artist Allan Kaprow (1967) denounces museums as "fuddy-duddy remnant(s) from another era" which "should be turned into swimming pools and night clubs . . . or . . . emptied and left as environmental scultpure."

Understandably, museum personnel are unwilling to take as radical a step as Kaprow proposes. However, some museums are attempting to alter their exclusionary image by facilitating public access. One such group is the Department of Urban Outreach of a major art museum. Organized in 1971, the DUO is:

> Dedicated to extending the experience of art . . . Its basic goal is to make the encounter with art a more familiar experience and to foster the growth of awareness and creative talent inherent in every individual . . .

To this end, the Department of Urban Outreach has developed a program which entails opening the museum for the exclusive use of those members of the urban community who have traditionally had little museum experience. In addition, the DUO has mounted a vital outreach program — reflecting the other major concern of new artists: to get art out of the exclusive museum context — which provides neighborhood groups with the expertise and advice they might need to integrate art with everyday community life. Striking wall murals designed and executed by community members which reflect the experiences and concerns of urban life are the most visible outcome of this project.

Further instances of contemporary efforts to bring art directly to the public are seen in the travelling museum (a train touring the small communities of the South and Mid-west with painting and sculpture and providing an opportunity to see artists at work), televised programs in which conductors explain symphonic music to children and interested adults, and documentary films proposed by artists demonstrating art in the making.

Guerilla and street theater also aim to bring artistic experience out of the institutional setting, and more directly reflect new artists' concern with social change. As one of the contemporary pioneers of guerilla theater maintains:

> The motives, aspirations and practice of U.S. theater must be readapted in order to teach, direct toward change, be an example of change . . . It is necessary to direct toward change because 'the system' is debilitating, repressive, and non-aesthetic (Davis, 1966: 131; see also Brecht, 1967; and Lesnick, 1973: 25).

This reorienting emphasis upon the social change utility of art is a self-conscious reaction to the traditional "art-for-art's sake" belief that art has no real spiritual or social consequence (Ortega, 1948: 8-14). This perspective is repellent to a growing number of practicing artists, who see it as removing art from an ethical, humanistic context (Tax, 1972: 16-17). The new artist is committed to incorporating art into the everyday growth experience of the society, "foreseeing a society in which there is room for play, in which art and entertainment and enjoyment are an integral part of daily life . . . " (Fox, 1972: 3).

The artist's position as an agent of social change has historical roots in the image of the artist as rebel, outcast, or social misfit. This image has been fostered by some traditional artists because of the commonly perceived link between creativity and deviance (Becker, 1963: 79-119; Hatterer, 1965: 34; Read, 1966: 117; Foster, 1974b; Gombrowicz, 1970). New artists gladly accept the label of "rebel," not because of its power to isolate from the social mainstream, but because of their concern with the precipitation of significant social change.

Finally, the "slick" finished quality of the art produced by traditional artistic professionals is looked upon unfavorably by the new artist. It is felt that a finely polished product encourages an unnatural and debilitating stasis. The rough edges of reality are polished off, new artists feel, in a desire to construct a pseudo-realistic product which is easily marketable:

> Professionalism and its price . . . all this ridiculous self-concern makes for the kind of show business that we have inherited . . . It wants to make something . . . tremendously smooth and balanced and fitting the occasion and fitting the enlightened stage or just the upholstered seat (Taylor, 1972: 262).

In order to avoid the creation or presentation of a traditionally polished ("plastic") product, new artists commonly emphasize spontaneous creative activities, improvisation, direct audience participation, and other techniques which ensure a loose artistic structure. It is essential that the member of the public is always aware that the work of art he/she is experiencing is produced by human beings essentially like her/himself. Art, they maintain, is ideally an interaction, a dialogue in which the humanity of the creators is clearly apparent. They seek art in which the old barriers between the producer and the consumer are broken down and which acts as a focal point for the development of community (Shank, 1974: 111; Kaelin, 1972: 380-381).

CONCLUSION

The activity of the new artistic professional is typified by demystification of creativity and the creative role, and by an increasing emphasis upon the development of alternative artisitic institutions. Those who are committed to the new artistic vision remain a distinct, but highly vocal, minority. While their impact is seen in a wide variety of artistic activities, co-optation is common and numerous problems remain. Poggi's (1968: 282) commentary on theater is echoed by the new artistic professional in other fields.

> The basic problem of the noncommercial theatre — how to achieve professional growth and economic stability without being absorbed by the established theatre — has not been solved.

New, humanistic artists, therefore, face the same problem of cooptation and conservatizing institutionalization which are encountered by their counterparts in other professionally related social movements.

BIBLIOGRAPHY

Baumol, William J. and William G. Bowen (1966), *Performing Arts – The Economic Dilemma*, Cambridge, Mass: M.I.T. Press.

Baxandall, Lee (1969), "Dramaturgy of Radical Activity," *The Drama Review*, 13 (Summer), 52-71.

Becker, Howard S. (1974), "Art as Collective Action," *American Sociological Review*, 39 (December), 767-776.

_____ (1963), *Outsiders: Studies in the Sociology of Deviance*, New York: Free Press.

Bongartz, Roy (1974), "Question: How do you Buy a Work of Art Like This?" *New York Times*, August 11.

Brecht, Bertolt (1967), "Theatre for Learning or Theatre for Pleasure," in James Hall and Barry Ulanov, eds., *Modern Culture and the Arts*, New York: McGraw-Hill, 305-316.

Bucher, Rue and Anselm Strauss (1961), "Professions in Process," *American Journal of Sociology*, 66 (January), 325-334.

Chagy, Gideon (1970), "Business in the Arts: Forms of Support," in G. Chagy, ed., *Business in the Arts '70*, New York: Paul Eriksson.

Chalupecky, Jindrich (1969), "Literature and Freedom," *Evergreen Review*, 13 (July), 51ff.

Davis, R.G. (1966), "Guerilla Theatre," *Tulane Drama Review,* 10 (Summer), 130-136.

Elkoff, Marvin (1960), "The American Painter as a Blue Chip," *Esquire Magazine,* reprinted in Milton Albrecht, et. al., eds., *The Sociology of Art and Literature: A Reader,* New York: Praeger, 499-517.

Estren, Mark James (1974), *A History of Underground Comics,* San Francisco: Straight Arrow.

Foster, Arnold (1974a), "The Dissident Trinity: Three Roles of the Artist," paper presented at the 44th annual meeting of the Eastern Sociological Society, Philadelphia.

(1974b), "The Slow Revolutionary: Role Restrictions on the Artist as a Change Agent," paper presented at the annual meetings of the American Sociological Association, Montreal.

Fox, John (1972), "Theatre to Liberate Fantasies," *Theatre Quarterly,* 2 (October-December), 3-17.

Goldman, William (1969), *The Season,* New York: Bantam.

Gombrowicz, Witold (1970), "On Art and Revolution," *The Drama Review,* 14, 102-112.

Greenwood, E. (1957), "Attributes of a Profession," *Social Work,* 2 (July), 45-55.

Griff, Mason (1968), "The Recruitment and Socialization of Artists," in David Sills, ed., *International Encyclopedia of the Social Sciences,* 447-454, Reprinted in Milton Albrecht, et. al., ed., *The Sociology of Art and Literature: A Reader,* New York: Praeger, 145-158.

(1964), "Conflicts of the Artist in Mass Society," *Diogenes,46 (Summer),* 54-68.

Gross, E. (1958), *Work and Society,* New York: Thoman Y. Crowell.

Halprin, Ann (1968), "Myths," *The Drama Review,* 13 (fall), 163-175.

Hatterer, Lawrence J. (1965), *The Artist in Society,* New York: Grove Press.

Herman, William (1965), "Theatre as Enterprise," *Tulane Drama Review,* 10 (Fall), 110-135.

Hirsch, Paul M. (1972), "Processing Fads and Fashions: An Organization-Set Analysis of Culture Industry Systems," *American Journal of Sociology,* 77 (January), 639-659.

Kaelin, Eugene (1972), "The Social Uses of Art: A Plea for the Institution," *Arts in Society,* 9, 370-386.

Kaprow, Allan (1967), "Death in the Museum," *Arts Magazine,* 12 (February).

Katx, Elihu and Paul Lazarsfeld (1955), *Personal Influence,* Glencoe, Ill.: Free Press.

Kirby, Michael (1965), ed., *Happenings,* New York: Dutton.

Lahr, John (1969), "The Arts and Business," *Evergreen Review,* 13 (July), 64ff.

Lesnick, Henry, (1973), ed., *Guerilla Street Theater,* New York: Avon.

Little, Stuart and Arthur Cantor (1971), *The Playmakers,* New York: Dutton.

Lyon, Eleanor (1974), "Work and Play: Resource Constraints in a Small Theater," *Urban Life and Culture,* 3 (April), 71-97.

Merriam, Alan P. (1964), *The Anthropology of Music,* Evanston, Ill.: Northwestern University Press.

Ortega y Gasset, Jose (1948), *The Dehumanization of Art,* Princeton: Princeton University Press.

Pellegrini, Aldo (1966), *New Tendencies in Art,* New York: Crown.

Perrucci, R. and Joel Gerstl (1969), *Profession Without Community: Engineers in American Society,* New York: Random House.

Poggi, Jack (1968), *Theater in America: The Impact of Economic Forces, 870-967,* Ithaca New York: Cornell University Press.

Rea, Charlotte (1972), "Women's Theatre Groups," *The Drama Review,* 16 (June), 79-89.

Read, Herbert (1966), *Art and Society,* New York: Schocken.

Reeves, Richard (1974), "The Trouble with Lawyers: The Case of James St. Clair," *New York Magazine,* 7 (July), 27-31.

Reiss, Alvin H. (1968), "Who Builds Theatres and Why?" *The Drama Review,* 12 (Spring), 75-92.

Rosenberg, Bernard and Norris Fliegel (1970), "The Artist and His Publics: The Ambiguity of Success," in Milton Albrecht, et. al., ed., *The Sociology of Art and Literature: A Reader,* New York: Preager.

Rosenberg, Harold (1972), *The De-Definition of Art,* New York: Collier.

(1969), *Artworks and Packages,* New York: Dell.

Roth, Julius A. (1974), "Professionalism: The Sociologist's Decoy," *Sociology of Work and Occupations,* 1 (February), 6-23.

Sanders, Clinton R. (forthcoming), "Icons of the Alternate Culture: Themes and Functions of Underground Comix," *Journal of Popular Culture.*

Shank, Theodore (1974), "Political Theatre: The San Francisco Mime Troop," *The Drama Review,* 18 (March), 110-117.

(1972), "Collective Creation," *The Drama Review,* 16 (June), 79-89.

Shattuck, Roger (1968), *The Banquet Years,* New York: Vintage.

Simmons, J.I. and Barry Winograd (1966), *It's Happening,* Santa Barbara, Cal.: Marc-Laird Publications.

Strauss, Anselm (1970), "The Art School and Its Interpretation," in Milton Albrecht, et. al., ed., *The Sociology of Art and Literature: A Reader,* New York: Praeger.

Suvin, Darko (1969), "Organizational Meditation," *The Drama Review,* 13 (Summer), 26-42.

Tax, Meredith (1972), "Introductory: Culture is not Neutral, Whom Does It Serve?" in Lee Baxandal, Ed., *Radical Perspectives in the Arts,* Baltimore, Md.: Penguin.

Taylor, Karen Malpede (1972), *People's Theatre in America,* New York: Drama Book Specialists.

SOCIAL CHANGE AND THE ATHLETE[1]

Richard N. Juliani

In recent years, the world of professional sport in America has been literally rocked by a series of events which would have been unthinkable in earlier years. In particular, the open expression of radical dissent and acts of rebellion by athletes have become common features of the professional sport scene. In the past, individual athletes, from Babe Ruth to Duane Thomas, occasionally rebelled; in rare instances, even a group of athletes may have displayed some "ad hoc" resistence to a particular, concrete crisis. But always such events represented a departure from the normal routine of professional sport. The traditional submissiveness of athletes as a group has also "spoiled" many American fans into a complacent expectation that regular season schedules must begin nearly as a matter of natural law.

But today we have witnessed an unprecedented explosion of organized, collective dissent and revolution on the part of professional athletes. Both major league baseball and football, perhaps the foundations of professional sport, have been disrupted by threatened strikes. The unity of particular teams has been shattered by disagreements and even outbursts of violence among players holding different viewpoints on these issues. Further, the fragile relationships of owners, managers, and coaches with their players have been aggravated. Numerous players have displayed their discontent by massive defections to precarious new leagues. Owners have retaliated against the organizing efforts of players by summarily releasing or trading veterans.

Much to the chagrin of anxious fans, the current troubles (and uncertain future) have revealed, without any question, that the social structure of professional sport contains the same inherent potential for con-

[1] I would like to thank my colleagues, Joel E. Gerstl and Glenn Jacobs, for their constant encouragement as well as their helpful criticisms in preparing this essay. It is important to note that numerous assertions, basic to the argument here, lack adequate documentation. Rather than accepting these points as demonstrated conclusions, the reader should regard them as hypotheses for later research. If this essay provokes criticism which, in turn, generates critical testing and even some rejection of these assertions, the author would welcome and applaud such efforts as genuine contributions to the empirical study of sport.

flict as any other employer-employee situation. The primary purpose of this essay is to explore some of the structural conditions which characterize modern sport and which have simultaneously served as the sources of radical dissent and rebellion among professional athletes. In addition, it is possible to offer some appraisal of future prospects for the continuation and development of these trends toward the radicalization of sport.

The scholarly analysis of athletics as an American institution has, for the most part, only recently begun. We are experiencing a rapid acceleration of interest by historians, social scientists, and social critics in the subject of sport in America (Page, 1973). Parallel to this discovery of sport as a suitable subject for scholarly analysis, and probably of far greater significance for general audiences, a number of popular writers have also begun their own examinations of sport (Bouton, 1970; Flood, 1970; Meggyesy, 1970; Amdur, 1971; Oliver, 1971; Hoch, 1972; Gent, 1973). The latter group, in sharp contrast to the generally dense language and clinical analysis of the intellectual, have emphatically offered clarity as well as critical ideology whether in fiction or non-fiction in the substance and tone of their writings. The result has been a series of essays and books which present an uncomplimentary indictment of sport at all levels.

This growing criticism should not, by itself, be totally surprising, because most of our cherished institutions — organized religion, the democratic state, economic capitalism, the family, and the educational system — have been subjected to extensive criticism in recent years. In fact, social criticism is so much a part of the modern temper that one recalls Henri de St. Simon's assertion that society experiences alternating "organic" and "critical" philosophical periods, and concludes that we are simply in a "critical" period.

But attacks on organized sports by intellectual critics are not new phenomena either; the novel aspect of the current criticism is found in the specific critics. The most salient feature, perhaps, of the new sports-criticism has been the conspicuous part played by the athlete and the former athlete. It is difficult to recall any time when so many "insiders" turned so boldly against the hands which once fed them. There is an obvious sense of betrayal in the writings of Jim Bouton, Dave Meggyesy, Chip Oliver, Curt Flood, and Pete Gent, and the growing list of others. This fact makes their "treason" immeasurably greater in the eyes of many, because these renegades have revealed secret truths which only a select few are ordinarily so privileged to share. It was as if we had bestowed upon them a sacred trust, only to discover in their revelations a world filled with immaturity, corruption, debauchery, and exploitation, a view which so much of the public finds so hard to accept. Simmel has provided some insight into the acerbity of this criticism by his reflections on the "renegade":

> This is particularly true of the renegade because of his sharp awareness that he cannot go back: the old relationship, with which he has irrevocably broken, remains for him, who has a sort of heightened disciminatory sensitivity, the background of the relationship now existing. It is as if he were repelled by the old relationship and pushed into the new one, over and over again (Simmel, 1950).

In short, the former athlete has realized that his playing career is irreversibly over, and as he assumes his new role as critic, he also reveals a unique enthusiasm for disclosure and condemnation.

The emergence of the athlete-critic is largely a function of rapid changes in society which have had repercussions throughout various institutions including sport. Of particular importance are those changes which bear upon the social character of the athlete and upon his relationship to the public. Specifically, several dimensions of change in the relationship of athletics to society in general appear significant: the legitimation of sport as an institution and as an occupational career; the role of the mass media in bringing sport to the public; the development of new patterns of recruitment practices; and, finally, the changing personal character of the contemporary athlete.

The most significant change in professional sport has been its moral integration within American culture. While participation in collegiate athletics has been respectable for quite some time, professional sport existed outside of the boundaries of social acceptability until fairly recently. As late as the 20th century, for example, the lifestyle and individual character of the professional athlete was often regarded as unsavory. The professional athlete was not ordinarily drawn from the ranks of conventional, main-stream families. Hard-working parents of Middle America, caught up in the Protestant Ethic, were not likely to encourage their children to waste too much time developing abilities and skills which could only lead to blind allies (and unrespectable ones at that) in adulthood. Going away to play professional baseball was much like running away to join the circus, primarily a fantasy of immature years. It meant a radical separation from one's family and community in moral as well as physical terms. It meant, in fact, an outright rejection of the norms and values of the conventional community. Consequently, professional sports were dominated by questionable characters and "tough guys" who were hardly the ideal role-models which parents wished their children to emulate. These social definitions became a part of a self-fulfilling prophecy which restricted the recruitment of professional athletes precisely to this undesirable population. The negative image of athletic careers held by Middle Americans served to contain and depress professional sports within the occupational hierarchy of the society. As long as this situation remained intact, so did the low prestige and social backgrounds of professional athletes. At the same time, these conditions should have created a gap in the structure of working opportunities, in which less integrated groups within the American population such as blacks or the foreign born might pursue careers less monopolized and controlled by native Americans. While this consequence did occur in some sports, notably boxing, it is interesting to note that in other sports, such as baseball and football, minority group members were routinely excluded.

But professional athletics began to pass through a great period of re-definition and re-evaluation by the American public, particularly in the period of general social upheaval which followed World War I. During this time, the moral valence attached to professional sports shifted dramatically. From a sociological point of view, the real significance of great athletes such as Jack Dempsey, Gene Tunney, Red Grange, Babe Ruth, Lou Gehrig, and Bobby Jones was their contribution to the moral legitimation of professional sports, both in terms of spectator interest and as occupational careers. But the mass media provided the key role in the cultural diffusion and moral acceptance of professional sports in America. The irony, here, is that the personal character of professional athletes was not changing as quickly as the tendencies of sportswriters in characterizing them. In the 1920's, professional athletes were not much different than they had ever been, but the growth of sports coverage by the media generated a glorifying mystique around them. Under these conditions, professional sports matured into respectable occupations and experienced a new mode of integration with the normative order.

Media coverage began in the newspapers in 1831 with the first of a series of weekly publications devoted entirely to sports.[2] By 1835, the major daily newspapers of New York City covered boxing, racing, track, and other sports. As early as 1862, regular coverage of baseball can be found in the *New York Herald*. William Randolph Hearst, however, is given credit for the radical changes in the newspapers coverage of sport after his purchase of the *New York Journal* in 1895, which created the sports pages as we know them today. Until that time, other papers devoted only three to seven columns to sport news. Hearst introduced as much as a fourfold increase in sports coverage in his daily editions, and innovated the special sports section of his Sunday editions, with a 12 page supplement. He also began to hire well known athletes as sportswriters. The widespread acceptance of sports by the American public was greatly facilitated by the sportswriter, who became both a cause and an effect in this process. As the sports pages became as much an integral feature of the newspapers as obituaries, classified advertisements, and the "funnies," the sports writer thrust athletics into nearly every American home. In the years immediately after World War I, however, a number of changing conditions, such as the return of the veterans; a tremendous spurt of concern by colleges and universities for sport, particularly for football; the prosperity and gaiety of the 1920's; and an unusually talented and colorful group of athletes, destined in many instances to become immortal heroes of the sport scene, generated an explosive resurgence of enthusiasm for sports among Americans. One correlate of these changes was an enormous expansion, again, of the newspaper coverage of sports. A staggering illustration is provided by the 800 newsmen from the United States, South America, Mexico, Cuba, England, France, and Japan who covered the 1923 Dempsey-Firpo fight, with 675,000 words transmitted by Western Union from ringside over 70 leased wires. Three years later, the 1926 Dempsey-Tunney fight produced two million words by the journalists assigned to cover the match. Moreover, by the 1920's, previously neglected sports

---

[2] The discussion on the development of sports coverage in the modern media is primarily a paraphrased summary of an excerpt from Frederick W. Cozens and Florence Scovil Stumpf, *Sports in American Life* (Chicago: University of Chicago Press, 1953) which appeared as "The Sports Page," (pp. 418-432), in John T. Talamini and Charles H. Page, editors, *Sport and Society* (Boston: Little, Brown, 1973). An excellent essay on the general influence of technology on sport is John Rickards Betts "The Technological Revolution and the Rise of Sport, 1850-1900," in M. Marie Hart (ed.) *Sport in the Socio-Cultural Process* (Dubuque, Iowa: 1972) pp. 116-139.

were now routinely reported, and the sports pages had finally become a year round segment of the newspapers.

Soon to follow the sports pages into the American home was the invention and diffusion of electronic communication which complemented the role of the press by providing the unprecedented excitement and suspense of play-by-play broadcasting. In 1899, hired by the Associated Press, Guglielmo Marconi used his recently invented wireless to report a news story for the very first time, and it was, ironically, a sports event, the America Cup challenge race between the English yacht, "Shamrock," and the American boat, "Columbia." Unwittingly, Marconi was opening a monumental chapter in the history of sports in this country. An older device, the telegraph, was also diverted to the transmission of sports news; by 1913, the telegraph was delivering sports reports to the newspapers. In 1916, the Associated Press did the first play-by-play transmission of the baseball World Series without any interruption or delay to the newspapers on its circuit. Twenty years later, on the eve of the Southern Methodist-Standord Rose Bowl game, the Associated Press used the wirephoto to send a special sourvenir edition from Los Angeles to Dallas, the first time that an entire page of a newspaper had ever been transmitted between two cities.

If these two great molders of public opinion and morality, the press and radio, were willing to accept, endorse, and promote sports, how could the rest of the community not do likewise? Moreover, these new sanctions also meant that it was no longer necessary (nor perhaps even possible) for any boy to run away from home, separating himself physically and socially from family and community, to join a professional athletic team. Since the press and radio now allowed him no place to hide, but provided, instead, a position of fame, respect, and honor, he could now become the pride of his local community and, in fact, carry the hopes, dreams, and name of his home town to meet the glamorous challenge of the big city. But an even greater development in the relationship between sport and the mass media remained in the future, one which would, indeed, alter much of the basic nature of sport itself.

On May 17, 1939, Princeton beat Columbia by a score of two to one in a ten inning baseball game, with nothing more at stake between the two teams than fourth place in the Ivy League (Johnson, 1973). Yet, it was truly a historic game and moment for all of sport. For less than one month after it had inaugurated regular television broadcasting, NBC had sent a crew to Columbia's Baker Field to cover this game, the first public telecast of a sports event. Did Columbia leftfielder Ken Pill realize that his home run had a significance, by being the first ever on television, that none by even Babe Ruth or Henry Aaron could ever have? The day of the Tube had arrived.

It is impossible to precisely measure the impact of the mass media upon organized sport in America; however, we can provide some suggestive data.[3] An examination of the television sports scheduling for a single month for an American city such as Philadelphia is rather revealing. Of course, October may not be an ordinary month, but instead an extraordinary month because so much sports activity occurs at that time. But no month is an "ordinary" month since each time of the year has its own peculiar qualities in terms of our social customs. Therefore, October is deliberately chosen because it may be the busiest month for sports, and permits us a certain degree of hyperbole in making the point. In any case, during the month of October, 1973, the Philadelphia television sports viewer had the opportunity to witness a live schedule of 48 hours of professional football; 42 hours of play-off and World Series baseball; five and one-half hours of NHL hockey; and eleven and one-half hours of professional basketball. In addition, there were six more hours of NFL highlights and 20 more hours of college football on film or tape. The calibre of telecast football varied from the Dallas Cowboys vs. the Washington Redskins to Kutztown State College vs. Montclair State College. Roller derby was scheduled for 13 hours; wrestling for twelve and one-half hours; boxing for three hours; and horse racing for one-half hour. The viewer could also watch five hours of pre-game "warm-up" shows; two and one-half hours of exclusively sports news programming; and eight hours of sports "specials" (such as *Wide World of Sports*), all in addition to the sports segment of the regularly scheduled early evening and late night news broadcasts. Every day had at least one sports program; bowling alone was on every day of the month, totaling 29 hours. The sports special brought to the viewer such sports as table tennis, stock car racing, gymnastics, surfing, wheel chair basketball, fencing, track, and roller skating. In addition to all that television offered, radio must not be entirely overlooked. On the first Saturday in October, for example, local radio stations broadcast to

[3] These data were compiled from the television programming on the Sunday and weekday editions of *The Philadelphia Inquirer* for October, 1973.

Philadelphia the baseball playoffs, the feature races from thoroughbred and harness racing tracks in the area, and 10 college and 13 high school football games. The autumn of 1973 also saw several feature films, made for television, which dealt with sport themes: George Plimpton's *The Great Quarterback Sneak; Rookie of the Year,* an afternoon presentation dealing with a young girl's efforts at success and acceptance in the Little Leagues; and *Blood Sport,* an exceptionally candid examination of a "blue-chip" high school football star. Certainly no one could accuse television and radio of ignoring sports in the fall of 1973.

It is difficult to know with absolute certainty what the future holds for the relationship between sports and the mass media. The clues provided by the media are rather ambiguous.[4] The 1974 Super Bowl game attracted 42 percent of all television sets, representing approximately 27,540,000 households across the nation. The 1976 Olympics are expected to produce about $100 million in advertising revenues. The three major commercial networks presently schedule about 1,000 hours a year for all sports, totaling 11 percent of all TV sports in 1964. The much publicized tennis match between Bobby Riggs and Billy Jean King attracted 37 million viewers. Yet, contrary signs are also apparent. The average sports telecast fell from 13 million viewers in 1972 to 12,740,000 in 1973, with significant declines in professional football, college football, professional basketball, and hockey. The only important increase came in the ABC Monday night pro football telecast, with Nielsen ratings up from 18.5 in 1970 to 21.2 in 1973. The World Team Tennis canceled four prime-time national telecasts because of unfavorable ratings and poor financial conditions. Similarly, low ratings have made the National Hockey League reconsider its Sunday national telecasts. Despite the negative trends, the *New York Times* still regards television as the primary factor in the changing economic and social aspects of sports today: "It has stabilized whole leagues, created events and personalities and emerged as an intensely competitive medium that often sells itself as much as its feature attraction." (Amdur, 1974). The *Times* goes on to quote Ronald E. Bain, director of sports for CBS-TV: "From what we've been able to determine, it does not appear that we've reached the saturation point yet." What this paradoxical situation could mean is,

---

[4] The bulk of the information on television and sports in this section comes from Neil Amdur, "Changing Face of U.S. Sports: T.V. Saturation and Its Effects," *The New York Times* (July 23, 1974).

simply, that certain sports are more compatible with television and contemporary tastes, while others are not. Some sports will continue to attract audiences and grow, while others become stagnant or decline. The American public, whether attending in person or vicariously through television, is still trying to sort out its sporting preferences. Consequently, it becomes rather difficult to generalize to all sports.

In addition to this interaction with the media, a parallel process of integration occurred over the same period between the growing popularity of organized sports at all levels and other communal institutions. The moral legitimation of the newer sports of the early 20th century was reflected by their increasing interdependence with respectable community institutions. For instance, baseball leagues sprang up in every small town and large city in the nation; and various local organizations rushed to their material and moral support. Church and civic organizations offered their endorsements of the game through the sponsorship of teams. The high schools adopted baseball as a major spring activity. In amateur leagues, retail merchants enthusiastically provided financial aid in return for the modest acknowledgement and advertisement value of having their commercial names emblazoned on the uniforms. Veterans groups, such as the VFW and the American Legion, offered a moderately sacred sanction to the entire enterprise of amateur baseball, by the establishment of a network of competition which ultimately produced a national champion each year. The minor league system of organized, professional baseball capped a continental complex of community-supported baseball. From coast-to-coast, spilling into Canada and Mexico, literally hundreds of North American towns proudly embraced minor league teams. And millions of Americans turned out during warm summer evenings to root for the home team. Few American boys by the 1930's and 1940's, regardless of social backgrounds, could resist the aspiration, at least in fantasy, of triumphantly batting and fielding their way through this system to the fame and glory of the big leagues.

Not only baseball, but other sports as well, soon developed the functional capacity to integrate entire communities. In their classic study of small town life. *Middletown,* the Lynds graphically demonstrated the role of basketball in uniting traditionally hostile economic classes and religious groups in common support of the local high school team (Lynd and Lynd, 1929). While even the Depression could not significantly reduce the importance of basketball in Middletown, this effect was eventually produced, ironically, by the increased popularity and growth of other facets of sport.[5]

Sport in America, in general, endured the Depression and, then, an even greater crisis. World War II imposed severe restrictions upon the character and organization of sport at all levels in the country. Fuel shortages, travel restrictions, internal security problems, and the great manpower demands all limited such non-essential civilian activities as sports.[6] Unquestionably, the calibre of performance among profes-

[5] In 1890, high school sports did not exist in Middletown; by the 1920's, according to the Lynds, the "Bearcats," particularly in basketball, represented the dominant activity in the life of the local high school. Organized sports, in general, increased fourfold in the news space alloted by the Middletown press from 1890 to 1923. Not only the high school, but the entire Middletown population supported the Bearcat teams in one way or another. Indeed, the Lynds found that more civic loyality and community cohesion came from basketball than from anything else. "North Side and South Side, Catholic and Kluxer, banker, and machinist," wrote the Lynds, "their one shout is 'Eat 'em, beat 'em, Bearcats." By 1931, the Depression did not deter the citizens of Middletown from rewarding the Bearcats with gold watches for having won the state championship in basketball. However, the Lynds reported that the Depression did result in somewhat reduced enthusiasm for basketball in Middletown, patricularly after the investment into a 9,000 seat field house, built in the late 1920's, turned into a financial disaster. Ironically, the other reasons cited by the Lynds for reduced interest and support for the Bearcats, actually involved the growth of sports in other respects. These other factors included the beginning of radio broadcasting of high school games in 1930; the establishment of other teams at a new high school, as well as the junior high schools, and at the local college; and the growth of intramural and other interscholastic sports at the schools. The Lynds concluded that basketball was no longer, in 1935, the singular attraction for Middletown's citizens as it had been ten years earlier. But it was, obviously, the growth of other forms of sport which was largely responsible for this change. Nevertheless, even in the 1970's, many Indiana communities still have a way of closing down other activities during the spring of each year in order to fill state basketball arenas with capacity crowds for the high school championship tournament. Despite the growth of other sports, the annual statewide epidemic of what the local press uniquely identifies as "Hoosier hysteria," indicates that high school basketball remains a very special passion for natives of Indiana.

[6] Fuel shortages limited high school football schedules; a team could be matched to play games with the same opponent during the same season. Because of war-time restrictions on the Pacific Coast, Oregon State played Duke in the 1942 Rose Bowl game at Duke Stadium in Durham, North Carolina. In 1943 and 1944, the volume of war-related travel on the railroads of the nations forced major league baseballs teams to locate their spring training exercises in the North for the first time in modern baseball history.

Similarly, the war made great manpower demands which acutely reduced the civilian population available for sport. For the 1943 season, the Philadelphia Eagles and the Pittsburgh Steelers merged to play as the Steagles. In college football, West Point capitalized on the draft exempt status of its students to form an awesome juggernaut which demolished most opponents. Overnight, the Great Lakes Naval Training Station also fielded a powerhouse, composed of many of the better college and professional football stars in the nation and began to batter various major university teams. In professional baseball, the draft and enlistments took so many regular players that many minor leaguers prematurely found themselves in the major leagues, and a number of previously retired

sional athletes reflected these conditions. At the same time, however, the historical situation produced a period of unsurpassed excellence among military athletic teams. Despite the poverty of talent within professional sports during these years, President Franklin D. Roosevelt recognized the importance of sport to the morale of the American people (and perhaps as well as a subtle sign to the Axis Powers of the strength and mood of the nation) by his emphatic request of major league baseball to continue to operate throughout the war. When the war finally ended, sports in America remained reasonably intact and evidently not seriously damaged by the hardships of the war years.[7]

In the post-war years, sport resumed its growth in America. However, not all aspects of sport have fared equally well during the last 30 years. Professional and college boxing and minor league baseball were notable victims of the post-war period.[8] But by most measures, sports in general became more solidly entrenched than ever before as prominent features of popular culture in contemporary America. Attendance or

players returned to active careers. As a peculiarly dramatic indication of the situation, a one-armed outfielder, Pete Gray, appeared with the St. Louis Browns. From 43 leagues with 296 teams in 1940, the minor leagues reduced their operations to nine leagues with 62 teams in 1943.

[7] It is more difficult to say how the actual quality of performances in sport were affected by the war; a deterioration of the calibre of play may be suspected. In 1944, Nick Etten of the New York Yankees hit only 22 home runs, but it was enough to lead the American League with the lowest winning total since 1918 when Babe Ruth and Clarence Walker had tied with 11 homers. Another Yankee, George "Snuffy" Stirnweiss, led the American league in batting with an average of .309, the lowest figure to ever win this title in either league. Despite the suggestive nature of these facts it is not possible to know conclusively how the war influenced performance in baseball or any other sport.

[8] Professional boxing, at first aided by television, and by a group of talented and exciting fighters, such as Sandy Sadler, Willie Pep, Kid Gavilan, Sugar Ray Robinson, Tony Zale, Rocky Graziano, Jake LaMotta, Marcel Cerdan, Archie Moore, Jersey Joe Walcott, and Rocky Marciano, boomed for a while. However, overexposure by television, along with internal problems of corruption and control, began to undermine the popularity of professional boxing. In recent years, except for the heavyweight championship, the American public seems to have lost much of its interest in boxing. After some tragic fatalities, college boxing itself literally died in the ring. Local professional club fighting is also all but extinct. Yet, is must be noted that the number of boxers, according to *The Ring Magazine,* who actually participated in at least one bout has gone from 3,940 in 1950 down to 2,202 in 1965, but more recently climbed up to 5,783 in 1973. In the same years, gross receipts from professional boxing have gone from $3,800,000 in 1959 to $10,237,000. While inflation may account for the increase in receipts, it cannot explain the rise in the number of boxers. Minor league baseball represents another well-publicized casualty of the post-war period. After reaching a peak of 59 leagues with 448 teams in 1949, the minors have diminished steadily to merely 17 leagues, including three rookie leagues by 1973. In what appears as a rather shabby effort to reassure the American public that quality has not been sacrificed, organized baseball replaced the traditional designations of minor leagues as D, C, B, AA, and AAA, with a new scheme consisting only the rookie leagues and AA and AAA. See *Information Please Almanac* for 1974.

participation figures reveal rather healthy conditions for baseball, soft-ball, golf, basketball, football, horse racing, and bowling.[9]

Within this context, the growth of professional sports in the past decade or so has been particularly striking, and is unquestionably evident in an entire series of impressive developments. The same events, however, at the same time, make it equally obvious that the continued evolution of professional sports contains another dimension as well, and that has been as an important new industry within the system of economic capitalism. And as these enterprises continued to grow and prosper, professional sports assumed all the basic attributes of economic competition as any other industry. Older leagues, such as the National Football League, and the National Hockey League success-fully spread their operations into newer territories with rapidly growing cities and suburbs, and without the fatal dilution of talent which pes-simistic opponents of expansion so confidently predicted at the time. Correspondingly, expansion triggered a sometimes nearly-mad compet-ition among cities and prospective owners for the new franchises. Sev-

[9] Attendance at major league baseball games increased from 17,659,000 in 1950 to 29,544,000 in 1971, despite a widespread rumor that the national pasttime was dying. The Amateur Softball Association of America reported a growth from 355 teams in 59 leagues in 1950 to 796 teams in 274 leagues in 1971; in the latter year, 18,000 participants played in organized amateur softball. According to the National Golf Foundation, 3,215,000 golfers played on 4,931 courses in 1950; but in 1971, 10,000,000 golfers played on 11,174 courses. During the 1959-60 season, 1,986,000 fans watched games in the National Basketball Association; eleven years later, in the 1970-71 season, attendance at NBA games reached 6,195,000, while 2,529,000 other fans saw games in the newer American Basketball Association. In 1950, 674 member schools of the National Collegiate Athletic Association played in football games before 18,962,000 fans; in 1971, while the number of teams had declined to 618, attendance had reached 30,455,000. In 1950, 2,008,000 fans of professional football watched the teams of the National Football League. In 1969, 6,351,000 fans turned out for NFL football, while another 2,983,000 saw the rival American Football League, while still in its first decade of existence. In 1971, the combined attendence totals for the now-merged professional football leagues reached 10,560,000. The National Association of State Racing Commissioners reported, between 1959 and 1971, that attendance at all types of race tracks increased from 28,291,000 to 73,619,000; the number of racing days was up from 4,018 to 10,792; and the parimutual turnover climbed from $1,638,000,000 to $6,326,000,000. Between 1950 and 1971, the American Bowling Congress showed an increase in bowling establishments from 6,325 to 8,922; of bowling lanes from 52,488 to 139,483; and of ABC members of bowling lanes from 52,488 to 139,483; and of ABC members (an all-male body) from 1,417,000 to 4,000,000. Although the number of ABC members is substantially down from the peak of 4,944,000 reached in 1965, the membership of the Women's Bowling Congress had grown steadily from 496,000 in 1950 to its 1971 figure of 3,000,000. Similarly, the membership of the American Junior Bowling Congress has steadily increased from 24,000 in 1950 to 610,000 in 1971. In almost all of these cases, the more recent figures represent new high, reflect tremendous growth, and are continuing to rise in each of these areas of sport. *Information Please Almanac* (1974).

eral city administrations, despite facing severe financial problems for other municipal services, nevertheless plunged into efforts to construct costly new stadiums to accommodate the newly-acquired franchises or to placate older organizations which threatened to move elsewhere. At the same time, professional football, basketball, and hockey have seen the introduction of entire new leagues which not only hired away many established stars of the older leagues and signed many younger players first, but also achieved financial solvency as well, despite the enormous costs of these efforts. The American Football League, of course, also achieved final recognition and integration with the NFL, and, at this writing, the same pattern is about to repeat itself in both professional hockey and basketball.

Although some poorly-operated franchises turned into financial disasters for specific owners, on the whole, the value of professional franchises has grown astronomically. All the while the fans have poured out a generous financial contribution to the success of these franchises by their enthusiastic willingness to purchase season tickets for football, the club could sell out the entire stadium through season ticket sales alone, but often finds it preferable to retain a small number of seats for single game sales. In cities with professional hockey, even ones which had expansion franchises awarded not so long ago, such as Philadelphia, the entire arena can be filled by season ticket sales alone. In cities with the older hockey franchises, such as Montreal, Toronto, and Boston, only the season ticket holders can count on having game tickets; and, according to local legend, the only way someone can obtain a season, ticket is by having it left to him in the will of a deceased ticket holder. Occasionally, fans have reacted against some conditions to which they have been subjected in recent years by the professional clubs. For instance, fans in several NFL cities organized (and with surprising success) against the insistence of club officials that the purchase of exhibition game tickets be included in season ticket plans. But, regardless of how tickets for such games are sold, capacity crowds for supposedly unimportant and meaningless pre-season games have become common. Recognizing their economic potential, the NFL has rather shrewdly succeeded in shifting the popular designation of such contests from the traditional "exhibition games" to the more marketable "pre-season games". Similarly, sponsors are quite willing to spend the high price of commercial advertising for local and national telecasts of even pre-season games.

On the whole, however, the fans have rather submissively accepted the harsh economic realities of sport as mass entertainment. The price of tickets, in all sports, whether for pre-season or regular season games, whether for a single game, some combination plan of games, or for season ticket plans, has steadily risen to a rather expensive scale. The day of the fifty cent (or even $1.00) bleacher ticket in baseball is all but gone; in football and hockey, the price scale may begin at $4.00 and $5.00 for seats which, in some of the newer stadiums, might as well be in the next country. Yet, the fans continue to come. Picking up these cues, investors and promoters have turned recently to the establishment of professional track, tennis, soccer, and lacrosse teams. In the cases of the latter three, teams representing various cities will compete in leagues spanning the entire continent in an obvious attempt to duplicate the success of the older and more successful professional sports. By the end of 1974, signs of crisis were unmistakeable. Economic hardships threatened the existence of the World Football League, World Hockey Association, and World Team Tennis. Similarly, the ABC telecast of Monday Night Football had declined 11% from the previous year. Whether or not success will result in the newer leagues, only the future can tell.

Through the glorification of sports by the media and the astounding salaries associated with athletic careers, the professional player has emerged today as a part of a highly esteemed and handsomely rewarded occupational elite. Although the performance standards are high, only a few other vocational careers are comparable to professional sports in terms of fame, attention, and cash. If he is good enough, a professional career may begin while the athlete is still in eighth or ninth grade. It is a well established practice in cities such as New York and Philadelphia that basketball coaches in private prep schools begin to compete with each other in attempting to recruit the best players, particularly from black neighborhoods where local public high schools are not well regarded. Dean Meminger, the New York Knicks guard admits: "I was a pro when I was 14 years old and Rice High School recruited me. They gave me tuition, room, and board" (Durso, 1974a). The talented black ghetto youth who ends up playing basketball at an exclusive private suburban prep school is not there because of any particular altruism on the part of the school. If he is wanted enough, over 60 college coaches may see him in the first week after his last high school game. If he has great talent, over 200 colleges may offer him scholarships. If he is the best prospect, a professional contract worth $1-million may even be offered him while he is still a teenager and before he has even attended college (Durso, 1974a). The athlete is often a "blue chip" prospect in football or basketball, but today, he may be in swimming, lacrosse, wrestling, rodeo, golf, tennis, baseball, or hockey. The much sought after recruit could even be a baton-twirler, or increasingly, a woman athlete. When Miami University recently made available 15 scholarships for women, there were 400 applicants (Durso, 1974a).

It is at the college level that the whole process reaches incredible proportions. In October, 1929, the Carnegie Foundation for Advancement of Teaching issued its sensational report on the corruption of college sports, charging that: ". . . college sports have been developed from games played by boys for pleasure into systematic professionalized athletic contests." Today, over 45 years later, the *New York Times,* in a series on the big business of college sports recruiting concluded that it had reached a point of crisis. The *Times* described a "slave market" which approached a national scandal in terms of the corruption of high school athletes, the distorted role of sports in education, and the moral climate surrounding all schools (Cady, 1974a; Durso, 1974a). Bob Cousy, the former basketball star and ex-coach at Boston College candidly admits: "You can't recruit on a major college level in basketball or football without cheating" (Heisler, 1973). Joe Paterno, the very successful head football coach at Penn State, says: "It's the worst I've seen in my 23 years of coaching" (Durso, 1974a). The excellent six-part *Times* series reaches the conclusion that a runaway attitude of "win or else" has produced five major consequences (Durso, 1974a.):

1. Increased competition for high school athletes who might give national prominence to a college have doubled recruiting costs in the last ten years, and 90½ of all colleges now maintain sports programs operating at a loss.

2. Increased pressures have forced 41 schools in the last decade, eight in 1973, to abandon football, increasing the possibility of a "super conference" of the few big powers who may be able to retain the sport.

3. Colleges and universities are increasingly ignoring the major recruiting rules of the NCAA.

4. Violations include financial payments to athletes; altered grades and transcripts; substitutes for exams; jobs for parents; cars; and providing football tickets which can be resold for as much as $8,000 over four years.

5. Only four investigators are available to keep up with 664 member schools of the NCAA.

Moreover, when caught, the sanctions for violations by the NCAA turn out to have little effect. In the last 17 years, Oklahoma University has been put on probation three times; Southern Louisiana twice in six years for basketball violations during a meteoric rise to power; and Cornell for hockey violations, while it continues to break the rules in basketball (Durso, 1974a).

The techniques of recruiting are of particular interest. One coach advised, "If you want a winning team, you'd better build some dorms and fill 'em up with booze and broads" (Cady, 1974b). Rather than the "booze and broads" approach, other schools rely on celebrities: astronaut Frank Boarman for West Point; ex-Secretary of State Dean Rusk for Davidson; actor Moses Gunn for Grambling; ex-governor John J. McKeithen for LSU; Bing Crosby for Gonzaga; Robert F. Kennedy for Harvard; and even the racehorse, Secretariat, for Kentucky (Eskenazi, 1974a). Matt Snell, the former All-American fullback at Ohio State and New York Jets star remembers: "I had offers of everything from girls to wardrobes to freezers stocked with food . . . And the only one who was straight with me was Woody Hayes of Ohio State. So I went there" (Eskenazi, 1974c). Somewhat paradoxically Coach Hayes responds to criticism against college sports with the observation: "I honestly think there's a great movement on campuses today to undermine athletics. Some of these psychology and sociology professors we can do without" (Cady, 1974e).

The great interest in the athlete, however, lasts only as long as his utility as a competitor. And his interest in college education, similarly, frequently lasts only until he is trained enough to make the final jump to the professional ranks. For instance, the *Times* also reports that only 62 percent of the players in the two major basketball leagues stayed around long enough to obtain their bachelors' degrees; 129 graduates among the 200 players of the NBA; and 62 graduates among the 104 players of the ABA. The worst record in this regard belongs to the Kansas City-Omaha Kings of the NBA with only two college graduates among the 12 players on their 1973-74 roster (Goldaper, 1974a). Yet, ironically, Otto Moore, a reserve player with the Kings, is reported to have drawn a $120,000 salary for the season. Some athletes such as Bill Bradley of the New York Knicks, who suggests that college players should be allowed to represent their schools in return either for money or for their education, are quite outspoken in their criticism of the system. The state superintendent of public instruction and an ex-officio regent of Arizona State University, Weldon P. Shofstall, has offered the sardonic suggestion that the hypocrisy should be removed from college football by the schools hiring of professional teams: "Why don't we just make it professional . . . I guess that's just as legitimate as preparing doctors and lawyers" *(Sports Illustrated, 1974).* [10]

The principal pay-off for the professional athlete comes in the staggering salary scale, from the super-star to the bench-warmer, which places him in one of the highest paid occupations in the labor force today. The *New York Times* reports that each field goal in the 1973-74 season was worth $431 to Kareem Abdul Jabbar who earned $400,000. Tom Seaver's $175,000 salary for 1973 meant $163 for each out in the 290 innings he pitched in 1973. Joe Namath's $250,000 in 1973, a season shortened by injuries, made each pass worth $3,671. The salaries of professional athletes today represent a tremendous increase, which occurred mainly in the last few years. In 1967, for instance, the last year in which the NBA was the only professional basketball league, the largest payroll for any team was the $500,000 paid out by the Knicks. Of the 12 teams in the league, five had payrolls below $200,000. Today, many players are paid more than $200,000 in a single season; some stars make twice that amount; and a superstar such as Wilt Chamberlain was reported to have a contract worth $600,000 a year. Even untested players with little or no professional experience can command an enormous price. Although the ABA was willing to offer Bill Walton a five-year package for $2.5 million, he signed with Portland of the NBA for a relatively modest $1.9 million. Similarly, Julius Irving was worth $1 million in salary to the New York Nets, after having some previous

[10] The incipient scandal of college football is symptomatically related to the fact that sports has become a big-time business at both the college and the professional levels. Furthermore, it is quite evident by now that college and professional sports as business enterprises are inextricably linked to each other. Otto Moore's salary with the Kings reveals that the primary value of attending college for the talented player is not to secure an education, but to display his athletic skills. (For the not-so-talented player, an education provides something to fall back upon, if success in the professional ranks does not come.) The Bradley-Shofstall view further reveals that college sports have become the major training grounds for professional athletes. Moreover, the consequences of sanctions for violating NCAA rules, as in the cases of Oklahoma, Southern Louisiana, and Cornell, further indicated that whatever scandals may be eventually revealed, the resulting sanctions will not be likely to seriously alter the structure of big-time sports at any level.

professional experience. Another rookie, Ernie DiGregorio, despite some reservations about his abilities as a defensive player, obtained a $400,000 a year contract with the Buffalo Braves in 1973-1974. According to the *New York Times,* the average salary in professional football is over $32,000; in professional baseball, over $40,000; and in professional basketball, over $85,000. (Goldaper, 1974a; Durso, 1974b).

Some credit, of course for securing these contracts must go to the players' agents such as Bob Woolf who earned $800,000 last year by representing stars· such as Jim Plunkett, Calvin Murphy, and Derek Sanderson. Woolf's 300 clients gives him the largest stable among player representatives. But the largest operation in actual dollars is that of Mark McCormack, who represents Arnold Palmer, Pele; Larry Csonka, Jim Kiick, and Paul Warfield. A smaller, but obviously choice stable is run by William Morris who serves as agent for Mark Spitz and Henry Aaron, among others, Sam Gilbert, who specializes in former UCLA basketball stars, for whom he has often served as a father-figure as well, handles Kareem Abdul Jabbar, Bill Walton, and Sidney Wicks. The accomplished agent can expect to earn about $100 an hour (Eskenazi, 1974d). There can be no question when remembering the unethical, brutal, and dishonest tactics which general managers traditionally utilized in contract negotiations with professional athletes that the players' representatives are worth every penny of their expensive fees to the athletes.

All these changes of the professional athlete in an occupational role reflect the continuing integration of sports into American institutions, but most emphatically into the economy. In a similar manner, as the athletes individually develop more and more an awareness of the business aspects to their careers, so too the teams as organizations also become commercially viable enterprises. It is no longer unusual but rather increasingly common that professional teams are extensions of business empires. In fact of the 120 professional teams in the major leagues today, perhaps no more than 12 are exceptions to this norm and are still owned by someone whose principal business is that team. Similarly, as the *New York Times* has correctly pointed out, the major problems of professional teams today are basically business problems, with players striking, teams moving, leagues expanding, television sales growing, lawsuits increasing, and Congress investigating (Koppett, 1974). But the most serious consequences in the analysis offered by the

New York Times are results of "interlockism," that is, the overlapping ownership and control of athletic teams and other business ventures. This situation means that basic decisions made by management are less subject than ever before to the "checks and balances" which fans provide by their attendance or lack of it. In addition, it can also mean that a winning team (the prime interest of the fans), is no longer necessarily the prime interest of ownership. Consequently, management is liable to make decisions which may weaken the team on the field, but may strengthen the enterprise as a business venture (Koppett, 1974). While this is not new, one has only to remember the sale of Babe Ruth by the Boston Red Sox to the New York Yankees over 50 years ago; the likelihood of such practice goes way up when it is built into the very structure of professional teams. The *Times* points out that a decision by CBS executives, in their capacity as the owners of the Yankees, was the critical factor in the move from Kansas City to Oakland by the A's which in turn created the need for new franchises in Kansas City and Seattle, as well as new National League teams in San Diego and Montreal. The initial move led to the eventual division of each league into east and west, and thus led to the disruption of a century of cherished baseball tradition (Koppett, 1974).

In light of this tremendous integration with business, the current economic condition of the country must have serious implications for the future of professional sports. Sensitive to the possibility of an economic crisis, a sportswriter recently asked: "Is the professional sports bubble ready to burst — or is it just inflating along with everything else in the economy" (Durso, 1974b). The signs of inflationary growth are everywhere: there are three times as many teams in major sports today as there were 25 years ago: The World Football League began play before suprisingly large crowds; the WFL founder announces his plans for eventually establishing franchises in Mexico, Japan, and Europe; the NFL about the same time revealed its plans for a "satellite" league during the offseason with teams located in Istanbul, Rome, Munich, Berlin, Vienna, and Barcelona; some kind of football became available on TV six days a week in the fall of 1974; box lacrosse opened successfully on the east coast and Canada as a professional sport; a record 135 million fans paid their way in 1973 to watch professional games in baseball, football, basketball, and hockey, and to the races; world team tennis attempted to survive in its first year of play; world team boxing announced its plans to begin in the near future; and women's professional basketball also revealed its intention to begin league play in 1975, with its first team, the Phoenix Pink Panthers.

From a sociological point of view, these economic facts are more significant because of the interrelationships of modern sports with other major societal institutions. In this regard, perhaps the most interesting issue is the possibility that sports may have even evolved into one of the principal integrating mechanisms of our culture. By the 1960's, it was increasingly evident that big-time sport could function as a worldly substitute for organized religion. Moreover, particularly during the worst period of the Viet Nam war, with the nation experiencing its most serious internal dissension in years, it became equally obvious that sport could be readily converted into an instrument of particular political values and interests. Althoug patriotic themes had been regularly incorporated int various aspects of athletics long before this time, during the late 1960's and early 1970's, sport provided numerous opportunities, rather one-sidedly, to the supporters of U.S. involvement in Southeast Asia. During their off-seasons, outstanding professional football and baseball players were sent by the State Department to visit American troops in Indochina, presumably to bolster military morale and to give sanction to many young Americans for their presence in Viet Nam. The much-publicized draft resistance and opposition to the war by Muhammad Ali led to the stripping of his heavyweight championship title by boxing officials. Returned veterans were invited to throw out the first ball in opening ceremonies for major league baseball. But the most garis and tasteless examples of this usurpation of sport by politics came in football, where pre-game and half-time activities at college and professional games began to look more and more-like nationalistic rituals — sacred celebrations of supposed political unity (in support of the war) among all Americans. It is difficult to erase from the memory the scenes which were so typical of the period, with their peculiar combinations of elements: the clergyman offering his solemn invocation, asking "God's blessing on the great nation and her people, particularly our boys in Viet Nam;" the military color guard raising the flag; the playing of the Star Spangled Banner and other patriotic anthems; the releasing of 10,000 red, white, and blue balloons; the "sensational pride of the South (or East, North or West)," the marching 200 with their Graustarkian uniforms and "the largest working bass drum in the Western Hemisphere;" and, finally, the chorus line of semi-nude, ever-smiling coeds doing a "bump-and-grind" routine which has, somewhat suddenly, become quite acceptable to Middle America, as least as long as it is performed in the Orange Bowl and not the local burlesque house — and all this to express, somehow, what it means to be an American.

Expression of dissent from the "official" values of the nation or of opposition to the war, at the same time, were carefully excluded from these public ceremonies. Occassionally, antiwar protesters surfaced before national TV audiences, but such events were, ordinarily, disruptions of the formally scheduled program of "patriotic" exercises. Toward the end of the war, some changes were faintly noticeable. An Ivy League band might play some music associated with the anti-war movement; players in a college all-star game wore the peace symbol on their helmets. The most chilling abasement of sport, within the context of political events, came much earlier when professional football conducted business as usual on Sunday, November 24, 1963, just two days after the assassination of President John F. Kennedy. Althougm most Americans, regardless of political views, numbed by the awesome tragedy in Dallas, suspended the normal activities, the games went on. An NFL defensive halfback later told of being totally oblivious to the game in which he played as his mind constantly swelled with grief. But what all of these events suggest is the evolution of sport into an important component of popular culture and, perhaps more interestingly, into a powerful ordering and integrating mechanism among contemporary American Institutions.

Perhaps nothing, however, has revealed the political implications of sport as popular culture with any greater symbolic significance than the ardent attitudes, activities, and friendships displayed by recent American presidents. To be sure, from George Washington's time, the American chief executive has been known to indulge, occasionally, in various uporting activities; Theodore Roosevelt comes quickly to mind here. Similarly, American Presidents have been participating in the opening game ceremonies of major league baseball for some time. Nonetheless there appears to have been an unprecedented, qualitative break with the past in recent administrations. Of our six presidents since the end of World War II, Truman and Johnson expressed only modest interest in sport. Truman seemed to prefer poker, the piano, and his famous morning walks for leisure. Johnson was known to attend a University of Texas football game, from time to time, but it seemed more in his years after retiring from politics that "Hook'em, Horns" became significant for LBJ. In the case of the other three presidents, however, each has displayed intense interest and conspicuous participation in sport. Eisenhower suffered a broken leg as a member of the West Point football team. Much later in life, he was also an avid golfer with a passionate interest in the game. His friendship and occasional rounds of golf with Arnold Palmer were widely publicized as was his use of White House grounds for practice. Kennedy had played a bit of football in prep school and enthusiastically enjoyed swimming, sailing, and golf as an adult. One can also recall the genuine smile of an obvious fan in photographs taken of President Kennedy at the Army-Navy football game. But it was the touch football games, particularly at the family compound at Hyannisport, which provided so much of the athletic component to the Kennedy mystique.

But no president had ever gone so far in openly acknowledging his passion for sport than Richard M. Nixon, the former scrub football player from Whittier College. His own ardor, coupled with the power, prestige, and public visibility of his office, made Nixon into the number one fan in the nation. And possibly no more important figure in America had ever so vigorously embraced the role of "super-fan." It is well known that Nixon turned to the distractions offered by televised football during urgent political moments. Similarly, he made the well-publicized telephone call to Coach Darrell Royal after Texas beat Arkansas in a crucial game a few years ago to congratulate the winners and to award them with the President's vote, at least, as the top team in college football (much to the expressed annoyance of Joe Paterno, coach of rival claimant Penn State). In addition, Nixon made public his Super Bowl prediction on the eve of the professional championship game. He even had the temerity to suggest plays to some of the most successful coaches of professional football. While these actions have stirred up modest controversy among his detractors, they also probably reinforced his appeal among his supporters. Not even his successor as President, Gerald Ford, although an outstanding college athlete, seems likely to surpass Nixon as an ardent fan.

It is also quite clear that disgruntled Congressmen, unable to secure tickets to see the resurgent Washington Redskins, were primarily responsible for the lifting of the television blackouts of home games by professional football teams across the nation. The public demonstration of interest by the political leaders of the nation further contributes to the sanctioning of professional sports as legitimate careers. Moreover, as the increasing integration of sports and politics proceeds, it should no longer be surprising to discover continued convergence of career patterns — such as Wilmer "Vinegar Bend" Mizell, once an outstanding National League pitcher, now a member of the U.S. House of Representatives or Justice Byron White, a former All-American football player, on the U.S. Supreme Court. The wide publicity given to the distinguished playing (and brief coaching) career of President Ford similarly underscores this point. Such facts also indicate that suggestions of New York Knickerbocker star Bill Bradley running for Congress, or either Joe Paterno or Arnold Palmer running for governor in Pennsylvania, may not always be amusing nonsense. In an age when former executives of the J. Walter Thompson advertising agency can make a U.S. President, the fame of well-known sport figures gives them a running start toward political victories as well.

With the growth in popularity in the second half of the 20th century, various "internal" features of social organization correspondingly adjusted to the cultural acceptance of sport. The emergence of new recruitment patterns is one conspicuous illustration of these processes. For instance, in contrast to earlier years, at the present time, not only are college sports more prominent as significant national events, but there also has been a substantial increase in lhe proportion of college-trained athletes now finding their way into professional sports careers. For axample, with the tremendous reduction of the minor leagues in baseball, the colleges have taken up the slack and have become, in recent years, of primary importance as training centers for aspiring major league players. Lee MacPhail, the baseball executive, recently stated that 1,000 baseball players have signed professional contracts during the last three years. Not so long ago, many baseball people derisively regarded the collegiate level of play to be of a relatively inferior calibre, certainly no better than perhaps the old Class C or even D leagues of the minors. Most players recruited from the colleges today, however, are assigned only a step or two away from the big time, and a few outstanding collegians may even go directly into the major leagues. In response to these conditions, the colleges have cooperated by a substantial expansion of their baseball schedules and programs. Were it not for the introduction of large numbers of blacks and Latin-Americans into organized baseball during the last 25 years, the increased importance of the colleges would be even more salient.

But other professional sports have an even greater proportion of ex-collegians within their ranks. Professional football, which in its earlier days may have been commonly defined as a competitor to college football, has become today totally dependent in recruitment upon the latter. There is, virtually, no other alternate source of talent for professional trams than the colleges. Although many athletes may fail to complete their educations, the professional football player who has not, at least, attended some college or university is a very rare individual at the present time.

Professional basketball, largely popularized in the last decade or two, presents a very similar parallel to football, in regard to recruitment. As in the case of football, in terms of the manpower supply, basketball is almost totally dependent upon the colleges. In both of these cases, with a rather negligible minor league system, it is difficult to see how either sport could continue at the professional level without the formidable support provided by the colleges.

It is interesting to note how fragile the boundary is which separates the professional and the collegiate. Competitive pressures occasionally induce professional teams to attempt to prematurely lure college athletes to sign professional contracts before their college status runs out. Oddly, the three major professional sports of football, basketball, and baseball, have established three entirely different codes in this regard. Professional football teams have solemnly regarded the inviolability of amateur athletics by refusing to raid the campuses. Professional basketball, on the other hand, has permitted itself to rationalize the early signing of so-called "hardship cases," players from poor families. Even this has not prevented secret drafts and clandestine uignings of "amateur" basketball players by professional teams before the college season has actually ended. Ironically, professional baseball teams permit themselves the signing of college players at any time during their undergraduate careers, and their coaches regularly accept and tolerate this situation. Obviously, the three sports differ in important ways which may be used to account for these three distinct situations. Among these varying conditions are: the presence or absence of rival leagues; the established draft and contract procedures for each sport; and probably most important, the level of skills developed by the college athlete in comparison to the demands of professional standards of competence in each sport.

Since the expansion of the National Hockey League, hockey has emerged as one of the more firmly established and popular professional sports, with a future as bright and promising as any other in America. The growth of the NHL has also triggered a great increase of interest and participation in amateur hockey in the United States. But, as expansion and national television has moved hockey very much into public view, ironically, the sport remains very largely in the grip of traditional recruitment patterns. Talented young Canadians are still recruited for the junior leagues where their demanding apprenticeship is served with considerable sacrifice in terms of education, since many professional hockey players never even finish high school. But again, the popularity of pockey has transformed Bobby Hull, Bobby Orr, Bobby Clarke, Gordie Howe, and Phil Esposito into public celebrities. Two small signs, however, suggest that the legitimation of hockey may have similar consequences as the public acceptance of other professional sports. First, collegiate hockey is steadily growing in the United States, and the first collegians are now beginning to appear in professional hockey. In fact, a few seasons ago, Ned Harkness, a former college coach became the new head coach of the Detroit Red Wings, although his tenure was short, unpopular, and unsuccessful. The thought of his appointment itself probably still distresses many hockey "traditionalists." Second, the NHL has recently announced plans to establish its own secondary school system to insure, at least, a high school diploma for the professional player. Here, one cannot help but ask what significance the player being interviewed on national television, particularly as he reflects upon the league itself, have had on these NHL plans.

With the exception of hockey, then, which is apparently trying to close the gap somewhat, professional athletes in the major sports are increasingly recruited from the ranks of former college students. Moreover, it is obvious today that many college athletes were exploited by their schools, given the benefit of "gut courses," special tutors, unlimited absences, and other devices which enabled them to stay around as long as they were needed by the institution, but also academically be abandoned when their playing eligibility ended. For their part, the players largely cooperate with this system, because they, too, get what they came for; that is, the opportunity to bid for a professional career as an athlete. Despite these abuses, the traditional stereotype of the "jock" with his questionable intelligence and "learning," slightly above that of the higher apes, is woefully obsolete. Many ex-collegians, now performing as professional athletes, were also good students whose grades equaled or surpassed the campus average. Because of this fact, we should stop distinguishing between "students" and "athletes" when talking about any college population. But also, even in the most notorious "football factories," there is considerable exposure and contact of the athlete with the civilized world. Intellectually and socially, he cannot help but be touched, at least slightly, by it. And, more important, if he takes advantage of the opportunities there, he can secure an education comparable to any other student at the same institution. So, the "animals" and "missing links" can still be found among the athletes, but the same kind of vulgar character will be discovered within the non-athlete student population as well. In addition, there is no intrinsic reason that participation in athletics, whether on the college or the professional level, cannot produce individuals such as Supreme Court Justice Byron White; or Frank Ryan, with his Ph.D. in mathematics; or Bill radley, another former Rhodes scholar; or John Wideman, the gifted novelist and University of Pennsylvania faculty member; or Pete Dawkins, the former West Point All-American. Perhaps it is more to the latter as norms that the student-athlete increasingly moves today.

There are more than intellectual implications in the changing role of the contemporary athlete. There have also been parallel, but interrelated transformations of other dimensions of individual character. For instance, the professional athlete traditionally was a man of relatively modest social origins, perhaps frequently of lower and working class origins, for whom a career in sports was an avenue of upward social mobility, a way out of an insignificant, uneventful, and meager material existence. Given the limited advantages and opportunities of his background, he was likely to be an individual of limited education, skills, and abilities. The restrictions placed on his aspirations and ambitions by his social situation led him to perceive a career in sports as a tremendous escape, provided he had athletic ability. His commitment to sport and his obligation to that opportunity made him enormously dependent upon that career as his only avenue toward success. However, the present-day professional athlete has socially evolved into a much more different type of individual. This historical shift is epitomized in the differences between, for example, Babe Ruth and Bill Bradley. A careful and candid examination of his life reveals that Ruth, perhaps the dominant sports personality of the first major era of modern professional athletics and a nearly sacred figure of popular culture, was actually a remarkably naive, crude, and oafish individual. In contrast, a person such as the urbane and scholarly Bill Bradely begins to typify the contemporary athlete. Of course, both periods have their exceptions. Ruth's own teammate, Moe Berg, was a veritable intellectual; and certainly more than a few troglodytes can be found today. But the general trend has been toward a population of professional athletes whose personal character is indistinguishable from their peers in any other career. Underscoring the importance of television in modern sports, the idea of the athlete as a Neanderthal is quickly dispelled while watching the articulate Larry Csonka, Roger Staubach, or Calvin Hill in a post-game interview.

But probably the most important source contributing to the changing character of the individual athlete is a major shift in his social origins. Although the point might be difficult to demonstrate, in terms of empirical proof, it appears likely that professional athletes of an earlier period came mainly from families with low incomes, education, and social standing in the community. Again, the compelling person of the motherless Babe Ruth, rasied in an orphanage, comes easily to mind as the archetype. Although athletes from minority backgrounds conspicuously continue to reflect similarly modest origins today, many others also come from affluent, middle-class circumstances. An important implication of this condition is that many professional athletes can pursue serious alternative careers besides sports. *Esquire* magazine showed this trend rather imaginatively in the selection of an All-Star Business Team, with each player chosen on the basis of his ability to earn money outside of sports (Hardin, 1973). Perhaps some of the *Esquire* selections involve a "showcase jock," with limited business abilities, who is employed by a firm, precisely because he is a celebrity. But, unquestionably, many of the business all-stars are, in fact, capable workers in their occupations quite independent of anything else. For instance, Nick Buoniconti, the Dolphins linebacker, is an attorney as well as president of All Pro Graphics, with over 100 NFL players as clients. Bob Lilly, the Cowboys tackle, is a partner in a real-estate investment firm and in an economy motel chain. Andy Russell, the Steelers linebacker, runs a Pittsburgh company which provides tax-sheltered real estate investments. Safetyman Dick Anderson of the Dolphins is president of an agency which sold over $1-million in group life insurance in 1972. Pettis Norman, the Chargers end, is a vice-president of a Dallas bank.

In the preceding pages, some description and analysis of change in sport as a social institution in 20th century America has been presented. With the endorsement provided by the mass media and by political leaders, professional sport has evolved into a lucrative and legitimate source of occupational careers for young Americans, while also becoming an important component of modern industrial capitalism. With shifting patterns of recruitment, the contemporary professional athlete has also emerged as a reasonably intelligent and capable individual off the playing field as well as on it. The latter development, however, has also served to push professional sport to a rather serious internal institution crisis. This problem stems from the inherent ambiguity in the organization of athletics as professions. Professional workers are defined partly in terms of the fact that they are provided a fee for their services. The athlete as a professional measures up to this standard quite well. On the other hand, another criterion in the definition of a profession, however, is relatively autonomous control and regulation of the organization and activities of the occupation. Because the free professional of the past is rapidly disappearing from the American occupational scene, however, it is better to compare the athlete with other professionals employed in formal organizations. On this score, not only do the athletes fail miserably, but they find themselves in a more feudalistic than capitalistic mode of economic organization. Most professional employees with large organizations have greater autonomy on their jobs, as well as in changing their employer, than do professional athletes. Despite their tremendous salaries and public adulation, most professional athletes find themselves bound into a rigid system of rules governing their contractual obligations as if they were serfs and their personal conduct as if they were children. Similarly, despite the frequent appearance of athletes as modern folk heroes, the maturation of sport as a professional occupation is a case of only partial evolution. No one is more conscious of this fact, today, than the professional athlete himself.

The contemporary athlete is frequently a college graduate and may perform quite skillfully during the off-season as lawyer, businessman, rancher, banker, broadcaster, or scholar. He no longer must retreat to the isolation and insulation of a provincial community to wait for the next season until he can again perform with his only talent. Increasingly, today, he has intellectual awareness, business acumen, political sensitivity, and social sophistication. Consequently, he cannot gracefully slide back into the bondage of professional sport when his season begins anew. For he realizes one basic fact today, that unlike very few other forms of employment in the modern economy, his personal services are owned and controlled by someone other than himself. Whether expressed through a sometimes acutely critical writer, as in the paramount illustration provided by a gifted Jim Bouton, or by direct political action, as in the recent player strikes, the current dissent and rebellion reflects the new social character and emerging political self-consciousness on the part of athletes. In particular, athletes now reveal their discovery of the fact that they were never anything more than psuedo-professionals — high-priced and glamorized prostitutes who had sold their freedom and autonomy to a repressive system of controls. The latter point becomes more obvious with the assumption that the militant organization of professional athletes has as its primary objective the securing of personal freedom and the stability of private lives rather than salary demands.

However, the validity of this assumption has not been convincingly demonstrated. The failure of the NFL players strike in the summer of 1974 indicates that the non-economic demands of professional athletes can still be bought out by increased salaries. But it also revealed the structural weaknesses in the social and economic positions of individuals in various sports which make the radicalization of professional athletes unlikely in the near future. First, the material security of individual players is too uncertain in too many cases; they are easily intimidated by the realistic prospect that other athletes can replace them. Second, their mobilization as a group proves very difficult; they are a highly individualistic collection of persons with widely varying backgrounds and aspirations. Third, their adherence to a militant ideology remains rather underdeveloped; they must forever struggle with their own intensely conditioned desire to be on the ball field or in the arena when the season opens. The latter problem, although not unique to sport, is a reminder that the career of a professional athlete is seldom merely a job, but is, rather, a way of life. The combined product of these factors destroyed the 1974 NFL strike; it also demonstrated that the players could form a workers' association, but not a genuine labor union. Consequently, the radicalization of professional athletes remains, at present, as only an incipient social movement.

But the conflict between players and owners will renew itself with increasing regularity in the future. And in this the players are bound to lock themselves into a difficult and protracted struggle with their proprietors over the structure of ownership and control. It remains to be seen just how far professional athletes will dare to organize themselves in collective bargaining and, similarly, how radical and militant a strategy they will adopt in future confrontations with management. It also remains to be seen whether any serious alteration of current property rules, such as giving players the right to acept or reject their being traded to other teams, would irreparably impair the nature of the sports themselves. But it may also be only a matter of time until some enterprising group of athletes attempts to organize a professional league on a model of democratic socialism in which franchises are owned by the players themselves; profits are distributed entirely to players' wages, strengthening franchises, or stadium improvements and amenities for the fans; and in which all operating procedures must be ratified by the participants themselves. Perhaps the full realization of this scheme is too utopian, but some modest movement in these directions would not be completely surprising.

In considering the effects of social change upon occupations, it is particularly instructive to examine the special case provided by the historical evolution of athletics in America. In a relatively short span of time, certainly not exceeding a century, athletics has undergone a massive and dramatic transformation in terms of its place within our cultural and institutional order. In an earlier period, athletics provided mainly avocational amusement for a wealthy and privileged elite, as well as leisure time folk culture diversions from the dreary routine of everyday life for immigrant and minority peoples. Actual careers within sport, however, were perhaps available only to an insignificant handful of individuals who belonged, in many cases, to pariah groups at the margin of respectable society. While its traditional functions for elites and minority groups continue today, sport has developed, in general, to a thoroughly pervasive and established set of institutions which permeates the entirety of the American population, social structure, and popular culture. In the 20th century, moreover, athletic careers, in particular, have emerged as very legitimate professions, indeed rather enviable pursuits, solidly entrenched in the values of most Americans. By the middle of the present century, athletics had arrived as an undeniably important component of contemporary American life.

As this transformation occurred, it has repeatedly interacted with other institutions, especially with the material realities of work and economic life in modern society. For instance, in recent years we have witnessed tremendous change in our leisure habits and recreational patterns; a revolutionary transformation of our media of information and communication; and an enormous growth of new industries. In each of these cases, sport has functioned as a contributing agent as well as a recipient of social change.

The legitimation of professional uports, ironically, has become a major source for the emergence of a critical perspective at the present time. Professional athletics passed through what almost appears to be an inescapable evolutionary process. In an earlier period, professional sports were first in a disreputable stage during which criticism and moral censure was quite obvious, and directed public attention to some very overt aspects of its organization — the modest social origins and character of professional athletes; the partial acceptance of athletic careers as legitimate occupations; the marginal integration of professional sports with the rest of the economy. Eventually, with the realization that these endeavors represented another wealth-producing instrument of industrial capitalism, professional sports also moved in the direction of legitimation, ultimately becoming a part of the sacred values and institutions of our society. The heroes of the sports world, despite their own obvious flaws, assumed god-like stature in the adulating minds of young and old Americans. One has only to recall the recent eulogizing of the late Vince Lombardi to recognize the idolatrous character which professional sports are capable of ultimately attaining. But, at the same time, when any institution becomes sacred, a new form of criticism may also arise — one that thrives on exposing the myths, contradictions, tensions, and deceptions that inevitably lie beneath the glitter. The institution may, then, enter into a third stage, one of critical reassessment.

Sport, at the present time, appears to have reached this point, in which even the desirability of the continued existence of the institution may be questioned. Much of the uncertainity and criticism of sports at the moment has this character. But a mechanical, evolutionary perspective on social change is not an acceptable analytical device in modern sociology. It is necessary to discover and examine the actual mechanistic theory. And it is seldom accomplished by any polemical orientation either and, unfortunately, much of what passes for sociological analysis in regard to sport is almost pure ideology. This is not to say that a critical perspective in the sociology of sport is not justified. In fact, an application of a materialist perspective, which attempts to show how the development of economic institutions in modern American life, has shaped sport at all levels, is a legitimate and fruitful approach. But what has frequently been offered to fill the gap in a largely ignored area of sociological analysis cannot begin to address the wide range of necessary and fundamental questions for an adequate understanding of sport as a social institution.

It should be readily apparent to the reader of this paper that numerous questions remain unanswered. Indeed, the most basic issues in the sociology of sport remain to be investigated by serious scholarship. Although it can fit reasonably well into several different specialized areas, it may be particularly valuable to see the analysis of sport as part of the sociology of work and occupations. Various research questions come immediately to mind: the relationship of sport careers as occupations, particularly as professions, to other occupations; the consequences of social change, particularly in economic institutions, upon the organization of sport as work; the nature of socialization into occupational subcultures; and, a particularly fascinating issue, the socioemotional consequences of retirement upon individual athletes. In this paper, we have attempted, in a rather sweeping fashion, to review the emergence of modern professional sport by focusing upon several important issues which are related, primarily, to occupational sociology. Yet, a profound absence of data, even upon relatively simple questions which many students of sport might be inclined to take for granted, encourages us to treat this discussion as a rather exploratory and heuristic exercise, intended to provoke a series of questions and hypotheses which may be more rigorously examined in more tightly designed and executed research in the near future. Certainly, for the enterprising sociologist with an interest in the social aspects of sport, the opportunities are limitless and inviting.

BIBLIOGRAPHY

Amdur, Neil
    1971 *The Fifth Down*. New York: Coward, McCann and Geoghegan.
    1974a "Pursuit: A Dirty, Dirty Job." *The New York Times* (March 11): 38.
    1974b "Recruiters Stepping Up Drive for Women Athletes." *The New York Times* (March 12): 24.
    1974c "Changing Face of U.S. Sports: T.V. Saturation and Its Effects." *The New York Times* (July 23): 45-46.
Bouton, Jim
    1970 *Ball Four*. New York: The World Publishing Company.

Cady, Steve

1974a "Educators Prepare for First Major Study of Sports in 45 Years." *New York Times* (March 10): 52.

1974b "Costly Business of Sports Recruiting Escalates Toward a Public Scandal." *The New York Times* (March 11): 1,38.

1974c "Meanwhile for the Brainy Nonathlete, a 'Financial Struggle.' " *The New York Times* (March 12): 42.

1974d "Sports Recruiting: For Every Winner, a Hundred Losers." *The New York Times* (March 13): 46.

1974e "Educators on Sports Recruiting: 'Roman Circus' Must Go." *The New York Times* (March 15): 24.

Cozens, Frederick W. and Florence Scovil Stumpf

1973 "The Sports Page." Pp. 418-432 in John T. Talamini and Charles Page (eds.), *Sport and Society*. Boston: Little, Brown.

Durso, Joseph

1974a "Sports Recruiting: A College Crisis." *The New York Times* (March 10): 1,52.

1974b "Changing Face of Sports: Bubble May Be Bursting," *The New York Times* (July 22): 1,38.

Eskenazi, Gerald

1974a "Governors, Actors and Secretariat, Too." *The New York Times* (March 11): 38.

1974b "Sports Recruiting: How Hunted and Hunter Play the Game." *The New York Times* (March 12): 42.

1974c "For the Superstar, a First-Class Ticket." *The New York Times* (March 14): 46.

1974d "Changing Face of U.S. Sports: The Agents." *The New York Times* (July 25): 39.

Flood, Curt

1970 *The Way It Is*. New York: Trident Press.

Gent, Peter

1973 *North Dallas Forty*. New York: William Morrow.

Goldaper, Sam

1974a "Pro Basketball: Diploma vs. Dollar." *The New York Times* (March 13): 46.

1974b "Changing Face of U.S. Sports: The Superstars." *The New York Times* (July 25): 39-40.

Hardin, Robert

1973 "Pro Football Special: Earnin." *Esquire* (November): 90, 94, 98.

Heisler, Mark

1973 "Looking at Sports: Colleges Cheat in Recruiting, Cousy Charges." *Philadelphia Evening Bulletin* (February 23).

Herman, Robin

1974 "How the College Crowd Feels About It: Jeers Outscore Cheers." *The New York Times* (March 15): 24.

Hoch, Paul

1972 *Rip Off The Big Game*. Garden City, New York: Doubleday.

Johnson, William
  1973 "TV Made It All A New Game." Pp. 454-472 in John T. Talamini and
        Charles Page (eds.), *Sport and Society*. Boston: Little, Brown.
Koppett, Leonard
  1974 "The Changing Face of U.S. Sports: Interlocking Interests Are Prob-
        lems." *The New York Times* (July 24): 51-52.
Lynd, Robert S. and Helen Merrell Lynd
  1929 *Middletown*. New York: Harcourt, Brace and World.
  1937 *Middletown in Transition*. New York: Harcourt, Brace, and World.
Meggyesy, Dave
  1970 *Out of Their League*. Berkeley, California: Ramparts.
Oliver, Chip
  1971 *High for the Game*. New York: William Morrow.
Page, Charles
  1973 "Introduction: The World of Sport and Its Study." Pp. 3-39 in John T.
        Talamini and Charles Page (eds.), *Sport and Society*. Boston: Little,
        Brown.
Searcy, Jay
  1974 "South's Signing Day A Football Jamboree." *The New York Times*.
        (March 13): 46.
Simmel, Georg
  1950 *The Sociology of Georg Simmel* (translated and edited by Kurt H. Wolff).
        Glencoe, Illinois: The Free Press.
Sports Illustrated.
  1974 "Scorecard: Arizona Idea." *Sports Illustrated* (February 24): 14.
White, Gordon S., Jr.
  1974 "Sports Recruiting: Odds Against N.C.A.A. Policing Unit." *The New
        York Times* (March 14): 46.

THE CASE OF ACADEMIA: DEMYTHOLOGIZATION IN A NON-PROFESSION

Morton G. Wenger

The basic themes to be dealt with in this essay are as follows: first, it is maintained that "professionalism" is an ideology, that is, a set of ideas that relies on normative support for its validation rather than on empirical verification. Second, it is contended that this ideology can function either as a support for any given occupation's movement toward substantial control of client relations **or** as a compensation for the lack of the above control. Third, it is centrally argued that when an occupation finds itself unable to utilize this method of controlling client relationships, and when compensatory ideology no longer satisfies occupational incumbents, alternative forms of occupational organization emerge. It is the position of this paper that these phenomena are present in the "natural history" [1] of academia, [2] and that these dynamic processes can be understood in terms of clearcut and linked changes in the social function of the academic occupations, the personnel base of the occupation, and alterations in the identity and activities of "proximal" and "distal" clients. These occupational relatities and the changes thereof will be discussed in the following sections. Quite simply, then, the crux of this consideration of academia can be seen in the title, wherein it is indicated that "professionalism" has served mythic functions for the occupation at issue, and more importantly, that academia is now undergoing a "demystification" of considerable dimensions, and perhaps most significantly that this developmental process can be seen to have profound impact on client relationships, as "professionalism" itself is seen here as a mode of client control. This then, is the direction being followed.

[1] See E. C. Hughes (1958) for a discussion of the natural history of professions, as well as Carr-Saunders and Wilson (1933).

[2] This includes all types of occupations which have teaching as the basis of renumeration, regardless of subsidiary functions (research, etc.). Significant differences between "levels" of the teaching enterprise will be noted where relevant.

PROFESSIONALISM AS AN IDEOLOGY

The question that must be confronted first is fundamental and two-fold: what has been the ideology of professionalism in academia, and in what way has it been "ideological"? There is no paucity of sources willing to answer the first query; when examining the relevant literature, however, certain points stand out as representative of "professionalized" occupations:

1. control of entry into the occupation by incumbments[3]
   2a colleague, rather than client orientation in terms of standards of performance[4]
   2b. an occupational code of ethics
3. "scientific-theoretical" basis for occupational activity[5]
4. high standards of remuneration[6]

These five criteria appear quite frequently in the literature on professions; most relevant to the current discussion is the common linkage among these five ideal-typical characteristics. Present in this list is a strategem for the maximization of rewards in a given occupational domain; not the only strategy available, but one that has proven effective under certain socio-historical circumstances and which has failed given others. Now, it should be recognized that viewing professionalism as a technique of reward-maximization is seen as "cynical" in sociology. In fact, such a view of professions was regarded by some, as in Wilensky (1970), as one of C. Wright Mills' heresies. This is noted not out of concern for the charge, but as an indicator of one of the primary ways in which definitions of "professionalism" become reified and in such a way reveal their ideological functions. It frequently occurs that after listing several characteristics of professions that lead directly to client exclusion from relevant occupational decision-making, students of professionals are presented with the statement that this is in the best interests of the client.[7] This assertioin by professionals about professionals in and of itself is indicative of what can only be called professional paternalism. Another related point of reification in the study of

---

[3] See Lieberman (1960)
[4] See A. M. Carr-Saunders (1928).
[5] See Ernest Greenwood (1957) or H. L. Wilensky (1970).
[6] See Ernest Greenwood (1957).
[7] Wilensky (1970) and Lieberman (1960) both stress this point.

professions is that "official" definitions of professions are themselves the product of academics, the occupational group that is at issue here. Thus, those definitions and conceptions prevalent in the sociological literature reflect the occupational status of academics rather than that of a "value-free" view of the phenomenon in question. This is of considerable relevance to the larger issue of the "professional" status of academics and actual and potential changes therein because of one major factor: those areas of special or peculiar emphasis should reveal points of occupational "sensitivity" or concern, areas in which academics may feel that they are professionally deficient or particularly blessed. When engaging in such an examination of definitions, several interesting avenues of investigation develop. First, there is the matter of "scientific-theoretical" bases for true professions.[8] This seems plausible on the surface; critical examination of this criterion may not result in the same judgment. (The relationship of this occupational characteristic to client-relationships, the major focus of this volume, will become evident as this discussion continues.) Second, there is the tenet of intra-occupational control of norms of performance. The first of these characteristics is one with which academics are particularly blessed; the degree to which academics possess the second "professional characteristic" is rather more questionable. Now, there is a potential flaw in this line of thinking that should be examined; simply, can one have this argument both ways? Can it simultaneously be said that academics construct their definitions of professions influenced by *both* occupational "inadequacies" and endowments? The response rests on an uncomplicated consideration and it is that the nature of arguments in which the two characteristics are discussed differ substantially: the theoretical/scientific issue is approached directly and with the assurance of widespread scholarly consensus. The following selection from Wilensky (1970:484) can be taken as exemplary:

> These two cases tell us not only that both scientific and nonscientific systems of thought can serve as a "technical" base for professionalism but that the success of the claim is greatest where the society evidences strong, widespread consensus regarding the knowledge of doctrine to be applied. In modern societies, where science enjoys extraordinary prestige, occupations which shine with its light are in a good position to achieve professional authority.

[8] Wilensky (1970) is only the most recent of a long string of authors emphasizing this point (see footnote 5).

This particular selection is chosen because of the "magnanimity" the author exhibits; he is even willing to extend the sources of professionalism beyond "scientific systems of thought." The question of the adequacy of other than "systems of thought" as a basis of professions is unframed, and more importantly here, seemingly unframable within the established parameters of discussions of professions. The central intent here, it should be noted, is not to "debunk" professional ideologies in whole or in part, but rather to establish that "professionalism" is a normatively supported system of ideas that has been effective in preventing the effective involvement of "lower participants," using Etzioni's (1969) felicitous phrase, in significant occupational matters. Of course, this contention debunks the "service ideal" tenets of professionalism, but this is incidental. "Professionalism" is being analyzed, not criticized. Admittedly, however, if "professionalism" is truly an ideology, the two forms of analyses become indistinguishable. This is noted at this specific point for a straightforward reason; namely, that Wilensky's statement reveals one of the accepted central criteria of "professionalism," and it is felt that certain questions about the "objective" worth of the criterion in question can be profitably asked. Even assuming that subsequent discussion will cast doubts on the adequacy of the criterion, there must still be the further question of why such a criterion developed. In essence, then, the answer to this "why" is the primary goal being sought. Therefore, of necessity, the first questions to be asked deal with the applicability of the criterion in question: Is a "theoretical" and/or "scientific" system of thought a necessary basis for a "profession"? In answer to this question, a further one can be asked: Is not the basis of all "occupations," i.e. task-oriented social roles, a "system of thought"? If the most "non-professional" of occupations is examined, given the symbolic base of human culture, is it surprising to find there too a "system of thought"? For example, in the assembly-line manufacture of automobiles, is there not a "system of thought" operant among the assemblers? Do they not follow some "rational," sequential, therefore systematic, series of visual-cerebral-muscular activities through space and time? The answer to this should be an obvious "yes," but it is equally obvious that when writers on "occupations" speak about "systems of thought" they have something quite different in mind. The question then becomes one of eliciting the *difference* between the systems of thought operating in professional occupations and those operating in non-professional occupations. Wilensky (1970) unlike others, has relieved the investigator of the task of opening the wormy can of distinguishing between a scientific system of thought and a non-scientific system of thought by allowing them both to serve as the bases for professions; it is in this way, though, that another thorny, or wormy, problem arises: if it is not "science" and "non-science" that serves as the categorizing characteristic of professionals, then what does? Wilensky indicated that the doctrine- or knowledge-at-issue here must possess strong, widespread consensus regarding it. Now, Wilensky is not a bit ambiguous in terms of what the social "consensus" is about: it is the "expertise" of the experts. This is not nearly so circular, nor half so confusing at it may seem; it is not the core system of thought that makes the profession, it is its accessability. We find this quite clearly in the following (Wilensky, 1970:484):

> Medicine, since its "reform" in the United States some sixty years ago, has emphasized its roots in the physical and natural sciences along with *high, rigorously defined,* and *enforced standards of training* to impart that knowledge. Among the dominant denominations in the ministry, *rigorous standards of training are also stressed,* and doctrines are well codified and systematized, providing a technical basis for practice . . . (italics mine)

Presumably, by Wilensky's definition, in medieval society alchemists were professionals; in ancient society, astrologers; and in "primitive" society, shamans. The criteria of consensus regarding worth and vigorous standards of training clearly obtain. Now, while well-constructed, highly plausible, and probably "true," in a scientific sense, this conclusion of Wilensky the sociologist-scientist leads to corollaries with which Wilensky the sociologist-ideologist seems uncomfortable. Wilensky, as have been others dealing with the same problem, is forced to contend with the type of question implied in the above discussion; that is to say, what about "craftsmen"? Take as an example printers; is there not a highly developed body of ideas that goes with the selection of inks, paper, type-face, and the utilization of a complex machine technology? Indeed, it is to treat this problem that Wilensky (1970) wrote the article cited above, titled "The Professionalization of Everyone?" Wilensky is enough aware of the implications not to raise the issue of control of entry into the occupation as a distinguishing factor between "crafts" and "professions"; the apprenticeship programs of plumbers and masons are just as effective in limiting numbers of incumbents as two years of abstract theory in medical school and little if any institutional financial support for students in medicine. What, finally, is the cutting edge of professionalism for Wilensky? The "service ideal" — the "norm' of selflessness." It is around this issue, as Wilensky notes, that Mills (1951) centered his most mordant criticisms of the ideology of professionalism, and to be sure, it is in this normatively supported idea (namely, that such a "service ideal" exists) that the ideological nature of professionalism is displayed most clearly. It would be superfluous to list that which several other articles in this collection have already discussed; the numerous "transgressions" of the "service ideal" by each of the various professions. There are, though, two issues which do bear mention in relation to *this* treatment of academia: first, why not assure the welfare of the client by allowing the client participation in occupational decision-making; and second, is academia the occupation in which the ideal type of the "service ideal" seems to make its closest approach to reality? [9] The answers to these two questions are crucially linked. The answer to the first consideration has been the focus of a great deal of the literature on professions; directly stated it is that by definition, a profession is an occupation which, among other things, has control over its standards of performance. Again, an apparent circularity has entered the discussion of professions, and this time it is as real as it appears. The rationale given for the exclusion of lower participants has been that they do not possess the requisite knowledge to judge the occupational performance of the professions. Decisions about surgical procedures, the entering of guilty pleas, the decision to withhold privileged information, and so on, are all supposed to be beyond the purview of any non-practitioner. The true significance of scientific/theoretical bases for occupations now begins to stand out in bold relief; it is a "ploy" or tactic for justifying the exclusion of lower participants from occupational decision-making. It is imperative that a certain understanding be arrived at here; basically, it is that such pleas for client-exclusion or the exclusion of other lower participants (nurses in a hosptial, police in court, low-level clergy in some religions, etc.) may well be valid and that the right to limit occupational decision-making to the "higher circles" of the practice may indeed be justified. Once this is granted, it might also be admitted that enforcement of these "norms of exclusion" be left to the State, the source of legiti-

[9] Witness the common refusal of teachers to acknowledge adversary relationships between faculty and administrations, as reported by Lieberman (1960).

mate societal coercion. Thus, medical licensing, admission before the bar and so on may be seen as both legitimate and societally "functional." Why then, is the issue of occupational control of occupational issues classified here as "ideological"? The answer is in no way mysterious — it is that an occupational necessity is carried into occupational issues of far greater scope than those referred to either above or in the usual discussions on the matter. These are issues of control of entry into the occupation, thus affecting the supply of new personnel and therefore standards of remuneration and availability of services; the amount and vigor of boundary maintenance, as in the delegation of peripheral or even central tasks to "para-professionals," and client involvement in decisions regarding the mode of delivery of services, i.e. neighborhood clinics, public defenders, and so on. No, or little, scientific/theoretical expertise is required to make decisions relating to areas such as these; involved are matters of utilization, and not of practice; ends, not means. Certainly, the dividing line between the two issues is not boldly drawn; nonetheless, it is equally certain that **no** participation by clients in such policy-making is not a *requirement* of practice, but rather is a *prerogative* of professions. Thus it is that "professionalism" is seen as an ideology, especially as it involves the question of professional autonomy — authority, which almost all the sociology on professions[10] regards as the fundamental issue in the area. Once more, blanket autonomy is seen not as a necessity for the efficient functioning of the occupation, nor primarily as a technique for preserving the interests of lower participants, but rather as a very successful ploy in assuring intra-occupational control over the occupational environment, and thereby an assertion of dominance in the determination of occupational rewards. This "conclusion" merely leads to further questions; however, these further questions begin to lead to the central concern of this paper, i.e. the position of academia as a "profession" and changes therein. The pivotal question, perhaps surprisingly, becomes one of the difference between a "craft" and a "profession."

In earlier discussions, it may have seemed that it was being maintained that there was no difference: in terms of the particular issue involved, the possession of expertise, it was decided that *fundamentally* the variance was minimal; that is, that "professionalism" and guild-

---

[10] See Hughes (1958) for a discussion of the natural history of professions, as well as Carr-Saunders and Wilson (1933) and Caplow (1954).

type "unions" were both ways of limiting access to an occupation, and thus maximizing the rewards to be obtained by the occupational practitioners. This is still seen to be the case, but an identity of goals does not necessitate, logically or otherwise, an identity of means. What is of central interest at this point is the difference between the means so employed. It is through this approach that the basic issues of professionalism and professionalization emerge and consequently the foundation of an analysis of academia and its extant and emerging client relationships can be established.

ACADEMIA AND THE CONTROL OF OCCUPATIONAL ENTRY

It was indicated above that both "expertise" and the associated phenomenon of codes of "professional ethics"[11] are occupational strategies for reward maximization. Leaving the second stratagem for a moment, it is also suggested that academia, although it requires expertise as an occupational entry requirement, has not been able to provide its incumbents with substantial material rewards, at least as compared to other occupations with similar educational requirements. Explanation for this anomaly can be seen to emerge from a consideration of the institutional milieux from which academia historically emerges, as well as the changing input characteristics of the personnel recruited as incumbents. Concern with the issue of the status and origin of academic intellectuals has existed at a number of levels in sociology, as can be seen in the theoretical works of Mannheim (1936), Merton (1949) and Michels (1935). But there has also been interest in the currently more central issue of the "professional" aspects of academic history. Wilensky (1970:486), in terms of the temporally more distant European experience, and Sirjamaki (1967:42) as well as Corwin (1965:72), in reference to the colonial and nineteenth century American context, have all observed the clerical and/or elite origins of academics. If, in fact, we return to some of the earliest critical commentary on modern academia, namely that of Veblen (1954:62), we find this church-school relationship again remarked upon:

[11]Insofar as they incorporate the idea of relying on peer accountability to protect the interests of non-peers.

At the same time it reflected the historical fact that the colleges of the early days had been established primarily as training schools for ministers of the church.

The perception of these facts is seldom accompanied by exploration beyond half-serious notes on graduation programs making reference to the priestly origin of academic garb. These origins are of considerable import in understanding the claims to "professional" status academia has traditionally put forth. What is of primary significance is that early academics **were** either churchmen or were former churchmen, or were sanctionable by clerics in the social context of the medieval estate system. Special normative-legal prerogatives attaching to distinct social groups are perhaps the hallmark of an estate system — the fact that one held a privileged position guaranteed that one was accountable only to one's peers; this was particularly so when it came to church vs. state, lords temporal opposed to lords spiritual. Affairs of the church were jealously guarded from interference by temporal authorities. In fact, the lack of "client" (aristocratic) involvement in church affairs was to no small extent a cause of both the English and German Reformations. As academia was born as an offshoot of the clergy, it retained some of the prerogatives of estate position; namely peer control of occupational affairs. This is so not only in a functional-occupational sense, where there is a marked similarity between clergy roles and academic roles, but also in terms of recruitment patterns in which early academics frequently had been or were clergymen. Again, a persistence of prerogatives is suggested here as the original source of an idea of academic-professional autonomy. Other professions can trace similar ancestry. Now, it is certainly true that the estate system does not persist, and that clerical prerogative does not persist into modern times. How to account for the persistence of professional privilege, given the rapid obliteration of estates as the organizational basis of Western society, is clearly a pivotal issue.

If one studies academic recruitment patterns in nineteenth century Europe and its cultural progeny in the Western Hemisphere, a clear-cut academic "labor-pool" can be seen to have emerged. This pool drew on one or both of two sources — young clergy waiting for a pulpit, the predominant American pattern, and in Europe, the sons of old aristocratic and new commercial elites that for reasons of taste or (in)ability "chose" not to enter the burgeoning marketplace of industrial capitalism. To this author's knowledge, no empirical research exists on the issue of whether the clergy "allied" with the rising business-industrial elites of the nineteenth century or in fact was already a part of it by way of common lineage. It is this author's assertion that the latter was the case, although this thinking will have to stand as conditional until further research in this area is conducted. If common origins do turn out to be the case, they can be seen to be of no small significance for four fundamental issues in academia, one of them central to this essay: remuneration, autonomy, unionism, and client involvement.

In the brief discussion above, it was asserted that some of the autonomous characteristics of professions can be traced to their historical origins, and notably in the case of academia, to its sources in the medieval estate of the church. Also, in yet an earlier discussion, it was indicated that "professionalism" was a potentially successful ploy utilized by occupational groups to maximize rewards, and that the "autonomy," i.e., peer-control of occupational practice, was the basic technique by which this reward maximization operates. It was further contended that one of the ways in which professional autonomy is "operationalized" is through control of occupational entry. This summary, it should be noted, does not represent a unique analysis of professionalism. In fact, Caplow (1964:102) provides us with the following that is of a similar nature:

> In the independent professions the entire recruiting process, from the initial choice of candidates for training to the bestowal of honors at retirement, is under the close control of the professional group itself. Although the right to practice is generally conferred by a governmental board, this agency normally represents the profession and has usually been kept free from "political interference," i.e., the intervention of laymen. In the case of the independent professions, the violation of the occupational monopoly is punishable as a crime. These circumstances comprise the essential strength of professional organization, and explain the yearning for professionalization which besets almost all technical, service, and business occupations.

Caplow's (1964:104) analysis does not end with description of a somewhat obvious social reality; the dual function of control of entry is also mentioned:

> The limitation of entry to an occupation has a double function wherever it occurs: first, the maintenance of standards of performance, both in the public

interest and in the interest of those concerned; second, the maintenance of standards of remuneration, both by the limitation of supply and by the selection of candidates with socially favored characteristics. It is usually argued by the spokesmen for successfully restricted occupations (which may lie as far apart as bricklaying and editorial writing) that high standards of performance can only be maintained by establishing a high rate of remuneration to attract superior recruits.

Caplow (1964:102-103) is also sensitive to an issue raised earlier: namely, the question of distinguishing between crafts and professions:

> Recruiting in the building crafts is equally formal and still bears many marks of guild ritual. As in the case of professions, the rights and duties of candidates are specified with precision at each stage of their advancement, and the power of the state is often invoked to prevent outsiders from practicing the occupation. The most important differences are that the ultimate judges of competence are members of "higher" occupations, such as engineering, and that governmental authority cannot be overtly exercised by the occupational association. The control of recruiting is seldom complete — apprenticeship has partly given way to trade schooling organized by outsiders; effective occupational monopoly is usually limited to a local community and ceases abruptly at the urban limits; and the penalties for violation are nominal, *unless they are reinforced by personal violence or by agreements with employers and suppliers.* (italics mine)

This last point brings us to a, perhaps the, crucial issue. It was suggested that both professionalism and unionism represent alternative ploys available to occupational groups seeking to maximize rewards. It was then capsulized into a statement that a similarity of goals need not logically necessitate an identity of means. The rudiments of an answer to the stated question of explaining this difference among means can be seen in the above citations from Caplow. Simply, the difference between tactics relies on different dimensions of power. This is neither as trivial nor as evasive as it may originally appear. In order to understand the implications of the answer, it is necessary to examine an excellent analysis of types of social power provided by Etzioni (1969:61):

> Power differs according to the **means** employed to make the subjects comply. The means may be physical, material, or symbolic.
>
> *Coercive* power rests on the application, or the threat of application, of physical sanctions such as infliction of pain, deformity or death; generation of frustration through restriction of movement; or controlling through force the satisfaction of needs such as those for food, sex, comfort, and the like.

Remunerative power is based on control over material resources and rewards through allocation of salaries and wages, commissions and contributions, "fringe benefits," services and commodities.

Normative power rests on the allocation and manipulation of symbolic rewards and deprivations through employment of leaders, manipulation of mass media, allocation of esteem and prestige symbols, administration of ritual, and influence over the distribution of "acceptance" and "positive response." (A more eloquent name for this power would be persuasive, or manipulative, or suggestive power. But all these terms have negative value connotations which we wish to avoid.)

In order to make Etzioni's typology serve present purposes, all that is required is the simple substitution of "client" for "subject." The means which a profession employs are quite clearly "normative." This relates directly to the earlier conception of professionalism as an ideology, a set of ideas relying on normative sanctions for support. It is unfortunate that the sociologically naive, when encountering the concept of ideological support, immediately assume that such support is "inferior" to coercive power in securing goals, either individual or social. While it is true that all exercise of power "ultimately" rests on coercive force, this search for first causes is as unprofitable in sociology as it is in any other field of intellectual endeavor. The reality of society remains, and it is that very rarely must "unequal," "unjust," or "oppressive" social situations be supported by the application of coercive force. Throughout most of human history, social systems and their elites have relied, and quite efficiently so, on normative support. A search need go no further than feudal society for an almost ideal-typical example of this. In fact, it might well be suggested as is commonly done by a great many sociologists, that normative, i.e. "internal" sanctions, being always present, are much more efficient as supports for social organizations than the necessarily sporadic application of external negative sanctions. Given the suppositions of Mead (1934) and Cooley (1909) that normative structures become the "self" during the process of socialization, there is also the persistent positive sanction of self-affirmation in conforming to socially accepted normative constellations, even given the lack of reward in "material" realms. This is of the utmost importance to this exposition: it is by this process that "professions" maintain their social position. It is by the manipulation of symbols at many levels, from the wearing of distinctive occupational garb, the use of esoteric tongues, the fact that in modern society the mass media are either willing to, or unable not to, present professions in an exclusively positive perspective, and through the careful cultivation of the public vis-a-vis the "professional ideal" of altruism that professions establish and maintain their autonomy in and control of occupational matters, which includes as a primary corollary the exclusion of all lower participants from participation in vital matters. Now, as was indicated previously, the fact that some professions emanate from the medieval clergy, an estate already heavily laden with normative power, is of considerable significance. However, it is also the case that modern professions have spared no effort to take on the aura of the sacred, especially through allusions to their scientific/theoretical underpinnings, which in modern secular society is as close to an appeal to the supernatural as is likely to occur.

How then to distinguish between professions and crafts/guild unions? The answer is implicit in the above discussion; that is, it is essentially through a combination of coercive and remunerative power. The "strike" which is the manifest exercise of power by such occupational organizations, utilizes physical force, directly, by halting the actual physical enterprise the craft is involved in, and thus, indirectly, by forcing the cessation of productive activity and thus the possibility of remuneration. How do professions limit occupational entry and thus maintain high remunerative standards? By excluding the "unqualified," which is of course done in the interests of the client. On the other hand, unions must exclude non-members ("scabs" that is), maintain occupational boundaries, by physically coercing them from participating in relevant occupational activities. The attempt is sometimes made to reinforce this unpleasant reality with the power of the norms, "closed shop" and "local agreements," but two factors inhibit these ploys from being effective. First, the powerful symbol of altruism is lacking; the above norms are in the interest of only one segment of the occupational situation, the job incumbents. Second, there is the fact that unions frequently do not have access to the sanctioning power of the modern industrial state that professions do. This can be understood in terms of the input characteristics of early academics referred to earlier in this essay. At least in the colonial period and the early nineteenth century, academics, both at the college and lower levels, were members of an already privileged class and/or profession — the early American clergy and the social milieux this clergy has as its source. Thus, whereas academics in earlier periods of American history first of all had open to them the symbolic-normative resources of the clergy, and secondly tended to possess advantageous ascribed status, most other occupations did not have this useful occupational arsenal open to them. However, this does not resolve a very inportant, and surely paradoxical issue — one that has been alluded to previously, and one that will be of primary value in developing an analysis of current and future relationships between academics and their clients. This issue is both obvious and subtle, and it devolves to the following question: if it is true that first, professionalism is an ideology; second, that this ideology allows for occupational autonomy; third, that this autonomy provides for control of occupational entry, client relationships, and remunerative standards; and fourth, that academics have "professional" origins, then how has it come to pass that present academics are poorly paid, essentially power-less, and in great, non-absorbable numbers? The answer to this crucial question will provide the springboard to the issue of the present and future status of clients in academic contexts.

SOCIAL CHANGE AND THE DECLINE OF ACADEMIA

Given the above discussion of academia, wherein it is noted that the occupation starts out with potent proto-professional resources in terms of functional occupational origins as well as in the origins of incumbents, it is necessary to account for academia's downswing in terms of remun-eration, autonomy, and prestige. In fact, most discussions of the current state of academia, e.g. Jencks and Reisman (1962), Lieberman (1960), have centered around the perceived unfortunate state of academia and proposed ameliorative measures therefore. There has been no defi-ciency of sociological studies attempting to understand this slide, and some of them will be cited here. First, however, a few basic orienting statements are in order. If we are to understand or to "explain" the nature of client relations in academia, it is imperative that the alterations in the social structure in which academia is immersed be understood. Gerstl (1967) has previously described the problem at hand as follows (p. 235):

> The characteristics of teachers and their occupational structure afford more immediate explanations of their social standing. First are the phenomena previously referred to of a female occupational image and numerical abun-dance. Furthermore, the social origins of teachers are more lowly than are

those of members of most other professions (Mason, 1961), as is their amount of professional training and level of intelligence (Liberman, 1956).

The occupational structure of teaching also has a mainly negative valence upon status, especially in contrast with that of other professions. Education associations are weak, the financial rewards of teaching are low, and autonomy is limited. Not only is the teacher an employee subject to the authority of direct supervisors and school boards, but those whose behavior she controls are mere children.

Although this represents an adequate description of the occupational status of teachers, and suggests proximate sources for some of them, significant questions are unanswered. How does an occupation arrive at a state in which most incumbents are female? How does autonomy fade? How does remuneration reach its current low level, and perhaps most intriguingly, how does an occupation alter the origins of its recruits within only several generations from "high" to "low"? All of these questions would seem to be related to the central phenomenon of alteration of task and the changing social identity of occupational clients. The tactic employed in answering these questions will involve a treatment of the more specific issues first, the general ones next.

Corwin (1965: 218) answers the question of the feminization of one segment of academia with the following:

> Because public school teaching salaries did not keep pace with salaries in other occupations open to men, what had been a male occupation at the beginning of the century began to attract disproportionate numbers of women, until elementary school teaching in particular became identified as a woman's occupation.[12]

Now, whereas this introduces a significant antecedent factor in the development of the present status of teaching occupations, it forces another question: why did salaries decline and thus contribute to the recruitment of members of oppressed segments of the labor market; i.e. women? When the answer to this question emerges, many seemingly diverse questions are resolved. In looking for such an answer, it is necessary to deal with the origins of the job locus for most (not all) of the incumbents in the teaching occupations, namely, "public" or state-financed educational systems.

---

[12] It is recognized that this does not speak to the college or university situation; this problem will be dealt with in a subsequent section.

In a recent and seminal work, Michael B. Katz (1972) indicates that the growth of public education in America[13] can be traced to two, somewhat related macro-social phenomena: the decline of child labor in America and the perceived need to counter the influence of a Catholic educational system. The second is the more interesting stimulus: the exclusively Protestant elite of the United States in the nineteenth century was anxious about the effects of a socializing apparatus beyond their control. Given the conditions of "their" workers and a lack of sure knowledge about the co-optative and mediating possibilities of the religion in question, the owners of the means of production resorted to what was to become a favorite ploy in their manipulative repertoire: the establishment of an institution under their control and financed by "public" funds. Thus, in what was soon to become a common occurrence, the "lower participants" of American society as a whole were made to pay for the instrument of their own subjection. While interesting, this ploy is not a primary focus here, however. Of real interest is the consequence of this policy of establishing public institutions of "education." Obviously, when such an institution is created, employees are needed to staff it, and the institution at issue being "mass" in character, many of them. If the historical, social, and economic constraints on this recruitment are understood, then the current realities of academia fall nicely into place.

First, and most importantly, the historical context in which the creation of this new occupation of public school teacher takes place was one in which economic conditions were still marginal, and tax bases were thus limited. Hence, occupational incumbents could not expect a great deal of renumeration. If for some reason this were "necessary," it is likely the entire process would never have gotten underway. Given this "requirement," it was necessary to turn to disadvantaged segments of the labor market for personnel, as was noted previously. This "necessity" was conditioned by another and conflicting condition: that these new teachers must possess the "right" values with which to inculcate

---

[13] Corwon (1965: 218) notes the origins for this phenomenon without comment when he states that:

During this same period the status of children rose as a result of various rapid social changes. As the status of children rose, the status of teachers declined. In short, the status of public school teaching has tended to change with existing conditions; it has been especially influenced by changes in the status of women and children in the society as a whole.

their pupils. Both of these problems could be, and were, solved by the utilization of female personnel emanating from "old" American segments of the population. This occupational development solved several problems that this stratum experienced. One, the movement from the rural hinterland to the industrial city that made many female personnel economically superfluous during their late teens and early twenties. This social problem was compounded by a deficiency in the marriage market during the period in question due to high casualty rates during the Civil War. This same deficiency, besides delaying marriage into the twenties for some, obviated it completely for others. This group of anticipatorily widowed women were probably those that formed the core of the profession throughout the late nineteenth century, and in fact the popular stereotypes of the dewy-cheeked school-marm on the one hand, and Miss Grundy on the other, probably have their origin in this historical circumstance. In any case, these incumbents were quite willing to take small amounts in payment for their services, either because these positions were seen as transitionary, as in the first instance above, or because there was a lack of alternative, "respectable" employment for those women of the "old middle class" finding themselves in the second circumstance. Also, given the further factor that those male occupational products of the neo-technic revolution, "clerical" and "retail," i.e. "white collar" workers were the "target group" for non-elite, non-rural, old-stock Yankee women, female marriage constraints increased as the men delayed marriage into their twenties due to similar economic constraints. Thus, the "femaleness" and the poor pay of public school teaching occupations can be accounted for by a set of related macro-structural factors: the Civil War and vast internal and external migrations.

Those segments of academia in which "real" teaching was supposed to take place retained their male, and privileged, character considerably longer than did the new and related occupation of public school teaching, which was neither male nor privileged, nor scarce, from the very start. Jencks and Reisman (1969: 204) recognize the problems for teachers implicit in these factors in the following observation:

> It seems to be easier to professionalize groups sufficiently small, powerful, visible, or all three, to form an in-group in terms of both communication and policing quakery and trespass. . . . Historical accidents also play a role. Engineering in America started with the military and grew with the railroads

and steamboats, and this history of dependence on big organizations may help explain the lack of professionalization even today. If doctors in this country had been employed in the early nineteenth century primarily by the Army, the states, and big hospitals, it might have been much harder to professionalize them.

As was indicated earlier, however, this relates to but the first, and more frequently discussed aspect of "professionalism": its function in the "successful" professions. There is, however, a second "professionalism," which can be seen as an *intra-occupational, compensatory* ideology employed as a surrogate for occupational autonomy, and the "positive" benefits it entails.

The process of interest here is one in which occupational autonomy becomes transformed into individual "independence." In order for this process to operate, several necessary conditions must be present. First, that the occupation suffer declining status and reduced autonomy; second, that the value-cluster "individualism" be present in surrounding social milieux; and third, that alternative strategies for intra-occupational controls be absent. It will be proposed that all three of these conditions were and to an extent still are present in public school teaching, and increasingly among the professoriate and their respective and increasingly similar social contexts. But before dealing with these specifics, it is necessary to clear up the conceptual issue residing in the distinction being made between occupational autonomy and individual "independence."

Obviously, given the context of the previous discussion, occupational autonomy refers to the ability to exclude clients from decision making in important occupational areas. Occupational independence, however, refers to the reality (and the perception thereof by occupational incumbents) of practice: the technique by which occupational duties are performed. In this sense, autonomy and independence evidence a relationship but perhaps not a perfect and necessary relationship to one another. For examples of this, one need only look over to occupations such as steel-workers, which have little control over task, but considerable control over occupational entry and remuneration; one could also look to engineers employed in large-scale organizations who possess considerable control over task, but little control over remuneration, entry and so on. It does appear that those occupations commonly called "professional" combine the two modes of autonomy/independence. As was noted above, however, this is not the case with engineers, nor is it the case with public school teachers. Examples are recent strikes such as those of autoworkers at General Motors Lordstown plant, in which incumbents attempted to slow the assembly line speed to a more desirable (from their perspective) rate, and also those of teachers in public schools who must use lesson plans, required texts, etc. These examples show that the distinctions commonly made among various occupational types may be becoming more analytical than real. This development is not really damaging to the exposition at hand, though, because the concern here is with the perceptions of incumbents, rather than of those studying them. Evidence of this concern can be seen in some of the idiosyncratic attitudes which teaching exhibits. For example, some of the arguments against unionization that have most perplexed those attempting to organize teachers have been those relating to a perceived loss of an autonomy which does not really exist. A particularly choice and anguished plea by Lieberman (1960: 156) illuminates this area quite nicely:

> Since acceptance of the check-off is always voluntary in public employment, it is foolish to contend that teachers would lose their freedom by paying their dues through a check-off. It would mean only that they would have chosen to exercise their freedom in this way.
>
> The fact that the check-off is more common among unions than among professional associations has nothing whatsoever to do with professionalism.
>
> The snobbery toward unions revealed . . . is made even more ridiculous by the fact that some professional groups which are on salary do accept the check-off.

In Seymour (1966: 127), we see a classic attempt to elide task independence, occupational autonomy, and professionalism:

> To continue our examination of whatever distinction exists between the professional teacher and other workers, we turn next to what appears to be the priceless characteristic of professional practice, that is, the manner in which the teacher accepts and carries out his responsibilities. Within the limits imposed by working as a member of an educational team, a teacher must do his own work and make his own decisions. He must see to it that his work is done, that it is done on time, and that it is always done to the best of his ability.

Nothing whatsoever relating to entry control, group autonomy, standards of performance, or remuneration is present. Seymour (1966: 127) also lays out the characteristics of teacher *cum* professional in a detailed, systematic manner; since the substance remains unchanged although the format alters, its inclusion would be superfluous at this point. What is *not* superfluous is the clear presentation of an ideology, and an ideology relating to occupations, specifically "professions"; the pivotal point in this paper is the realization that *this* occupational ideology relating to professionalism is substantially different in form and radically different in intent and function from the ideology of "successful" professionalism discussed here previously. The next issues of concern and the final ones anticipating a discussion of client relationships in teaching occupations center around a more comprehensive discussion of the second form the ideology of professionalism takes, the realities of the occupations which the ideology intends to obscure, and the social origins of this obfuscating ideology. In this consideration, it will be seen that the identity of "lower participants" both as roles and people alters, and it is this alteration which will form the transition to the discussion of client relationships.

THE MYTHOLOGY OF PROFESSIONS

It would seem that it is both possible and desirable to analytically distinguish between two distinct types of occupational ideology. A problematic situation arises from this though, basically due to the fact that both ideologies go by the same name; i.e., professionalism. As was suggested in the preceding section, the crucial distinction between the two ideologies is the target group at whom the normatively based power of the concept-set is directed. In the ideology of professions that exists in and is promulgated by such occupations as law and medicine (notably, but not exclusively), the group at the "receiving" end is composed of clients and subordinate functionaries. As important as this "targeting" is, the associated factor of the goal of the ideology is also significant. In the case of "real" professions, the intent would be to gain the "consent" and willing participation of the lower participants. Thus, the flow of this ideology is from "top to bottom," from *independent* practitioners (this issue of "independence," will be of central importance, and is somewhat variant from an earlier usage of "independence") to clients, and is used as a client-regulatory mechanism. Thus, the ideology is constructed **by** the practitioners **for** the furtherance of their goals.

The second form of occupational ideology taking the name professionalism can also be labeled "mythological." That is, the relevant idea-set has as its function the "making understandable" of reality. Its goal is to provide those whose existence is covered by the mythology with an image of the universe that affirms identity, gives constancy to "reality" as it is perceived, and provides the believer with a sense of order in the universe. Mythologies, it goes without saying, exist at many levels in society: at institutional, and in the present case, associational levels. In a sense, the purpose of mythology can be seen as the insulation of persons from unpleasant realities, and more so, unpleasant realities which require unpleasant measures if amelioration is desired. This differs from ideology, as it appears in our first instance, in that ideologies are externally directed by social groups towards other social groups as a tactic for the manipulation of social reality, whereas mythology is intragroup in nature, and serves as an explanation of reality that obviates manipulative action in terms of that reality. That which is an ideology for one group often becomes a mythology for another. The seminal issue here is that a mythology for another. The seminal issue here is that a mythology differs from a "true" picture of reality along one significant dimension — whereas both "true" and mythological images of the world, or aspects of it, provide the believer with a relatively invariant and thus secure *Weltanschauung,* only "true" images of the universe allow its satisfactory manipulation. When reality changes beyond the abilities of the mythology to adapt, or the identity of believers alters dramatically, the mythology will likely not persist. The way in which the occupational mythology of academics ("professionalism") has functioned is thus at issue here.

In the specific case of academia, the mythology of professionalism has been structured around one primary concept: the myth of the cooperative enterprise. In this view of the occupational world, the teacher is an independent professional practititoner engaged in the education of children, and primarily concerned with this goal. School boards, administrations, boards of trustees, are all seen as means to this primary end. In this picture of reality, all participants in the educational process are equals (except students) with teachers as the first among equals in deciding matters of educational policy and technique. As was discussed, this is an example of the attempted substitution of individual independence for occupation autonomy. Even this independence is questiona-ble, but it does serve as a transitional concept to the one in which task, and not its associated reward, is seen as occupationally primary. Of course, if the linked assertions were correct or true, the notion of mythology would be considerably diminished. A great many other sociologists, and academics at all levels have found that situations different from that described above have been the rule. Corwin (1965: 241-242) provides a cogent summary of this position, and Jencks and Reisman (1969) and Lieberman (1960) voice nearly identical views:

> Teachers have virtually no control over their standards of work. They have little control over the subjects to be taught; the materials to be used; the criteria for deciding who should be admitted, retained, and graduated from training schools; the qualifications for teacher training; the forms to be used in reporting pupil progress; school boundary lines and the criteria for permit-ting students to attend; and other matters that affect teaching. Teachers have little voice in determining who is qualified to enter teaching. Non-professionals control the state boards which set standards for teaching cer-tificates. In 1950, in only five states were all or a minority of state teacher licensing board members required to be teachers; physicians, attorney, and dentists constitute a majority of such boards in all states, and even barbers and beauticians constitute majority groups on such boards in forty-four and thirty-eight states respectively. Teachers are not represented at all on such boards in a majority of states, ten of which expressly exclude the professional educator from state licensing boards. In view of the enrollment pressures, these lay boards of education have been reluctant to raise standards for teacher certification. The reluctance has been detrimental to the status of teachers, for raising the level of admission standards not only increases professional competence, but it also simultaneously creates a scarcity of trained personnel, a condition which leads to higher salaries and greater prestige. It is never possible to know which of these desired effects constitute the underlying motive for raising standards. But in either case, control over admission standards is essential to any organization, and it is especially characteristic of professional ones.

Now, it might be argued that this addresses itself to the issue of occupa-tional autonomy, but not independence as it has been defined here. This aspect of professionalism is also dealt with by Corwin (1965: 242) when he states that:

> Teachers do not control important phases of their classroom work. In 1950, the adoption of textbooks was in the hands of state boards of education in

sixteen states, only two of which were required by law to have a majority of educators. In the majority of states the state boards of education have the responsibility for adopting courses of study, and seldom are these boards controlled by educators. Where textbook adoption and curriculum is in the hands of local authorities, the decisions are often made by the administration or supervisory staff. These decisions are often made in consultation with teachers; but consultation is not authority to decide, and decision is the crux of professional authority.

Given that both aspects of autonomy *and* independence are lacking in some sectors of academia (excluding some college and university teaching, to which we will be returning shortly), the questions might be asked as to what the function of this mythology is, and also, what is its source? Although they are specifically concerned with scientists in business contexts, Goldner and Ritte (1970) provide an interesting analytical perspective on the ideology of professionalism. It is their belief that professionalism can become, in certain occupational circumstances, a substitute for occupational "success" and an anodyne for "failure." It is this kind of adaptation that has been suggested here; a way by which ideational rewards are substituted for more concrete rewards. Earlier it was stated that in this way, scant remuneration can be offered for a socially valued task. This rather abstract process can be concretized by acknowledging that what the mythology of professionalism does is prevent occupational incumbents from seeking scarce rewards, mainly economic, by providing them with unlimited rewards, social prestige.[14] If part of the offered positive self-conception (the offerer being employers of teachers) includes a notion of independence of practice, this serves to maintain the economic *status quo,* as Marmion (1969: 3) has noted:

> . . . it is difficult for many college faculty even to consider unionism. The position of many is that they oppose trade unionism (for them) because they cannot accept the hired hand, employer-employee relationship upon which the whole concept of trade unionism rests. Yet the typical professor has as the basis of employment a binding personal services contract. Although one may balk at the terms "employer" and "employee" they certainly are not altogether inappropriate.

Thus, not only does the mythology of professionalism supplant material

[14] This "prestige" is unlimited in that it relies on no consensus from those external to the occupation, but is a matter of self-image.

reward maximization as an occupational goal, it renders it next to impossible to attain by excluding self-perceptions necessary for relevant collective actions. A major problem still remains to be solved, though, and it centers around the issue of demythologization; that is, why is this mythology seen to be disappearing in the leading occupations, and what has led to this change? We turn to these pivotal questions now.

THE DEMYTHOLOGIZATION OF ACADEMIA

To start this portion of our discussion, we must reiterate our earlier points in reverse order. First, professionalism was seen as a compensatory ideology as it is present in academia. Second, this compensatory ideology serves to prevent the development of occupational autonomy. Third, the reason autonomy does not develop in academia is because of the organizational context in which the occupation exists in modern times; the large public educational apparatus.[15] The crucial factor is that this occupation is *created* by a privileged elite for its own purposes. Fourth, the original group of occupational incumbents are "cheap" labor, members of large and disadvantaged groups. Thus, the inability to "force" autonomy and large-scale remuneration makes a compensatory ideology attractive. What should then be looked for as causes of demythologization are changes in the identity of occupational recruits, and changes in occupational function, a topic as yet untouched here. It is obviously crucial to our purpose to deal with these changes.

In the case of public education, the most important change in incumbent characteristics has been the "masculinization" of public school teaching. As cheap "higher" education has become available, and as growth in the number of white collar occupations has slowed, and even reversed recently,[16] the attractiveness of teaching as a career for men has increased dramatically. This trend is further supported by strong social values relating to social mobility. As the supply of labor continues to grow rapidly, especially as the post World War II age group matures, and the number of "true" professional positions are maintained by

---

[15] Both Jencks and Reisman (1969) and Elam and Moskow (1969) deal with this issue. It is their contention that first, there are too many teachers for truly professional organization; and second, that the fact that teachers are employees and not independent practitioners selling their scarce skills to many clients inhibits their ability to demand professional prerogatives.

[16] See Miller and Roby, "The Future of Inequality," (1970).

present incumbents at a more or less stable level, the attractiveness of even quasi-professions such as teaching increases. Although mobility drives relating to status may be gratified, or at least be mollified by entry into teaching occupations, the material rewards available are seen as inadequate. While teaching salaries may be adequate as supplementary incomes (in the case of married women) or as temporary incomes (in the case of the unmarried), they are clearly inadequate as primary sources of family income, especially for those who have been anticipatorily socialized to life-styles appropriate to other occupations requiring college training. Thus, in public education, it should be expected that demythologization will take place. There are two possible directions which this thrust takes. Before continuing, however, a brief discussion of the relevance of all this to college and university professors must be included. After this attempted unification of the future of separate occupational segments we will return to the control discussion begun above.

To this point, emphasis has been placed on public school teaching. At least as important, if not as large, is the occupational sub-group involved in higher education. The careful reader might well question the significance of our discussion to such a group. College and university professors have historically been better paid than public school teachers. They have come from privileged segments of society and have been male, white, Protestant, and upper-middle class in origin. College teaching has historically required credentials difficult to come by. The present situations are substantially altered. Since the origin of land-grant institutions in the nineteenth century, and the growth of prestigious private colleges into the nuclei of vast multiversities, the number of academic positions has increased enormously. With this increase in size have come other changes of similar scale. First, it is no longer possible to draw on "spare" members of social elites or sub-elites for personnel. Veblen (1954: 155) recognized this early in the century, when he noted that the economic lot of professors was a precarious one. Second, the birth and growth of secular institutions causes a major break away from the clerical traditions and sources of academia. Third, the previously mentioned impaction in other professions has caused more interest in academic occupations.

The question might aptly be asked why academic occupations have not been similarly impacted — that is, why haven't academics retarded entry into **their** occupation. A partial, though important, answer can be seen in the nature of occupational tasks involved. College and university professors serve dual functions — one is teaching, one is research. From Veblen (1954) on there has been argument as to which function is or should be primary in the occupation. One way in which these functions have been combined is that apprentice professors, "graduate students," have come to fill the role of assistants in the research process, either as direct adjuncts to it or as professor-surrogates performing teaching functions while professors perform the research. This phenomenon has played a crucial role in the supply of college teachers in that the professoriate has not sought to limit occupational entry because of the benefits of plentiful apprentices. Thus, the custom of more-or-less unrestricted entry into graduate schools and monetary support has become the rule.[17] This free-entry policy has attracted substantial numbers of members of large age-cohorts interested in upward mobility to these occupations. This places pressure on the occupation in two ways: the large number of incumbents available depresses the job-market, thus threatening already present practitioners (a much remarked upon phenomenon today) and secondly, causes the occupation to consider limiting occupational entry. Also, due to the fact that almost all of the modern professoriate is of non-elite origins, remuneration becomes of great significance. Hence, it can be seen that the occupational situations and prospects of teachers and most professors are the same with respect to *employment* in large-scale bureaucratically organized institutions, increasing concern with remuneration, and growing pressures towards asserting control over occupational entry. There have been alternative responses to these occupational pressures and the present and future consequences of these developments for client relationships are the matters remaining.

REPROFESSIONALIZATION AND UNIONIZATION

The compensatory mythology of professionalism is rapidly disappearing or has already disappeared in vast segments of academia. Where it remains, it is either among older teachers who acquired identity in earlier situations, or who exhibit the objective characteristics of earlier

[17] Unrestricted in that no supply-demand calculations are made; only those calculations relating to the maximal number of graduate students funding will allow have occurred.

incumbents, or it is within institutional contexts mimicking earlier forms — small private schools and colleges, especially those still recruiting personnel with elite or sub-elite origins. Many articles, "theoretical," professional, and popular have noted this movement away from earlier self-images in academia. In general, two occupational responses to the stated constraints have been identified; one consisting of an attempt to move towards the more successful type of professionalism, the other adaptation being a movement towards a more coercive form of occupational autonomy; i.e., unionism.

In looking for evidence of "reprofessionalization," it is necessary to consider several diverse trends. The first movement towards occupational autonomy has been in the attempt by certain fields experiencing a glut in potential incumbents to limit the number of graduate students in those fields.[18] This ploy, somewhat obviously, is being examined in the segment of academia employed in institutions of higher education. This, of course, is a tactic whose "benefits" occur in the future, and that cannot be precisely measured. It also can become counter-productive as undergraduate students become aware of dwindling opportunities in a field and make their career plans accordingly. This then decreases enrollments in a given field, or as more and more fields do this, higher education as a whole, which leads to decreases in faculty size. A similar, but distinct tactic has appeared at some recent scholarly association meetings, such as the 1971 American Historical Association meetings, in which a group of historians suggested that the association should limit faculty course loads in order to put pressure on institutions of higher learning to hire additional faculty. Again, these tactics bear the hallmark of professionalism; the attempt to further the interests of occupational incumbents through the manipulation of task-centered situations, and in a way which can be "justified" as client-beneficial also, as in this case the improvement of faculty-student ratios.[19] In toto, these types of actions are typical of policies coming from a rejuvenated American Association of University Professors, the over-arching professional association of those engaged in higher education. Of late, the AAUP has become more active in seeking the position of bargaining agent for

[18] This tactic is also being considered in the legal field, as can be seen in Volume 17, No. 2 of the Pennsylvania Division AAUP Newsletter (Fall, 1972).
[19] Movements against tenure can also be seen as paradoxically "professional" in the same manner.

organized college faculties. The issue that has persisted as the most sensitive and fundamental is still unresolved, and this is the issue of the power-base from which this segment of the academic profession can enforce its desires. Oberer (1969: 133) recognizes this problem and introduces a concept that leads to a further issue of interest:

> The dilemma of the professor is that he is both a member of a profession and an employee. In the former capacity he must set his own standards, or at least share in their setting. This is so because of the two factors which create the societal need for and which define a "profession": (1) the grave importance of the calling to the public . . . (2) the esoteric character of the calling and the consequent inability of nonmembers to set and enforce the necessary standards. In the other aspect of his dual capacity, that of employee, the professor's standards are set for him by his employer. The classical professions of law and medicine are not typically burdened with this ambivalence. . . . What self-employed doctors and lawyers can do because they believe it to be professionally right, professors can do only after overcoming opposition from the administrators and trustees who hire and supervise them.

A very important point is broached in the above selection, and it is that those academics employed in institutions of higher education, while professionals in terms of expertise, exist in an occupational milieu in which client relationships are mediate, not direct.

What has been suggested is that the issue of the identity of the "client" in academia is somewhat unclear. Whereas academics are employees in large-scale organizations, there are still lower participants, namely, students. In some sense, students are clients, but their remunerative contact with academics is minimal. The political unit or educational institution which hires academics is the actual purchaser of occupational services, in some instances serving as an intermediary between student and academic (in "private" institutions), and in most cases the sole remunerative agent (as in public institutions). When physicians or lawyers wish to increase remuneration, they raise *fees* which they then collect themselves. Academics face the dilemma of receiving income indirectly through an organization, thus, they must put pressure on an institution to change its policy — remuneration for academics is by salary, not fee; it is somewhat separated from practice. In academia, unlike in autonomous professions functioning on a fee system, the *academic* is contractually purchased for a length of time, whereas in medicine or law, a clear cut service is purchased — an examination, an operation, a consultation, or a court appearance. *The client contact is of short and well-defined duration;* in academia this is not the case. Thus, there arises considerable fuzziness about the "value" of the service being purchased, and concomitantly, difficulty in establishing "fair" compensation arises. Further, any demand by incumbents for an increase in remuneration has an element of arbitrariness, in that the ultimate clients, parents and/or taxpayers, are never quite sure what they are getting for their money. This problem, inherent in the nature of the occupation, ultimately leads to calls for "accountability" of various types: credit hour/student "units," student performance, and so on. This creates further problems, in that these issues are not strictly remunerative, and in fact are of great technical/theoretical interest. Thus, evolving client relationships in academia present what is apparently a far more complex set of issues than is the case in other "professional" occupations.

Returning to our point of departure, we can see the above complexity in attempts by the AAUP to cope with both types of issues, but as independent phenomena. More importantly, the employee status of the professoriate demands employee tactics as sources of occupational power. This necessity is accentuated by a task characteristic of medicine, law, and dentisty, which is that the services provided have an immediacy to clients that is not present in academia. Besides the fact that competition is eliminated by fee-setting and practitioner-scarcity, there is the crucial reality that when a doctor, dentist, or lawyer is needed, in most circumstances, the need is *now*. In education, on the contrary, the delivery of services is a years-long process, and its benefits are diffuse (although no less socially "important" than in the other professions) and not clearly linked to the delivery of services. In fact, the whole issue of strikes and unionism is only "possible" in a society in which teaching occupations serve vital *latent* functions of delaying entry into the job market for adolescents and child-care for younger children. When unskilled labor is scarce, and the place of women is in the home, coercive power is a dead-letter as far as academia is concerned. To a lesser extent this is still the case in circumstances, e.g. the recurrent strikes by public school teachers in urban areas, in which a not uncommon public response is "who cares"? A similar pattern can be seen in the refusal of certain electorates to approve school budgets thus forcing the closing of schools. Such client reactions can be generally expected in areas in which occupations are predominantly industrial and in which female participation in the labor market is limited.

Even if academics should decide on coercive tactics; i.e., unionism, as a means of controlling client relationships, such tactics may be ineffective in a great many contexts for the reasons just delineated. In any case, both professional associations such as the AAUP and NEA, and unions such as the AFT, are becoming progressively more similar in their reliance on the withholding of services as the ultimate source of occupational power. It might also be argued that in the future, as this tactic becomes more widely used, the gap between remuneration in the professoriate and among public school teachers, small to begin with, will diminish even more due to the fact that public school teachers play an increasingly more important social function, that of child-care. Withholding of services by public school teachers has more *immediately* serious social consequences than the same action by college professors. Now, this would be consistent with the argument that the position of college professors will likely become increasingly precarious as increasing automation and cybernetization continue to diminish jobs per capita, and thus diminish the value of a college education for a great many, although concomitantly increasing the value of the education for a select few — those entering "non-rationalizable" occupations. An opposing and perhaps dominant trend, however, will be the emerging need for institutional absorption of a new lumpenproletariat composed of unemployables with middle class origins. The only "acceptable" or ego-maintaining endeavor for such a social group would likely be "education," even when its "material" benefits are increasingly obscure. Thus, the willingness to withhold this service may well prove extremely profitable, especially if one considers the state of mind of middle-class parents whose college-age children are forced to return home with absolutely no immediate or long-term prospects of employment.

What is being suggested here is that as the functions of the various segments of academia become more and more similar, standards of remuneration and the tactics for increasing them will also move towards similar forms. Hence, what we have approached rather gingerly here is the question of evolving economic client relationships in academia, and in general, macro-social realities would seem to indicate that clients will have to expect an erosion of their position. What this means in concrete terms is that they will have to pay more, either through tuitions or taxes, for the same services rendered, however, by "demythologized" professionals. Every indicator available shows increasing willingness in academia to use coercive power, or strikes, to control economic conditions in the profession. This is especially true at the public school level where the torrent of newly-minted teachers is putting exceptional stress on established incumbents. Evidence for the trend towards unionization and strike is plentiful at all levels in academia.

At the college and university level, Lieberman (1971: 61) points out that although only six percent of the professoriate were collectively organized, and only six universities were among the 180 institutions of higher education so organized, past experience among public school teachers, where the NEA and AFT have come to represent 65 percent of said functionaries after a campaign of only nine years, would tend to indicate that future trends would be towards greater organization. Lieberman's prognosis would seem to be well founded, as since his article appeared, significant NEA and AFT gains have taken place, as can be seen if the house organs of the respective organizations are consulted. Of more importance than raw data on current percentages of unionized college faculties are twin trends: increasing concern on the part of the AFT with higher education, perhaps due to diminishing returns on "raiding" the NEA as well as the "ripeness" of the professoriate for organization, and concomitantly, increasing accommodation and joint action between the NEA and the AFT, a movement, it should be noted, yet to be joined by the increasingly militant AAUP. Perhaps the most obvious manifestation of this was the report in the *American Teacher* (1973a: 6) of joint NEA-AFT representation at the City and State University of New York systems. Also, this *entente,* perhaps ultimately consummated in merger, has been the major concern of the AFT for many months (*American Teacher*, 1973a, 1973b). Beyond the tactical impact of such accommodation, there is the more central matter of the abandonment of "compensatory" ideology by the NEA. Although there is and will be obvious revision taking place as to how collective bargaining is not *really* "unprofessional," and in fact really is "professional," it is not the revisions themselves that most support the arguments that have been made here, but rather their impact; the way in which organization has come to supersede "independence" as a legitimate occupational value. It is this transition that can be seen to most clearly exemplify both the dual ideologies of professionalism and the altering polarities in academia.[20] To be discussed next are certain extremely significant "non-economic" (though in many cases, economically related) issues that are of profound interest to clients, and that have already become *casus belli* in various client "revolts": tenure, "accountability" (touched upon briefly at an earlier point), institutional decision making, "community" control of educational processes, and classroom reform.

THE REVOLT OF THE CLIENT
AND THE ACADEMIC COUNTER-REVOLUTION

The revolt of the "client" (still an unclear social role in this discussion) in academia has taken place on a broad front, involving many issues relating both to task and occupation. The issue of tenure will allow a distinction to be made between the two types of "clients" academics serve in the modern world; i.e., those with whom a people-related occupation palpably deals, in this case teachers vs. students and their parents; and those who actually employ (remunerate) the practitioners of the set of skills involved, in this case, school boards, colleges, etc. As more and more "professionals" enter large-scale organizational contexts, it is likely that such a distinction will become of increasing value. In any case, what is being suggested here is that there are two types of clients with whom academics must deal: "job" clients that they meet in task situations and "occupation" clients that make out pay-checks. Both of these client-types are rebelling, or, in the latter case, resisting occupational gains in remuneration and autonomy. Although aspects of "rebellion" idiosyncratic to each sector can be analytically distinguished, often the effects of movement in one sector have consequences in the other; sometimes these dual currents move at cross-purposes to each other, and sometimes they are mutually reinforcing. As an example of this latter situation, the case of "tenure" will serve well.

Tenure. It would be possible to assemble a literally enormous bibliography on tenure composed solely of articles written in the last few years,

[20] It should be noted that the differential success of organization among urban and non-urban, state and private institutions tend to validate previous assertions regarding the role of input characteristics of incumbents, social milieux, and organizational context in determining which professional ideology becomes dominant at a given time.

both intra-occupationally and in the popular press.[21] Academic "professional associations" such as AAUP and NEA, and the pre-eminent teacher's union, AFT, have all spent huge amounts of energy in dealing with this issue. Much of the argument can be distilled to two central issues: academic "freedom" and job security. Both of these issues are of consequence to clients of both types, and both relate to further issues inherent in the ideology of professionalism, especially the primary ones of autonomy and remuneration.

The relevance of academic freedom can be seen in its existence as an ideology. As was previously noted, an ideology represents a means of exercising power through the use of normative force. Therefore, it is not unexpected that on a vital issue such as tenure, academia has developed a body of normatively supported ideas indicating to job and occupational clients why they *should want* to support the institutional norm of secure life-time employment of incumbents (after a "probationary" period of variable length). Certainly, in a self-professedly egalitarian society, no one wants to condemn "freedom," but this semantic manipulation is only tangential to the real issue here, which is in *occupational-client* terms what is this ideal's meaning? Academic ideologists would have it that in order to assure the safety and security of those holding unpopular, but perhaps "true" ideas, and thus to encourage the discussion of those ideas, employment must be assured to their holders. This sounds fine and commendable on its face, but there are several questions that need asking, and have in fact been sporadically asked in the past. First, given the existence of probationary periods of employment, what is the likelihood of a holder of unpopular ideas, presumably needing protecting, ever receiving tenure? What does such a set of concepts and norms mean to proximal clients; i.e., students, parents, and communities (as opposed to their employing political apparatus)? In a very real sense it means that academics hold that they have the right and privilege to remain aloof from the standards of those that succor them. This is clearly **not** a client-centered principle. When "liberals" advocating "community" control of education are faced with such questions as "What if a community such as X wished to teach racist thought in their classrooms"?, they are usually at a loss for an

---

[21] Most important and comprehensive has been the very recent AAUP and AAC "Faculty Tenure" (1973). This work in itself is a palpable response to attacks on tenure.

adequate answer. Usually, what emerges is a watered-down argument of the "free market-place of ideas" school which begs the Kantian question of how one entertains an idea to which one has never been exposed. To state that *ipso-facto* clients should thus be prevented from entering this realm of occupational decision-making puts the argument smack back into the middle of the paternalistic ideology of professionalism. Academic freedom and client control are not *necessarily* mutually exclusive — some proximal clients would presumably *choose* academic freedom and perhaps even tenure as a method of insuring it — it is likely, however, that a significant number would not. Thus, the revolt of task clients against "tenure" might be seen as having profound repercussions for the development of ideas *if*, and this is an extremely significant "if," one buys the idea that the holders of unpopular ideas receive tenure, and once they have it, can keep it. Since this is a questionable proposition, and unless one has a dangerously low opinion of non-academic participants in the academic enterprise, it is likely they will also question it, one might inquire as to other issues relating to tenure that are of interest to job or task clients. A primary one that has emerged is the question of "dead wood." This question is of significance not only to task clients and practitioners, but will also lead to a discussion of job clients and the "real" tenure issue — standards of remuneration and job security.

The issue of "dead wood," or of practitioners who are protected by tenure but who presumably no longer adequately fulfill occupational requirements, has emerged as a significant ideological counter-thrust by task clients in their "revolt." It is an "ideological" counter-thrust in that it too has some cognitive elements of questionable pedigree. One of these is that academia is one of the rare occupations in which life-time job security is guaranteed. But academia is also one of the few occupations in which (prior to the acquisition of tenure), yearly or bi-yearly contracts form the basis of employments. In the vast bulk of large-scale organizations, employment is open-ended and based on continued adequate, usually minimal, performance. If we look to the autonomous professionals, we find that once licensing, or admission before the bar is attained, only under the most esoteric of conditions is the privilege of practice removed. This observation allows at this point the beginning of a demystification of the ideology of *counter*-professionalism. Again, debunking such myths no more supports professionalism than does debunking professional myths support client-centered positions. In fact, what we have in any proper discussion of occupational issues is a question of the differential allocation of "scarce" societal resources for the performance of socially valued tasks. Thus it is possible to describe tactics, including normative-ideological devices, used to influence the outcome of struggles for these resources and for the observer still to maintain a stance of value-neutrality.

If one asks whose ox is gored by tenure, even given superlative performance by all occupational incumbents, the answer is, employing institutions. Tenure amounts to a substantial surrender of organizational power; i.e., the power to remove incumbents, and also, perhaps more importantly, leads to an increasingly expensive array of practitioners. That is, as incumbents remain in positions for numbers of years, they also tend to rise in rank and therefore the cost of their services rises concomitantly. To institutions attempting to minimize the costs of instructional staff, a consistent and appealing conjecture appears, e.g., why not trade off a teacher making $18,000 for one or two practitioners willing to accept half that amount? In terms of ideological counter-thrusts, academics might maintain that the quality of education is thereby damaged, that a trade-off of occupational expertise for occupational naivete is being made, and to the detriment of the educational process. An ideological riposte to *this* parry might involve the assertion that what one is in fact trading off is outmoded occupational material for that newly minted; the knowledge base of yesterday for the knowledge base of today, in addition to halving faculty/student ratios, which would be a "good" trade. Their issue of tenure thereby transforms itself into an issue of "accountability"; i.e., the degree to which the occupational enterprise achieves its goals, and the relative efficacy of alternative means to these ends. In reference to the question above, does classroom experience or contemporaneity lead to the more adequate fulfillment of desired educational aims? This question in conjunction with related ones, has application to both higher and mass educational situations, and indeed is already being asked with some frequency at both levels although often rhetorically and retroactively, following decisions made on the basis of other criteria, such as financial exigency and the anticipated readiness of incumbents to countenance unionism. Regardless of its current "relevance," this question still is intermediary to the fundamental issue of "accountability," and the causes by which this issue has emerged quite strongly in the developing battle between academia and its dual clients.

Accountability. "Accountability" has become an issue in academia; this is an induction that can be made by reading any newspaper, educational journal, or topical magazine. The interesting concern here, though, is the question of why. Resistance to "accountability" or client judgment of performance is to be expected in any profession — the very "soul" of autonomy, as was discussed at an earlier point, is the privilege of peer judgment — the belief that only peers known enough to adequately consider their fellows' conduct of occupational tasks. Although there have been mutterings by clients in this connection in other professional contexts, only in academia has the matter emerged with such force. Physicians have not been asked to provide morality statistics, dentist re-visit figures, or lawyers their won-lost record — why teachers? There seem to be three primary reasons for this: one dealing with the relative occupational "strengths" of professions; the second relating to the occupational context within which academics function; and third, goal-diffusion.

It is not difficult to argue that one of the reasons academia is subject to pressures by clients relating to "accountability" is that it is too "weak" to resist these pressures; that when the bulwark of autonomy, especially as it relates to occupational entry and decision-making is absent, then such subsidiary "assaults" on the occupation are bound to get by. In effect, this argument maintains that in an overall picture of weakness, a minor frailty should not be surprising. While in some sense true, such an approach does not serve as an opening for the more substantial questions of "why" and "now what" which this paper seeks to answer. For such an examination, the second and third points serve much more adequately.

As has already been suggested, teachers exist in the same occupational context as many other occupations; that is, academics are predominantly employed in large-scale, bureaucratically structured organizations — schools or colleges. One of the much remarked upon, and equally lamented characteristics of such organizations is a zeal, and occasionally a fixation, for quantification. In some contexts, this zeal can be easily, and sometimes usefully, satisfied; for example, in factories. In other organizations, where the product is not material, some difficulty arises. In government agencies where information is the "product" this can lead to goal-displacement in which record-keeping and related behaviors, rather than the activities they reflect, become the focus of the incumbents' activities.[22] This tendency is aggravated in institutions where there is the additional factor of public funds grudingly allocated, and thus the frequent need to justify the support provided. This situation exists in academia, and even more so in times of economic duress in which funders are especially loathe to finance let alone increase funds, without "good," which in most cases means palpable or tangible, reasons. This raises the third, and pivotal aspect of this explanation of the source of client pressure for "accountability" — goal diffusion.

A very real question in relation to academia is the question of what exactly it is that academia "produces," or in an archaic conception, what is its social function. Many easy answers, but few adequate ones, suggest themselves. "Education" is the obvious answer, but of course it begs the implicit question of precisely what "education" is. Given knowledge of large-scale social organization, it should not be surprising that opinions as to these functions differ as different levels of participation are examined. For task clients, teachers serve several apparent functions: child-care during the day, the imparting of valuable skills, and socialization to norms of the wider society. For employing clients, the main function of teachers is the maximally efficient organizational processing of students, and for society as a whole, the institution of academia provides an acceptable means of delaying entry into the labor market.[23] This last issue has not emerged as one of import in comtemporary discussions of accountability since to point it out would bring to light more encompassing ideologies, and a discussion of these would be uncomfortable for many important sectors of modern society. The other issues of a more intramural type have emerged, however, and thus deserve consideration of two counts: first, why have clients rasied such issues to which we have already alluded, and what effect would this movement have on academia if it were successful. Possible responses by academia will be discussed in a final section of this exposition.

Proximal clients, as has already been indicated, have centered their concern around two main issues: the adequacy of current educational practitioners as the teachers of skills, and as agents of socialization. On

---

[22] Merton (1949).
[23] See Collins (1971) for a discussion of this academic function.

both these counts, concern has emerged in the wake of apparent failure. First, there has long been a feeling among substantial segments of the American populace that the norms academics are imparting are suspect. Thus, when juvenile deliquency rates rise, or drug addiction among adolescents increase, or reformist political activity among college students become prevalent, questions almost always arise regarding the role of schools in these matters. Now, for the simple reason that it is nearly impossible to apportion the effect of peers, parents, and macrostructural pressures in producing "inadequate" socialization, it has caused discontent with academia and perhaps is the reason for "accountability" pressures among proximal clients, rather than being a manifestation of "accountability pressure itself.

On the other hand, concern over grade-reading level, percentage of students continuing their education, and the ability for newly minted students to enter the job market successfully have all provided nexuses around which calls for "accountability" have come. Again, the reason these issues seem to arise in academia has to do with diffuseness of goal and the related issue of method of financing. Regardless of success or failure, the actual performance of task by other "professionals" serves as an immediate satisfaction of the client's goal. This is not the case in academia, where the performance of task is distant in both time and space from the value of these performances as they are immediately experienced by the client. A physician delivers his services to the client in a way that is immediately obvious; the effect of a teacher, if any, [24] in getting a student a job may be lost amidst a vast number of other factors. Also, in other professions not predominantly operating in a publicly funded milieu (social work being another exception), "purchase" of services is discretionary — one cannot be forced to go to a private physician under most circumstances. One must, however, pay taxes. For those academics operating in a public setting, this serves to magnify the negative effect of goal diffusion on client relationships. The question remains, however, whether these demands for accountability by proximal clients are essentially inimical to the interests of academics. It would seem that they are, and for the primary reason that there now exists no effective body of theory or technique that when used in the academic context can "guarantee" results. Thus, accountability de-

[24] Jencks, et al (1972).

mands by proximal clients *are* inimical to academics because they can have little hope of demonstrating efficacy to these clients. Also, the question of sanctions also enters the picture; that is, what happens to teachers who do not perform up to these "standards" once they are established? Since teachers have no well-grounded strategy or set of tactics which will assure "success" in passing on norms or bodies of knowledge, accountability must be threatening to some extent to all those who are not the possessors of a bed-rock pedagogical "self-confidence," which almost certainly excludes the vast majority of academics. This is *not* to say that the vast majority of academics are incompetent; rather, it is being maintained that there is as yet no clearly successful and systematic set of pedagogical techniques which when utilized provide, if not necessarily the likelihood of success, at least reasonably accurate predictions of success. This is not the case in many other professions; engineering has a reliable knowledge base, as do medicine, law, and dentistry. In these occupations, when a practitioner says that he/she has done his/her "best," it can be said with some assurance that will generally be accepted as such by clients, even in the case of "failure" of practice, since some more or less crude notion of best is held by both client and practitioner. As this is not the situation in academia, a certain insecurity as to standards of performance established by proximal clients should be expected among academics. The threat of "accountability" as it relates to distal clients is of a somewhat more straightforward nature, and this is the next point to which we turn.

It was already suggested that as far as the employing institutions in which academics practice are concerned, the primary consideration of "performance" is the smooth "processing" of students at the lowest per capita cost possible. This is true of colleges, universities, public schools, parochial schools, and other educational institutions. There may be other goals which distal clients value, but none is as clear-cut nor of as immediate import as the very basic one just delineated. Thus, "accountability" in terms of these clients devolves to a very immediate occupational matter: maximization of class size. This has varying import in different institutional contexts: in "lower" education, where the supply of students is ample, at least in the immediate present, this amounts to progressive pressure for increasing class size. In higher education, this is true of publicly funded institutions, but not necessarily of private colleges, since many are faced with a decline in enrollment.

"Credit-hour-accountability" usually amounts to reductions in faculty size. Thus, in the first instance, "accountability" demands by distal clients amount to a decline in working conditions; more importantly, in the second context, "accountability" or cost per pupil analyses of individual professors and departments threaten livelihoods themselves. In the end, the same can be said for accountability demands by proximal clients; presumably, if no immediate positive benefit can be seen to accrue to proximal clients, pressure will be put on distal clients to reduce the financial burden placed upon them in the funding of educational institutions. It can therefore be expected that academics will generally oppose calls for accountability. In fact, this has been the case with the AFT and NEA in public school teaching, and with the AAUP at the level of higher education. The next "front" in the rebellion of clients to be considered is that of "community control," briefly alluded to in reference to the "academic freedom" argument for tenure.

COMMUNITY CONTROL

"Community control" of public educational establishments is perhaps the broadest thrust by clients for a voice in educational decision-making. It is a clear-cut and directly stated desire on the part of proximal clients, usually parents and significant figures in other community institutions such as churches to involve themselves in matters of incumbent selection and practice. The first of these, the selection of incumbents, seems at first glance to present a threat to academia in general and new occupational practitioners in particular. Rather than being a new development, community control is an old concept that is being diffused into new social contexts. Background for this contention is obviously required.

If by "community control," it is meant that parents and locally based representatives participate in the selection of curricula, texts, administrative personnel, and other task-related decisions, then in the majority of white, middle-class communities, such control has long existed. In fact, the existence of such an "infiltration" is one of Lieberman's (1960) primary complaints regarding non-professionalism in public school teaching. School boards, drawn from community personnel and often acting in public with the knowledge of parents are the predominant mode of decision-making in American public school administration. In fact, it is a further complaint by Lieberman (1960) that not only do proximal and distal clients "interfere" in matters of process and practice, but they additionally participate in setting the criteria for teacher education in states, thereby effectively controlling entry into the occupation and thus standards of remuneration. In most educational contexts, if demand for "community control" is seen as a client "revolt," then it is a battle long ago lost by academics. Why then the current focus on this issue? If one briefly examines the battle in New York City over community control, the issue clarifies itself. In fact, community control over educational policies has become a focus for client dissatisfaction in one particular context: large-scale urban school districts. This has occurred for three major reasons: first, the form of administration apparatus in effect in such areas; second, the social identity of decision-makers; and third, the changing ethnic composition of American cities.

By virtue of the fact that city school districts are of large, often immense size, three problems arise; first, the personnel who come to sit on local decision-making bodies, i.e. school boards, of any size are usually members of local elites. In small school districts, thus small towns and cities, these local elites are to some extent "plugged into" their constituencies. In large cities this is not the case, as substantial class and ethnic distinctions divide local elites from those they represent. Therefore, a conflict of interest often arises between the needs and desires of proximal clients, and the distal clients that represent them. It is not uncommon for the childless, the aged, or the non-utilizer of local school resources to sit on such school boards. Second, there is the problem of bureaucratic administration necessary to organizations numbering thousands of staff members and perhaps millions of lower participants. The problems and aspirations of communities numbering in the tens of thousands, are shunted aside or ignored in the interests of a smoothly flowing total organization. Given both of these factors, it is not surprising that those, especially those differing substantially from local elites, who are served by such a system would demand a greater voice in the education of their children. Although the solution to these problems via community control clearly portends a movement of power from an elite to a constellation of sub-elites, and also puts job pressure on those entrenched in the extant administrative bureaucracy, there should be some question as to the reality of the threat presented to actual academic practitioners. It might even be argued, as yet *in vacuuo,* that such decentralization would materially aid urban teachers in their tasks, and in any case, is little different from the condition of non-urban school teachers. It is a "small" difference, however, that often makes a great deal of difference.

Due to historical "accident," or to the movement of the dialectic-in-history, a significant problem has arisen in certain sectors of American academia. In certain communities, generally urban, a discontinuity now exists between the social characteristics of incumbents and the population they "serve." Further, this discontinuity is of a manifestly obvious type, based on ethnic, linguistic, and racial differences. It might be argued that a social class discontinuity has always existed between teachers and their students in urban areas, and that this was, in fact, "intended" so that immigrants would be "Americanized." While this may be true, it is equally true that earlier disadvantaged groups were entering an occupational structure wherein the benefits of acculturation were much more obvious than they are, given contemporary socio-economic realities. Also, the differences between incumbents and lower participants still stimulated conflict, but native participation in local affairs was still strong, and powerful national elites had yet to withdraw from local affairs. These factors are not present in today's urban areas. Perhaps most importantly, in the current context the disadvantaged groups, especially blacks, are already natives, and thus do not feel the pressure to accede to the wishes of extant power structures that many immigrant groups, unsure of their "belongingness" did. Also, as indicated, powerful elites with an interest in the cities and the assimilation of groups therein are rapidly absenting themselves and surrendering their positions to those with few more resources than more recent ethnic arrivals. In brief, what is being suggested is that whereas it was, with few exceptions (Jews, Chinese, Japanese), true that disadvantaged groups in American cities were resentful of the "alien" presence in their midst, one that often turned their children into equally alien creatures, there was a sufficient countervailing force in a native community and in powerful elites to "force" acceptance of schools independent of the communities in which they existed. As the native community has left the cities for the suburbs, and as power elites have broadened their purview to national and international affairs, the countervailing force disappears, and "inevitable" drives for community control assert themselves more successfully.

The problem for urban public school teachers is thus a novel one: although non-urban teachers are subject to community control, the communities in question are homogeneous in socio-economic status and ethnic background, and thus similar values are held by the teachers. Where points of teacher-community friction arise — they are usually of a financial nature. On the other hand, urban teachers today find themselves fully emboiled in the *kulterkampf* wracking American society — alien in status, background, and world view to those with whom they deal. Furthermore, as indicated above, they do not receive the forceful backing of powerful elites. Thus, conflict between clients and teachers becomes overt, and often vicious, since incumbents will more readily accept a loss of autonomy to those holding privileged status than to those who are perceived as being of lower status. This situation can be further inflamed when teachers in a given political unit are predominantly of an easily identifiable ethnic background themselves. Due to this, what starts out as an already significant issue of transference of control over educational decision-making becomes intertwined with macrosocial socio-economic and ethnic issues, so that it becomes increasingly unlikely that a simple solution will be found to client demands for community control in urban areas. The reaction by academics to this problem will be dealt with in a subsequent section.

STUDENT PARTICIPATION IN THE FORMULATION OF ACADEMIC POLICY

An analagous but even more important issue in higher education is that of student involvement in institutional decision-making.

One of the off-shoots, almost an afterthought, of the highly visible student activism of the late 1960's was the demand for significant student involvement in most of the important areas of higher education, specifically in the hiring and firing of faculty and in the structuring of curricula. Certain aspects of the situation are worth examining here, primarily the dynamic by which a revolt substantially of students against college administrations was converted into a conflict between students and faculty. In many cases, this transference or redirection of client revolt was intentional on the part of the administrations.

Quite simply the revolt of students against administrations was a dismal failure. This was partially the result of a willingness on the part of administrations to abandon untenable positions, such as various supervisory functions undertaken by the college *in loco parentis*. A withdrawal from attempts to administer the sensual, sexual, and stimulatory lives of students resulted in a reduction of overt conflict, removing from administrations some onerous overtones. If this was a revolution, then its victims were more than willing. On other, more central issues, such as institutional decision-making, the pattern was less uniform. In some contexts, administrations conceded token membership on boards of trustees, often without voting privileges; more frequently, students were appointed as voting or non-voting members of college-wide policy-making committees. It was at this juncture that student-faculty conflict emerged. Often, such committees form the major source of faculty input into broad policy-making. The administration normally is still the ultimate executor of policy. Thus, administrations surrender no power, while attenuating the force of faculty committees. This "let's you and him fight" tactic has been widespread, and in many cases has formed the basis for further faculty-student conflict. Once students participate on college-wide curriculum committees, and engage in the process of choosing high administrative personnel, the next obvious ploy is a desire for participation of this sort at the departmental level. This is a radical departure from the situation that has existed in most institutions of higher education in the United States, where typically such faculty matters are overseen by a dean, and rubber-stamped by a president, but where the actual policy-setting has been inviolate. Now, it might be contended that such "power" is illusory; that is, as long as deans must consent, the power of decision-making does not rest with the faculty. Even if this were so, given the compensatory function of the mythology of professionalism in academia, it is quite plausible that academics would fight all the harder to preserve what may well be a "necessary" illusion. When vital issues were involved, administrations seldom hesitated very long in calling on the power of the state to protect their prerogatives; no such backing is available to faculties other than administrations whose best interests may be served by throwing faculty prerogative to the wolves (students). Even if this ultimate support were available to faculties, there is some doubt that they would be willing to employ it as they must deal day-to-day, face-to-face with their potential victims, whereas administrations are often well-insulated from students. Another factor involved is a lack of unanimity among faculty as to the desirability of student involvement. This is the next point to be discussed.

It has been frequently observed that those faculty who do not have tenure, usually young assistant professors, are most prone to support student involvement in academic affairs. This may appear somewhat paradoxical in view of the fact that these same faculty members are those who support unionism;[25] that is, they hold to one position supporting client interests, and another that represents a counter trend to these interests. Ultimately, it is the differentiation among academic clients that is of explanatory power. If simplistic explanations were desirable, it could be argued that this paradox can be explained by a general "radicalism" among young academics which supports positions to the degree to which they represent anti-establishment trends. There is, however, an alternative explanation, both specific and complex, and it relates to the relative powerlessness of young faculty members in institutions of higher education. By supporting unionism, young faculty members without tenure are most probably seeking an alternative path to institutional power, and thus an improvement in their various deprived statuses, economic and otherwise. By introducing students into departmental decision-making process, they can become foils for young faculty who may feel insecure in espousing certain positions, and in a yet more covert Machiavellianism, these faculty members thus become the fulcrum of power in what most often becomes a polarization between students and tenured faculty on most issues. Thus, support for student participation by young faculty members can be seen as either idealistic or "cynical," as can their support of unionism; a more jaundiced view of human nature, besides being usually accurate in most contexts, in this case also allows a resolution of the paradox of support for unionism *and* student participation by certain faculty members. As to the ultimate efficacy of students in having their interests served through participation in intra-institutional decision-making, an equally cautious perspective seems in order.

Given the only moderate routinization of decision-making in higher education, in which policy flows from many sources and is in turn put into practice in varied institutional contexts, informal networks of influence and mutual interest form a sigificant aspect of "power." This, of course, is an application of Michels' "Iron Law;" in such a bureaucratic apparatus, tenure (in the sense of length of affiliation) and access to more-or-less covert knowledge of institutional realities, can become the source of "inordinate" amounts of influence. Those professors in the higher ranks, as well as department heads and chairmen, and committee

---

[25] Ladd, Everett Carll and Seymour Martin Lipset (1972).

chairmen, are the very ones most likely to possess these resources. Conversely, students, regardless of formal positional power, are least likely to develop such capacities, if for no other reason because their contact with the network of informal power is short in duration: a *maximum* of two to three years. It is difficult in that amount of time to *locate* decision-making centers, let alone enter them. Also, the differences in informal social milieux between professors and students further limit such contact. It is for these reasons that this particular revolt by clients, even when enjoying immediate success is doomed to long-range failure. Students, when granted formal institutional power, still seem destined to become little more than foils for *relatively* disadvantaged higher participants. A similar situation can be seen in the drive for "classroom reform" which is as close as academia seems to have come to an internal rebellion. This rebellion will also be seen as a revolt more chimerical than substantive.

Classroom Reform. Of all the changes, apparent and/or substantive, that are currently taking place in academia, the drive for classroom reform has been the one that has met least resistance by the extant academic "establishment."[26] The vast body of "new" writing in academia has concerned itself with the evils of the formal, pedagogically conventional, highly stratified classroom, and the concomitant promise of freer and more interactionally rich classroom environments. The substance of these discussions does not concern us here — its preponderance in current intramural academic literature and the positive light in which it appears, does. Although not a "reassertion of a professional ethic of client concern," which this author believes has never existed as other than ideology/mythology in *any* "profession," this manifestation is of interest in that it serves as an exception that proves a rule. By the absence of an internal move to "ethical" professionalism and the presence of the above *practical* focus of occupational interest, it would seem that academia is thus best revealed as a non-profession. Whereas intraoccupational moves toward client participation can be seen as supported by dissident groups in many other professions, in academia such a movement would be truly superfluous; there is little left that academics

---

[26] A discussion of this can be found in Kozol (1972), and evidence in Hapgood (1972).

could surrender to various client-types even should they so desire. On the contrary in the autonomous professions, law and medicine primarily, internal movements to surrender some of a vast reserve of power make sense. To suppose that academia *can* also do so is to reveal considerable naivete about the current state of the occupation. By way of the fact that in its internal "revolution" academia focuses down on issues of practice, it reveals what has already been described as a compensatory ideology. When a generalized societal movement towards client involvement in bureaucratically organized and/or fee-based remunerative occupations arises, all that academics have left to surrender is their authority relation with children. Occupational entry, broad policy, and standards of remuneration have been out of the control of occupational incumbents for a long period, if such control ever existed. In fact, this "practical" revolution is in some notable respects unlike what has occurred in "true" (or puissant) professions such as law and medicine. Although it can be seen that a generalized enchantment with participatory decision-making also exists in those contexts, far more serious thrusts relating to the availability of services and the remunerative standards for those services have seemed to predominate among rebellious clients. Whereas it *is* true that programs for change originating intra-occupationally in law and medicine have followed a pattern similar to that appearing in academia; i.e., wherein the client is prospectively seen as a full participant in the occupational enterprise, there has been a far more profound movement relating to delivery and remuneration emanating from legal and medical clients than seems to have existed among academic clients. What then is the further significance of the practical reformism so prevalent in academia today?

It was suggested previously that the focus on "independent" conditions of practice as the central characteristics of professions was a primary indicator of what was called a compensatory "mythology." Changing the body of practical techniques while maintaining the primacy of the teacher in the classroom presents no threat to anyone except the most hide-bound of occupational reactionaries. In fact, it *is* in this way that the thrust of classroom reform has penetrated into established occupational milieux; take the following as an example (Hapgood, 1972: 16):

> You also hear the underlying structure of the class in the teacher's remarks. There are reminders to children to wait their turn, to "get on with"

work, to help each other, to be self-reliant, individually responsible, concerned, careful, to respect their own and other's work. There is implicit in the quotations the belief that the class, as one head put it, is "not Liberty Hall" and that some children need more direction than others. People aren't naturally educated to freedom. They have to be educated. All the emphasis on order can lead to the kind of behavior from children that can allow them to use the whole school — the corridors, the outdoors, as a learning environment.

In a way then, a careful concern for order in the classroom can lead to more freedom rather than less for the child.

We might also examine the yet-more-saccharine and co-optive set of ideas below (Hapgood, 1972: 15):

> Teachers know so much that they can help children learn! They know how to bind books, how to weave and spin, and card, and dye wool from natural plants. They know how to do etching, linoleum blocks, and woodblocks. They know how to help and encourage a child to see and study a shell or a flower, or a bone, or a landscape. How many of us have such competencies — skills through which children can become involved in learning and from this proceed to involvement in books, books which are right for what they want to know?

Or (Hapgood, 1972: 15):

> What do you do as a teacher in the classroom if you really believe as the Plowden Report says . . . You do three things:
> 1. *You* give the child concrete situations to experience and develop.
> 2. *You* build on something about the situation with which he is already familiar.
> 3. *You* ask him to organize the learning material himself in some new form.
> (italics mine)

Now, it is not entirely fair to characterize the "radical" thrust for school reform by the above example. Nonetheless, it must be noted that it is in *this* way that the existing occupational organizations are using "radical" school reform. This usage parallels movement in society as a whole, a movement from overt forms of oppression towards "repressive tolerance" from malevolent to benevolent dictatorship, but still the context of authoritarianism is maintained. We should recognize again, however, that this is not necessarily the intent of the original reformers, but it is the way they and their ideas are being co-opted into the "system." Of late, there has been a counter-thrust by some of the more perceptive of the early reformers as they see what is happening to their conceptualiza tions. Kozol (1972: 37-39) provides us with an excellent example of this counter thrust:

> In the past two years there has been a massive media campaign to popularize the idea of a painless revolution in the U.S. public schools via something known as "open-structured education." The enthusiastic reception which this notion has received in liberal circles, above all in the upper-class schools which wish to have an innovative and attractive image, suggests the desperation that is felt by those who recognize incipient stirrings of an insurrectionary nature in the consciousness of children and young teachers. It is not possible to leave such stirrings undomesticated. Ethical strivings in the consciousness of youth constitue a solemn danger to an unjust nation. The public school, as the custodian of youth, cannot allow this kind of ferment to go unrecognized and unconstrained. . . . In most cases, what we do in public schools in the United States today is not to suppress but to buy out the revolutionary instincts of our children. We offer them "independent research," "individualized learning," "open-structured education," "non-directive class-discussions." Each child, in the standard code word of the fashion, learns "at his own pace." Teachers are present not as educators but as "resource-people." The children "do their own thing." Everybody "tells it like it is" and tells other people "where it's at." . . . It is all fashionable, fun and "innovative" . . . It is intelligently marketed and publicized. It is remarkably well-packaged.

So, although Kozol and others are not unaware of what is happening, they also seem equally unable to do anything about it. If the questions involved are reduced to their basics, it seems that no other alternatives can be expected. If we take the "truly" radical reformers like Kozol, or Illich (1971, 1973), or Henry (1969), what do they advocate? Well, Henry (1969: 95) asks the following questions:

> Radical reform of schooling — as distinguished from mere "innovation" in the organization or content of instruction — demands that basic postulates be re-examined, challenged, and where necessary, replaced. Is formal education necessary or desirable? Should there be schools? Should education be compulsory? Should teachers and school administrators run the schools? Should there be a curriculum? Should there be goals of education which are considered applicable to all normal children?

To believe that academics, or their organizations such as NEA, AFT, AAUP, or that physicians and the AMA, or lawyers and the ABA, will dissolve themselves when shown the inconsistencies between their practice and their self-proclaimed norms, displays an unrealistic romanticism common in liberal reformerism. The same tactics that were employed at a total social level in relation to the Southeast Asian War are being utilized once more in the context of conflict with more-or-less privileged occupational groups. It is probably safe to say that such tactics of idea manipulation will meet with little success. What strategic alternatives are available? Few, if any. In fact, it will be contended in the concluding discussion of this chapter that reformist efforts will have a precisely counter-productive effect; that all that will result from the ideational conflict now joined is a further retrenchment on the part of the great majority of occupational incumbents and a consequent movement towards more coercive forms of control such as unionism. Some on both sides of the question may welcome this "demystification" as air-clearing and more "honest." For those clients whose primary interest is community control, and not some ultimate sanctification of ideologies, such tactics in which words are primary weapons must be viewed with further cynicism. In discussing this set of assertions, we will also be able to justify an earlier observation left as established by *fiat*: that the likelihood of school reform in the absence of maco-level social change is practically nil. In any event, there are two issues to which we must address ourselves before this discussion is complete: first, we must investigate reason(s) why, unlike in other "professions," such as medicine and law, movement for client control has been internally supported by dissident groups, whereas in academia (and in some ways similarly, in social welfare) movement has been basically external in its source. Second, and perhaps most importantly of any issue in this paper, what will the consequences of these various client rebellions be for the status, absolute and relative, of incumbents and clients. The answers to these questions will be seen to be highly inter-related.

The Academic Counter-Revolution. In each of the previous considerations of the different aspects of client revolts, it has been implied that they are counter-productive; that rather than bringing about substantial changes in the position of clients in academia, somewhat paradoxically, these thrusts seem to be bringing about the "demystification" of a compensatory "mythology" of "professionalism." Further, it has been suggested that as this demystification takes hold among occupational incumbents, willingness to reject previous occupational self-conceptions specifically excluding unionism will increase, and in the face of low remunerative standards, will become the rule in time. This is seen to be true at both academic levels, but as progressing even more rapidly among public school teachers than among college professors. This is seen as true for two reasons: one, the standards of remuneration are lower among public school teachers, often approaching the marginal, and two, due to the differing recruitment patterns of the two academic sub-types. This latter point is of considerable significance. Whereas the professoriate continues to draw on the socially mobile as new incumbents, it still exhibits a predominantly upper-middle class recruitment pattern. Even where this is not true of the social origins of participants, occupational constraints as well as income tend to move academics towards interaction patterns and status communities that are distinctly different from those of young male public school teachers. Both by heritage and milieux, public school teachers are more "susceptible" to "unionism," and the material pressures on them are greater. Besides this, the covert, sometimes overt, ethnic conflicts lying behind community control demands threaten those employed in public institutions much more than those in private ones. Demands for "accountability," especially credit-hour accountability, are an economic threat of at least as great proportions as low salaries among primary bread-winners, a social type new to "lower" education. Compounding and interacting with these social factors are the fact that many first-generation college students end up in teacher-training curricula for two reasons: the types of colleges attended are often "state colleges" with perhaps a patina of the liberal arts to provide respectability; and there is the reality of a constrained white-collar labor market in which teaching, a previously scorned profession, looks increasingly attractive, especially due to its well-established white collar status. Such new and potential incumbents are ripe for unionism, an occupational strategy in which task clients are seen as necessary evils, and neither as charges to be protected, nor as co-equal participants sharing goals in a common enterprise. It is interesting to note that even the enthusiasm for the practical reform of the "open" classroom has been tempered with caution among the vast body of young teachers. In higher education, the response has been more enthusiastic, at least at a "theoretical" level, if not in actual usage. In any case, the open classroom concept is being sanitized and de-radicalized by the educational establishment to the point where it is threatening to few, if any. Given the numerous variables seemingly exerting pressure in the direction towards unionism, it is difficult to see how such pressures can be resisted, barring any question of why they should or should not be resisted. If such unionization is fully accomplished, whether through the AFT, or through a revitalized NEA, (Shanker, 1972), or through the likely combination thereof, the status of clients in the occupational contexts will probably be similar to that of clients in relation to any other unionized public service occupation — only occasionally threatened, but always external to occupational decision-making. This is the essential paradox that was referred to earlier: that pressures produced by client responses to dissatisfaction with "professional" performance will force the rapid development of yet more exclusionary occupational organization. Even had these forces not been present, economic realities would probably have "demanded" a unionistic solution anyway. The situation in higher education, though, is in some respects different.

There exists in the upper reaches of academia, in the small private colleges of good reputation, in the large state-supported universities, and in the handful of elite institutions, a privileged "class" of professors. These are senior professors, with low course loads, high salaries, and tenure. Their contact with students is limited; in the classes that they do meet, frequently they confront only small groups of graduate students. For such a group of advantaged practitioners, unionism has no obvious value, and in fact, given their secure positions may represent an ambiguous and ill-defined threat to the status quo which rewards them so richly. It is the existence of this group in higher education that makes the prospects of unionization less likely; whether this will benefit clients in the short or long run will be considered, but for now a more obvious question presents itself: Why should the existence of such a group, numbering no more than a few thousand nationally, have a significant effect on an occupation with hundreds of thousands of incumbents? Again, the crux of the matter is one of differential power.

This group of "mandrarins," as they are sometimes called, control two primary power bases: the graduate programs and the learned associations, both specific and generic. The latter resource is mainly one with an ideological underpinning, but the former is a source of substantive power. By controlling admissions *policies* in graduate schools, though never necessarily participating in actual admissions decisions, this elite in fact controls the size of the profession, and thus standards of remuneration. Given an earlier discussion of the vested interest this group has in producing large cohorts of graduate students, whether positions await them or not, it is likely that this group would resist strenuously any super-ordinate occupational organization seeking to limit this manpower supply. Does this mean that upper academia will resist unionization? In many places, it is true, due to the ethnic and socio-economic backgrounds, the local conditions, large scale universities have gone for a collective-bargaining position on localistic issues and issues of direct remuneration, either through AFT, AAUP, or NEA. These, however, are not the monolithic organizations necessary to deal with total social issues of labor supply and training. In fact, such issues remain as jealously guarded local prerogatives. What then of the pressure of other client demands for change? Do these not place as much pressure on "mandarins" as on the academic "proletariat"? The answer to this pivotal question must be selective in nature.

"Accountability," at least in its predominant form in higher education, credit-hour accounting, is a "threat" to all incumbents, that is, it impinges on all. However, for those who are basically engaged in teaching small graduate seminars, it presents an especially sensitive point. Now, even if tenure remains in force, these privileged professors are still threatened: the available tactics open to college administrations to cope with a poor credit-hour profile reduce to one — reduction in departmental size, even if it is "only" among junior faculty. Besides the reduction in departmental "status" such a tactic results in, it also directly affects the material conditions of senior faculty, in that they then must take up the "slack" produced by reduced faculty size, forcing them back into the undergraduate lecture context. It is therefore likely that credit-hour accountability will be a potent factor in reducing the traditional reticence of senior faculty to unionization of the professoriate. There is, however, an even more potent pressure, and that is the "client" drive against tenure.

This threat to senior faculty is so direct, and of such magnitude, that it really needs little discussion, even more so due to its conjunction with accountability moves. It is those very professors who have tenure that generate least credit hours per dollar. Thus, if traditional "professional" defenses against client demands for the cessation of tenure fail, it should not take long before senior faculty fall into line. On the other hand, younger faculty are not as threatened by credit-hour accountability as the tenured: in fact, in any tenureless situation, it is bound to increase their stature. Also, the fact that younger faculty are closer not just in age, but also in outlook, to their students, in combination with the earlier discussed power benefits that would accrue to them, probably accounts for a considerable amount of sympathy for client rebellions among this group. Thus, there seem to be counter-pressures existing in this academic group — some, such as poor remuneration standards, working towards unionism and adversary client relationships, another set working against coercive forms of occupational organization. The existence of these cross-pressures in higher education probably means that clients in higher education stand a much better chance of achieving their demands than do those in public education. If, however, the continued over-production of occupational incumbents in certain academic fields continues, the material interests of young practitioners in higher education may overwhelm other factors and thus bring unionization. A further projection into the future will serve as summary for this exposition.

PROSPECTS FOR THE FUTURE

It would seem that the broad thrust of client-centered action in academia over the past years has produced, and will continue to produce, a paradoxical result: increasing exclusion of clients from occupational decision-making. The causes of the demystification of academic mythology, and the consequent movement towards "coercive" forms of intra-occupational control were discussed at length; they will not be reiterated here. What still remains, however, is a fundamental "constructive" question: Is there no way in which clients can participate in the determination of their destinies while still not threatening the livelihood and security of occupational incumbents? Are not academics just as "oppressed" by the closed classroom, tenure, and ivory tower isolation from their supportive communities as clients? If one answers "yes" to these questions, it is obvious that a "positive" strategy must be suggested. This is both possible and not possible. It is *not* possible if suggestions are confined to alternative strategies which seek to change the inequities of the occupational structure of modern industrial society one occupation, and one inequity, at a time. As has so often been the case in recent history, a "backlash" of one unpleasant sort or another seems to be the reward reformers obtain for their efforts. "Deprofessionalization," if successful, will serve for clients only as an intermediate stage between a normatively-supported frying-pan, and a coercively-enforced fire. This is "inevitable" because of the social context within which both occupational practitioners and clients must function; a social milieu in which social rewards are distributed to those with the most social resources to back up their claims on them. In such a situation, the same small piece of a very large pie is recarved endlessly; a social drama in which wage earners of various sorts persistently replay the tragedy of Sisyphus, with only the roles of rock and pusher changing. If the "revolt" of clients in academia succeeds, what are the consequences? For academics, they are not necessarily pleasant. Unless vengeance of some diffuse sort is the goal, this should not be gratifiying to clients or anyone else. If, on the other hand, the desire is to provide liberation for both academics and their clients, and for many of the most thoughtful of radical occupational reformers this is the case, then the strategy to be followed is simple: a social context must be created in which reward is not scarce, in which equally deprived ethnic groups need not scramble for the control of cities and their institutions, cities which were the subject of an orderly evacuation by elites many years before, in which classrooms contain not 50, which is the ultimate product of credit-hour accountability, but ten; and finally, a social context must be created in which the war of all against all finally ceases. The strategy is simple; the tactics are not.

BIBLIOGRAPHY

American Association of University Professors.
   1972 The Pennsylvania Division AAUP Newsletter.
       Volume 17, No. 2 (Fall).
American Teacher.
   1973a Volume 57, No. 5 (January).
   1973b Volume 57, No. 7 (March).
Caplow, Theodore.
   1964 The Sociology of Work. New York: McGraw-Hill Book Company.
Carr-Saunders, A. M.
   1928 Professions: Their Organization and Place in Society. Oxford: The Clarendon Press.
Carr-Saunders, A. M. and P. A. Wilson.
   1933 The Professions. Oxford: The Clarendon Press.
Cole, Stephen.
   1969 The Unionization of Teachers: A Case Study of the UFT. New York: Praeger Publishers.

Cooley, Charles Horton.
   1909 Social Organization: A Study of the Larger Mind. New York: Charles
      Scribner's Sons.
Corwin, Ronald G.
   1965 A Sociology of Education: Emerging Patterns of Class, Status and
      Power in the Public Schools. New York: Appleton-Century-Crofts.
Elam, Stanley and Michael H. Moskow, eds.
   1969 Employment Relations in Higher Education. Bloomington, Indiana:
      Phi Delta Kappa, Inc.
Etzioni, Amitai, ed.
   1969 A Sociological Reader on Complex Organizations. (Second Edition)
      New York: Holt, Rinehart and Winston, Inc.
Gerstl, Joel E.
   1967 "Education and the sociology of work." Pp. 224-261 in Donald A.
      Hansen and Joel E. Gerstl (eds.), On Education — Sociological Per-
      spectives. New York: John Wiley and Sons, Inc.
Goldner, Fred H. and R. R. Ritti.
   1970 "Professionalization as career immobility." Pp. 463-474 in Oscar
      Grusky and George A. Miller (eds.), The Sociology of Organizations.
      New York: The Free Press.
Greenwood, Ernest.
   1957 "Attributes of a profession." Social Work 2, No. 3 (July): 44-55.
Gross, Ronald and Beatrice Gross, eds.
   1969 Radical School Reform. New York: Simon and Schuster.
Grusky, Oscar and George A. Miller, eds.
   1970 The Sociology of Organizations. New York: The Free Press.
Hansen, Donald A. and Joel E. Gerstl, eds.
   1967 On Education — Sociological Perspectives. New York: John Wiley
      and Sons, Inc.
Hapgood, Marilyn.
   1972 "Open classrooms: stimulus/order/beauty." New Jersey Education
      Association Review (May): 14-17.
Henry, Jules.
   1969 "In suburban classrooms." Pp. 77-92 in Beatrice Gross and Ronald
      Gross (eds.), Radical School Reform. New York: Simon and Schuster.
Hughes, E. C.
   1958 Men and Their Work. New York: The Free Press.
Illich, Ivan D.
   1971 Deschooling Society. New York: Harper and Row.
   1973 After Seschooling, What? New York: Harper and Row.
Jencks, Christopher and David Reisman.
   1969 The Academic Revolution. New York: Anchor Books, Doubleday &
      Company, Inc.
Jencks, Christopher, M. Smith, et al.
   1972 Inequality: a Reassessment of the Effect of Family and Schooling in
      America. New York: Basic Books.

Katz, Michael B.
　1972　Class, Bureaucracy, and Schools. New York: Praeger Publishers.
Keast, William R. (Chairman, Commission on Academic Tenure).
　1973　Faculty Tenure: A Report and Recommendations by the Commission
　　　　on Academic Tenure in Higher Education. San Francisco: Jossey-
　　　　Bass, Inc., Publishers.
Kozol, Jonathan.
　1972　"The open schoolroom: new words for old deceptions." Ramparts
　　　　(July): 37-41.
Ladd, Everett Carll and Seymour Martin Lipset.
　1972　"Poisoned ivy — McGovern's campus report." New York, Volume 5,
　　　　No. 42 (October): 43-50.

Lieberman, Myron.
　1956　Education as a Profession. Englewood Cliffs, New Jersey: Prentice-
　　　　Hall.
　1960　The Future of Public Education. Chicago: The University of Chicago
　　　　Press.
　1971　"Professors unite!" Harper's Magazine, Volume 243, No. 1457 (Oc-
　　　　tober): 61-70.
Mannheim, Karl.
　1936　Ideology and Utopia. New York: Harcourt, Drace & World.
Marmion, Harry A.
　1969　"Faculty organizations in higher education." Pp. 1-39 in Stanley Elam
　　　　and Michael Moskow (eds.), Employment Relations in Higher Educa-
　　　　tion. Bloomington, Indiana: Phi Delta Kappa, Inc.
Mason, Ward Sherman.
　1961　"The beginning teacher: status and career orientations." U.S. De-
　　　　partment of Health, Education, and Welfare, Office of Education,
　　　　Washington, D.C.
Mead, George H.
　1934　Mind, Self and Society. Chicago: The University of Chicago Press.
Merton, Robert K.
　1949　Social Theory and Social Structure. New York: The Free Press.
Michels, Roberto.
　1935　"Intellectuals." Encyclopedia of the Social Sciences, Volume VIII.
Miller, S. M. and Pamela Roby.
　1970　The Future of Inequality. New York: Basic Books.
Mills, C. Wright.
　1951　White Collar: The American Middle Classes. New York: Oxford Uni-
　　　　versity Press.
Oberer, Walter E.
　1969　"Faculty participation in academic decision making; as to what issues,
　　　　by what forms, using what means of persuasion?" Pp. 132-180 in
　　　　Stanley Elam and Michael Moskow (eds.), Employment Relations in
　　　　Higher Education. Bloomington, Indiana: Phi Delta Kappa, Inc.

Seymour, F. J. C.
   1966 "Occupational images and norms." Pp. 126-129 in Howard M. Vollmer and Donald L. Mills (eds.), Professionalization. Englewood Cliffs, New Jersey: Prentice-Hall, Inc.
Shanker, Albert.
   1972 Weekly Column. Sunday New York Times.
Sirjamaki, John.
   1967 "Education as a social institution." Pp. 36-68 in Donald Hansen and Joel Gerstl (eds.), On Education — Sociological Perspectives. New York: John Wiley and Sons, Inc.
Smith, Bardwell L. and Associates.
   1973 The Tenure Debate. San Francisco: Jossey-Bass, Inc., Publishers.
Veblen, Thorstein.
   1954 The Higher Learning in America: A Memorandum on the Conduct of Universities by Business Men. Stanford: Academic Press.
Vollmer, Howard M. and Donald L. Mills, eds.
   1966 Professionalization. Englewood Cliffs, New Jersey: Prentice-Hall, Inc.
Wilensky, Harold L.
   1970 "The professionalization of everyone?" Pp. 483-501 in Oscar Grusky and George Miller (eds.), The Sociology of Organizations. New York: The Free Press.

LAWYERS FOR THE PEOPLE: DILEMMAS OF LEGAL ACTIVISTS

Robert L. Kidder

PROFESSIONALISM IN LAW

The purpose of this paper is to examine the common features shared by radical and conventional patterns of law practice; since radical professionals are normally thought of as deviants from conventional practice, an analysis of conventional legal practice is in order.

A. The Professional Model

Law is one of those occupations which is normally accepted as typical of professional work. As such, it seems to share many features which are thought to characterize the professions. Above all, professionals share a common identity of *expertise*. The professional is looked upon as the possessor of an extra measure of knowledge and skill which separates him from the layman and legitimizes his claim to special status.

The process of professionalization is regularly identified with expertise. Firstly, professionals have their own academies portrayed as centers for the transfer of expertise. Efforts to "upgrade" an occupation usually include the expansion of academic requirements. Those who pass through the academy are welcomed into a kind of fraternal order. Those who do not are denied the right to practice either by prevailing community norms or by law.

Legal requirements indicate a second feature of professionalization — the use of licensing as a barrier. The theory of expertise justifies the use of legal restrictions so that the public will be protected from "quacks" — i.e., those whose skills have not been proven against prevailing methods of evaluation and/or those whose practice violates the paradigms of expertise of the dominant professional community. Licensing can, of course, be responsive to norms other than expertise (e.g., considerations of supply and demand for the service), but in the licensing of professionals, expertise is the sole "up front" justification.

A third characteristic of professionalization in Western countries is the apparent allegiance of professionals to a rational model of problem solving. Sociologists are beginning to rediscover a charismatic element in the apparently rational procedures of scientist.[1] But the model of rationality based on expertise still seems to predominate in conventional conceptions of professional work, and probably in the self-conceptions of those considering themselves professionals.

Expertise is also related to the second feature of professionalism, the *group solidarity* which leads to a discrepancy between what has been called the Cosmopolitan vs. the Local Role Identity (Gouldner, 1957, 1958). Professional identity constitutes a behavior system which may draw a professional's loyalty and dedication away from any particular clientele being served, whether institutional or individual. Demands of the client are tempered to some degree by norms of the profession. Indeed, the professional's distance from the client is taken as a measure of his objectivity or ability to decide rationally. It is therefore counted as a positive characteristic, a sign of a "true professional."

This potential schism relates to the general question of client characteristics and status. Clients of professionals are defined in the relationship as lacking in the essential skill and knowledge possessed by the professional. They are therefore subordinates in the relationship. They are dependents in an essentially dyadic relationship. The professional model also defines the "problem" as an individual's dilemma rather than a collective phenomenon. The client buys the services of the professional for his "own" problem.

In this kind of one-to-one marketplace, the professional has a problem of salesmanship. His marketability depends on the degree of expertise he possesses as perceived by clients. To clients, expertise ultimately means "results" — can the professional produce the result the client wants. Among the professionals, these lay concepts are often an annoyance, a form of "ill-informed pressure" which ignores the professionals' "true" contributions. If the market is competitive, the image of expertise cannot rest on academic qualifications, since all practitioners have them. In such a market, therefore, the pressure will exist to control the interpretation of results so that the image of expertise can be preserved (along with the flow of clientele). Control of interpretations varies with the degree of client ignorance in the sphere of the professional's practice.

[1] See Gustin, 1973; and Kuhn, 1962.

B. The Conventional Legal Model

Institutions of law constitute the work setting of legal professionals and therefore exert a powerful influence on the characteristics of all legal practice. In most Western societies, and in former British colonies, certain common characteristics are especially relevant to a discussion of radical lawyers. In these systems, law theoretically treats citizenship as meaning "equality of all in the eyes of the law." The existence of inequality in a society is divorced in theory from legal action — if differences exist in the society, they are due to the operation of societal forces rather than law, and law should operate as though ignorant of those differences. That is, the law must act as though all differences in wealth, prestige, education, etc. can somehow be parked at the courthouse door and resumed only after legal actions have been completed. In practice, this theory includes the very important assumption that all actors possess the same access to the services offered by the legal system.

These legal systems are based on a critical distinction between the domains of law and politics. Collective action is defined as political. The law is to serve as a forum for the expression only of individual claims of right and duty. It has been assumed relevant only in its application to "specific cases," meaning specific dyadic relationships. Following this theory, collective action is to be expressed through political action in the creation of legal norms, while their interpretation and application is to apply to cases brought by individuals. In action, this has meant resistance to the idea of the "class action lawsuit" on the grounds that the legal forum is appropriate mainly for the expression of individual grievances.

C. The Profession of Law

Combining the professional and legal models, we have the basis for a conventional model of law practice. The lawyer's expertise is assumed to be concerned mainly with the formally guaranteed rights and duties of the individual. He is expected to know the various parameters of those rights and duties, the range of permutations and combinations which may affect his client. He must further have a special grasp of the procedures by which rights and duties are asserted.

The lawyer is a middleman in several ways. He is at once both advocate for his client's interests and "officer of the court." Ideally this means that he gives the most vigorous presentation of his client's case while keeping it within the restraints of legal norms. In addition, however, he is expected to comply with the norms of his profession, many of which concern his behavior in the professional marketplace.

The marketplace is basically understood as involving "skill for hire." It is organized according to the model of "free market competition" where each practitioner's expertise "speaks for itself." As in other professions, the law frowns on active solicitation of business, such as through advertising. Such solicitation is generally considered unprofessional, but in law it has a special significance because it may give the appearance of "stirring up trouble." Ethical proscriptions are based on the assumption that legitimate grievances will find their way to lawyers while solicitation might simply generate frivolous claims and conflict.

In keeping with the hypothetical distinction between law and politics, the behavior of lawyers is supposed to be determined by whether they are acting in their capacity as lawyer or as politician. The conventional model asserts that any correlation between law practice and political activity is purely coincidental, and that individuals can and do clearly compartmentalize their activities in these two fields.

The legitimate opportunity structure of the lawyer, then, is one founded on assertions of expertise within an institutional framework of individualized legal claims. It is a competitive situation involving a close correlation between success and the expertise image. And the tools of competition consist mainly of the rules of existing or "established" legal order.

THIRD WORLD AS LEGAL CLIENTELE

As stated above, an assumption of Western legal systems is that all citizens have equal access to the means of legal redress. In practice of course, legal services of all kinds have gone to the highest bidders. Carlin (1962, 1966) and Smigel (1969) have argued that this imbalance has been true of legal professional assistance. Following the expertise model described above, they submit that the "best legal talent" goes to support the interests of corporate wealth in the U.S. They present evidence that all conventional measures of legal expertise show the wealthiest persons and corporations receiving highest quality advice. The inference is that the poorest in our society, our "third world population," receive the poorest legal advice.

In recent years, the term "third world" has been used as an all-inclusive label for powerless, exploited elements of society. It has included that class known as the "poor," specifically depressed minority groups, welfare recipients, ex-colonial, colonial, and neo-colonial "native" populations, the proletariat, and peasants. It has also been applied to society's "deviants" (prisoners, mental patients, radicals and dissenters, and homosexuals, among others), as well as powerless groups generally, such as youth, women, and draftees

It is probably safe to assume that "third world" terminology has arisen as part of the atmosphere of political mobilization centering on powerless elements of society. For that reason, radical lawyers and their third world clientele bear a special relationship to legal institutions. Specifically, there is usually a collective aspect to the claims of such clients. Grievances tend to be referred to general social injustices rather than to the individualized conflicts around which the law is formally tailored. The trial of the Chicago Seven dramatized this clash by pitting the judge, bent on hearing only the individualized facts about specific personal acts, against a group of persons who collectively identified themselves as oppressed, and who saw the trial as an expression of a political message. As with other third world cases, these clients looked on the judge's restrictions as threats to the solidarity and integrity of their collectivity. The law's individualistic approach translates into offers of individual solutions which leave the collective problem unsolved. Wexler neatly summarizes this view when he states that:

> Poor people do not have individual legal problems; the problems that they have are common to them all, are the product of poverty, and are not legal problems in the traditional sense at all. (Wexler, 1971)

A third world client, then, brings to the radical lawyer a dilemma not usually faced in conventional legal practice — i.e., the choice between maximizing the client's personal interests or pressing the cause of the group. The two options are often incompatible. Wexler brings this into sharp focus with his advice: "When an organization (of poor people) exists, a lawyer must strengthen it; he should refuse to handle any matter for anyone who is not in the organization." (Wexler, 1971, 216). Arguing that all the lawyers in the country could not even begin to handle the legal problems of the poor, Wexler concludes that "the object of practicing law for poor people must be to organize the poor people rather than to solve their legal problems." (216). In one way or another, all third world clients bring radical lawyers this dilemma.

Radical practice also raises a dilemma peculiar to law. The goal of mobilizing and organizing those who "share the oppressed status and lack of rights consciousness" directly clashes with the profession's ban on the solicitation of clientele. Lefcourt speaks of having "Canon 28 of the Canon of Ethics" (a ban on stirring up litigation by expanding an individual's legal problem into a group test case without the consent of the individual) "thrown at him (the poverty lawyer)" by controlling groups who resist aggressive legal advocacy for the poor (1971, 136-137). Lawyers in the Chicago area organized neighborhood law offices, but discovered a reluctance among the public to approach them. They responded by developing a network of "ropers" whose contacts with people in the community helped overcome the barrier of mistrust and started channeling clients to the offices. Had it been detected, such a practice could have been construed as solicitation and advertising, and might have led to disbarment for the participating lawyers. One response to this dilemma has been to exploit specific cases for their proselytizing potential. The publicity of a legal action (e.g., trial) is used to heighten the awareness of common identity and the potential of radical lawyers in furthering common interests.[2]

THE RADICAL LAWYER

A. Modes of Radical Practice

"It doesn't take a radical to defend one, any more than it takes a murderer to defend a murderer." (Axelrod, 1971, p. 72). The truth of this comment intrudes itself on any attempt to identify *radical* law practice or *radical* lawyers. Since legal advocacy incorporates a formal ethic of neutrality concerning type of client served, we cannot simply look at lawyers who have served radicals. Nor do radical lawyers necessarily service only radical clients. Often a conventional clientele is used for support of a "movement practice."[3] Hair and dress styles have long since ceased to convey information about one's political inclinations.

[2] See, for example, Fitzgerald, 1975, for a discussion of these kinds of decisions made in the midst of the campaign of the Chicago Contract Buyer's League to renegotiate the conditions of sale on their houses.
[3] See, for example, James, 1973, for descriptions of several groups with a mixed practice.

Furthermore, the legal profession is an especially difficult area in which to define boundaries. For centuries it has been a marginal occupation heavily dependent on innovation as a means of sustaining a unique role in society. Succeeding generations of lawyers have shown remarkable entrepreneurial ingenuity in carving out new niches among the shifting patterns of economic and social organization.[4] The result has been a constant series of new lifestyles made necessary by the changing demands of the work.

In determining what makes radical lawyers different, it is necessary to describe those individuals most clearly identified in the popular media as radical lawyers, in order to compare their work with that of some other new professional forms. When people hear the phrase "radical lawyer," they may envision hippies in communes, and in fact the commune is one form of radical practice. The commune has taken many forms, and like communes with less specific identities, has often had a tenuous lease of life. In form, the communes are considered radical because many are organized around the goal of democratizing the profession. This involves eliminating both explicit and invidious status differences between degree holders and others working on cases, ideally demystifying the expertise of degree holders by weighing the opinions of all commune members equally. This has led in some cases to periods of group introspection where the practical advantages of division of labor are discarded in favor of equal participation of both trained and untrained members in decision-making.[5]

The clientele of the law communes has been diverse. Some communes have worked primarily on the problems of the poor and oppressed in large cities. Such groups also tended to become involved in the more publicized political trials, such as that of the Panther 21 in New York (Lefcourt, 1971a, p. 313). Other communes formed during the height of the Vietnam War in conjunction with radical-sponsored coffee houses near military bases, especially the basic training camps. During this period, legal assistance was a key device in the campaign to radicalize the grass roots within the military system. It was designed to provide the recruit with alternatives to submission to military authority.[6]

---

[4] See, for example, Bazelon, 1960; Hale, 1970; and Rueschemeyer, 1973 (Ch. 1) for discussions and descriptions of the entrepreneurial character of the profession.

[5] See, for example, Biderman, 1971, (286); Lefcourt, 1971, (312-313).

[6] See Coulter, 1971 (167-175) for description and explanation of aims.

Commune practice is, of course, not the only mode of radical law work. The mass media have also given wide exposure to a few solo practitioners, such as William Kunstler, whose work takes them all over the country in the service of particularly conspicuous cases. Supported by special defense funds, their involvement helps to designate particular cases as especially significant. Their main function, in other words, lies in the realm of the political and public relations goals of "the movement." Victories for these movement lawyers are measured particularly in terms of proselytic success. The trial of the Chicago 7 becomes a success because of its effect on the public image of the court and judge, not because of acquittal. The Attica prison riot saw Kunstler and others drawn in to dramatize radical inmate reaction to prison authority. Such "name" lawyers, then, provide a significantly different function in the movement from those carried on in the communes.

Another category of practice has been called the "movement" law firm. These differ from communes by having more involvement with conventional practice and by emphasizing the priority of legal effectiveness over that of alternate or more humane lifestyles. Such firms define their primary function as serving "third world" clients, but they finance such service by carrying on a survival level of ordinary lawyering. They tend to reject "democratic, communal" modes of operation as inefficient, a luxury they and their clients cannot afford.[7] Many such firms have become involved with one particular kind of clientele or legal problem, and this involvement becomes a defining characteristic of the firm. Such, for example, was the case with the lawyers pressing the cases of the Contract Buyers' League in Chicago (Fitzgerald, 1975).

We have not yet mentioned the "public interest" law firms, the unique phenomenon known as Ralph Nader, nor other manifestations of change in the profession, such as pressure for "released time" practice within conventional law firms and the work of the O.E.O. legal services lawyers. All of these are trends which coincided with the birth of the law communes, and are probably explainable as outgrowths of a combination of factors converging during the 1960's: 1. The War on Poverty, which saw relatively large sums of money being channeled into attempts to bring law to the poor; 2. the civil rights movement, which involved a whole cohort of young Americans in an "unfinished crusade"; 3. the

[7] See James, 1973 (232-255) for an example of this type of firm.

Vietnam War, which generated a relatively rapid rate of economic expansion (thereby creating a high demand for lawyers) while producing widespread political awareness and fiddsyidgsvyion. The law market during this time was one which allowed fresh law graduates to demand free time from their law firm employers to work on public interest cases (Marks, 1972, 256). Law firms yielded because the alternative was to lose the most qualified graduates to O.E.O. programs, public interest firms, or rival conventional firms. The unprecedented autonomy given to O.E.O. lawyers (since taken away) simultaneously led to a period of widespread challenges to local authorities over the interests of poor clients. The class action suit became a weapon of unprecedented potency. "Public interest" firms concerned with questions of consumer rights, environmental protection, civil liberties, and other more localized issues[8] grew up in association with the politicization of those issues. Getting their support from foundations, from coalitions of conventional law firms, [9] public solicitation, the American Bar Association, and sometimes through partial involvement in conventional practice, these firms leaned toward the class action suit and the test case, seeking to establish precedents protective of some classes of clients. Their heavy reliance on student volunteers to do important basic work on cases means that they have played an as yet unmeasured role in the socialization of future lawyers (Marks, 1972, 148).

Supporting many of these moves in the profession are various committees and associations with regional and sometimes national ties, such as the Emergency Civil Liberties Committee, Community Law Offices, the Southern Legal Action Movement, and the Lawyers' Committee for Civil Rights Under Law. According to one view:

> A new network of exchange is emerging . . . based on a set of principles, loyalties, commitments, and experiences seemingly far removed from commercial law practice and economic incentives. (Marks, 1972, 121).

These networks support efforts at legal change by serving as brokers between lawyers and potential clients or classes of clients. That is, they help to insulate the concerned activist practitioner from the ethical problem of "chasing" clients who are unaccustomed to legal remedies. But they are not neutral brokers; they intentionally seek to link lawyers

---

[8] For example, the Boston Lawyers for Housing (Marks, 1972, 144-146).
[9] For example, see the Sunday Philadelphia Bulletin, August 8, 1971, Section 2, Page 2.

with clients meeting their criteria of need. They also provide new sources of information exchange that prove useful in building new cases.

Finally we should mention the "counter-bars" which have grown in a number of cities. These are local associations of usually young lawyers who seek to promote public interest types of issues as they relate to the profession (Marks, 1972, 147-148). They constitute an intentional bypassing of traditional bar associations at the local level on the grounds that they are incapable of promoting change.

B. Problems of Definition

The preceding section covers a broad spectrum of activities and ideological commitments all of which relate to seemingly unprecedented changes in the profession. The actual numbers of persons involved in these kinds of activities is debatable, in part because few actual counts have been made,[10] and in part because of the difficulty of capturing a rapidly changing set of relationships. Most published material on the subject has been content to simply itemize the tremendous range of activities and groups which have made themselves known in recent times.

The range of activities which most studies mention, however, illustrates the problems in defining the term "radical lawyer." Many "movement" activists would object to the inclusion of public interest firms, Ralph Nader, or O.E.O. under the radical heading. And their objection goes much deeper than a mere claim for sole possession of a title. For they would argue that true radicalism is aimed at bringing down an entire socio-legal system, while most of the activist lawyers discussed above are only involved in tinkering with what they believe to be an essentially sound mechanism. Some would assert that the term "radical lawyer" is a contradiction in terms because following the lawyer's role is a fundamentally nonradical act. Still others acknowledge that they admire the elements of the legal system, but see little hope that present society can permit it to function.[11] Many tend to see their own position

---

[10] See Simon, Koziol and Joslyn (1973, 95-108) whose survey of two law schools indicates just barely noticeable changes in job preferences and actual career patterns over a twenty-year period. However, the questionable representativeness of the two schools makes the study of limited value. Even Marks (1972) whose study is the most systematic recent work on "public interest" practice, includes not one table dealing with the scope of the phenomenon.

[11] For example, see the discussion of Southern legal activists in James (1973, 232-255).

as transitional — they are lawyers for the sake of the movement whose success should eliminate the need for their skills.

The contradiction is much more than mere semantics. Movement literature on radical lawyers is pervaded by introspective observations on the problems of reconciling the conflicting demands of the two roles. One says the self-image of expertise must be exorcised in favor of recognition of the people's common sense. Another counters that if you are to serve the people, you must acknowledge your expertise and maximize its effectiveness. And so on. Wasserstrom summarizes some of these tensions:

> . . . the advocate's role runs afoul — at least potentially — of the revolutionary's interests and desires. The attorney's role is intimately connected with securing for his client the greatest possible advantage that can be wrung for him from the institutional system. Paradoxically enough, this leads not to the singlemindedness of purpose that so typically characterizes the revolutionary and the radical, but leads rather to the penchant for compromise, accord and accommodation. (1971, 80-81)

The dilemma alluded to is a structural fact peculiar to the legal profession. To a very great extent, the lawyer's ability to serve his client depends on his ability to convincingly relate the specific case to a more general social context. This may mean openly appealing to general societal values, whether expressed in the law or not. Or it may mean covertly arranging compromises or exchanging "favors" with other actors in the legal system with whom the lawyer's role brings him into regular contact. In all cases, the validity of some mutually recognized social context must be asserted as a means of leverage on behalf of the client. The wider the scope of social contexts rejected by the radical, the narrower the range of resources available to the lawyer, acting *as lawyer*, for asserting his client's case. Thus, for example, William Kunstler speaks of his criticism of movement lawyers who appear in court wearing blue jeans and work shirts because he feels that such expressions of solidarity hurt the client's case (Kunstler, 1971, 302). At issue is the question of whether or not the symbolic system that objects to jeans in court should be accorded the deference and implied legitimacy symbolized by the three-piece suit. So, the personal interests of the client have probably been better served, but at the expense of reasserting rejected values. All legal practice is similarly interwoven into the general social fabric, and is thereby set apart from the other professions where the *product* of expert treatment can be separated from the facts of social control by which the product is distributed.

It is this close relationship between law and social system which makes it difficult to isolate clearly the line between radical lawyers and all others. The order of presentation in section A above moves from most to least radical in the sense that is moves from highest to lowest degrees of overt rejection of existing social contexts. Correspondingly, therefore, it moves from the least to the most effective forms of practice from the point of view of the individual client's personal chances for success. But in both cases, it is a continuum of opposition to the status quo and the supportive role of the lawyer in that status quo. The deeply committed commune laywer may see his service to a client as a means of politicizing a whole class of persons, or of giving already politicized persons temporary legal shelter from a hostile social environment. But the means available to him are not essentially different from those of the O.E.O. lawyer or a Wall Street business advocate.

All of the activist lawyers, then, share in a general lawyers' dilemma, that their role is defined and legitimized by the very legal structures being attacked. The history and predominant pattern of the profession provide the basis from which action can be generated, but the action springs from a definition of that tradition as at best inadequate, if not fundamentally corrupt. The response to this dilemma is what seems to differentiate the radical lawyer from the mere activist. The activist is likely to treat expression of the dilemma as a problem of role definition, asserting new practices as valid new facets of the role. He is liable to argue that the new facets strengthen the existing structure by eliminating neglected weaknesses. The radical on the other hand, looks on his actions as no more than stepping-stones to a new social order. He uses the inertia of existing rules and official attitudes to create temporary niches for those working to overturn the system. He may use the events of law as a means of politicizing whole classes of persons and teaching them how to use that law to create their own protective niches. And he constantly wrestles with the choice between niche-making (which protects the individual at the expense of obeisance to the law) and politicization (which is likely to require actions sacrificial of an individual's interests and perhaps the lawyer's accumulated sources of leverage).

While activists and radicals would differ in explanations of their tactical decisions, they both share with the conventional lawyers a set of dilemmas that seem inherent in the role and are illustrated in part by the radical's choice as described above.

BASIC DILEMMAS OF LAWYERING

As basic as the above described dilemmas are, they derive from the shared decision to work for change. Even more basic, however, is a set of problems which appear to plague all lawyers, regardless of their acceptance or rejection of the status quo. These problems revolve around the question of expertise described earlier. The analysis which follows is based on a year-long study of the legal profession in action in India. It is useful here because it reveals patterns of lawyer-client relationships which can be found as a common theme running through scholarly studies and professional self-criticisms of advocacy wherever it is practiced.

The situation of the lawyer in India is well-suited for comparison with the profession in the U.S. because so much of the legal systems of the two societies is derived from common roots and shares basic institutional features. The Indian citizenry engages in a notably high rate of interpersonal litigation, and its legal profession is one of the largest in the world. The most significant difference between the professions is that the American profession is more highly differentiated into solo practitioners and groups of specialists in law firms. In India, the profession remains almost exclusively composed of solo practitioners who must single-handedly develop their own clientele. And in India, the profession derives almost all of its income from the processing of litigation. As we shall see below, this exclusive attention to litigation makes the Indian lawyer an excellent source of comparative data suggesting the universality of the kinds of dilemmas to be discussed here. The reason for discussing Indian lawyers here is not that they practice law in an area considered to be "third world," but rather because their problems are the problems of all lawyers who must deal with the uncompromising expectations of clients seeking legal redress.

One of the few constants emerging from the great complexity of law-related events in the Indian setting was the personal uncertainty of lawyers about their own skill, their "expertise." From all quarters came evidence that the legal profession predictably fails to offer practitioners solid evidence on "where they stand" in relation to other lawyers. Most lawyers admit, for example, that they attended law school only after failing to gain admission to medical or engineering school, or some other advanced school offering more assuredly lucrative and secure life chances. Few expected to practise law even after they entered law school. Most drifted into law after concluding that they had no other options except for dead-end bureaucratic jobs. Most therefore were accidental and reluctant recruits who chose law as a last resort, and entered it burdened with unfavorable definitions of their own competence. Law school does nothing to bolster their self-confidence, because it is generally regarded as irrelevant to the demands of the "real world." Most lawyers look on law school as a ritual ordeal which must be passed but which contributes nothing to their ability to succeed as lawyers.

Evidence accumulates that these lawyers are uncertain about two aspects of expertise: 1. They do not feel certain that they even know what criteria should be used to measure it; 2. They have strong doubts as to the nature of the connection, if any, between expertise and professional success. Almost without exception, respondents placed "luck" among the top three features explaining degree of financial success and command of regular clientele. When pressed to describe how "luck" works, respondents generally described chance social encounters which led to valuable "contacts" and networks of clientele. Such explanations came equally from struggling marginal lawyers and those considered most successful in the bar. This view of success places it in contrast with an explanation based on skill, expertise, and other controllable processes. Almost none of the lawyers want their sons to become lawyers. Even the most successful lawyers are still uncertain about what they have done to achieve their prominence. But they are certain that there is little wisdom or reliable advice they could pass on to their sons which would overcome the pervasive element of luck. Nor do they consider it adequate to simply pass along their own clientele. They have strong doubts about their own abilities to please the clients, and they view clients as fickle customers looking for a personally possessed quality called skill rather than a diffuse relationship with a family. So they prefer to direct their sons into the more secure professions so that they, at least, would be spared the lifetime of anxiety experienced by the father.

The sense of insecurity has even become recognized as a normal feature of lawyering in the jokes that lawyers tell. One living legend was an aged Supreme Court advocate who, though he commanded a fee of over $500 per hour and turned away more clients in a day than most lawyers see in a year, lived in a low-rent one-room apartment and slept, so it was said, with his pants folded under his pillow so he would not have to pay to have them pressed. His exaggerated concern for financial security strikes a sympathetic note with most lawyers who describe their own uncertain careers by noting that one month filled with business may be followed by another with none.

The reaction to this occupational situation is ambivalence — a mixture of approach and avoidance. On the one hand is the experience of insecurity. On the other is evidence of considerable opportunity for "good luck." The attraction of the work is that you are "your own boss." There are no supervisors or fixed schedules. Courtroom lore is full of stories about the spectacular successes of some previously unknown young lawyers. To some extent, the attraction of the work resembles the enticing insecurity of the gambling casino.

Expertise and Bargaining

The overall picture of lawyering in India indicates that something about the institutions of law creates very special problems for those seeking to project an expertise image as legal professionals.[12] The search for reasons for this dilemma leads to an analysis of the modes of operation made available to the lawyer by the system. The obscurity of indentifiable (and therefore usable) expertise arises out of the nature of the client's problem and the nature of society's proffered solution to that problem. Society offers "the law," with its courts, judges, juries, and enforcement apparatuses, as a resource for assertion and vindication of claims and grievances. In theory this is a search for "truth" and the one correct way of applying the law. That is, the law offers the promise of adjudication. But, as this author has argued elsewhere (1973), the finality of the law's actions is actually determined, in routine cases, by the willingness of disputants to cease their pursuit of total victory. The elaborate apparatus of due process, rules of evidence, rational deliberation, and right to appeal transform the law court into an arena of threats and opportunities whose use is best described as <u>negotiation</u> rather than <u>adjudication</u>. In such an arena, conventional legal expertise is only a facade masking the importance of tactical skill, relative bargaining positions, and "luck" (i.e., a condition of high uncertainty about outcomes because of the wide range of tactical opportunities open to both sides).

[12] The author has elsewhere (1974) dealt in greater detail with the evidence supporting the uniqueness of the lawyer's dilemma.

Innovation, both legitimate and illegitimate, becomes necessary as a means of overriding routinized disadvantages. The lawyer's role in litigation therefore takes on entrepreneurial characteristics. But this actual role must be performed under the critical scrutiny of a client who has been conditioned to search for expert command of a predictable field of knowledge and who tends, therefore, to interpret the events of law-work as reflecting the effects of relative expertise.

In India, this schism between the client's search for expertise and the lawyer's actual role as entrepreneurial negotiator in a highly uncertain structure of contingencies has produced conspicuous tension as a regular feature of the lawyer-client relationship. Recurrent expressions of mistrust of the lawyer characterize much of a client's discussion of his experience with the law. Doubts about competence are mixed with doubts about loyalty to the client's interests as opposed to those of wealthier clients, and even those of the opposition. These doubts are mirrored by expressions of frustration and indignation among lawyers over the fickleness of clients, the unreasonableness of their expectations, their pressure on the lawyers to act "unprofessionally," and their unwillingness to play the game as constructed for them by their lawyer. Much of the lawyer's attention in such circumstances becomes focussed on the problem of sustaining a client's trust so that present and future patronage will be guaranteed and fees will be paid. Stage setting of the professional office, the development of elegant rhetorical styles in court, the staging of elaborate shows of involvement in the case (e.g., conspicuous exploration and citation of voluminous references on "precedent"), and the insistence on public displays of deference by the client — all these common techniques reflect the lawyer's insecure positon in an entrepreneurial role.

Just as a patient looks to a doctor for a cure, the client expects vindication and legal "recovery." But much of what a lawyer does is to forestall even worse damage than the client has already experienced; the lawyer's ability to do that depends, not on expertise as esoteric knowledge, but on current familiarity and influence with the parochial social networks within which legal events occur. In India, the lawyer's manipulation of these relationships supplies the client with the defense of *delay* which usually leads to eventual compromise with opponents. When a system such as this operates as an arena for bargaining, its output reflects the relative abilities of the two sides to sustain the battle.

Missing, in other words, is the equalizing effects of the promised adjudicative process: a preset normatively regulated outcome based on the formal rights of legal actors.

Radical Lawyers and Client Ambivalence

The preceding analysis is presented as a way of dealing with some otherwise puzzling evidence about the relationship between radical laywers and their clients in the U.S. One might expect that lawyers doing "pro bono" work (i.e. legal work, usually voluntarily done, "for the good the public") would be immune to the kinds of suspicion expressed by the Indian clients. After all, much of the work being done for them is free, or extremely inexpensive. And "pro bono" lawyers offer many clients their first opportunity to assault entrenched injustices. Nevertheless, the literature on this kind of law practice is full of clues that radical lawyers are just as prone to client mistrust as are the most dedicated private attorneys.

Wasserstrom speaks of this tension, and relates it to the same kind of analysis of litigation and adjudication as we have derived for Indian litigation:

> Although there are, of course, some respects in which litigation is a 'winner take all' situation, we should not let these glamorous features obscure the far more significant respects in which the process of litigation and adjudication derive from and are infected by the model of the market place in which a good bargain consists in each of the parties making concessions and compromises. (Wasserstrom, 1971, 81)

Wasserstrom is emphasizing the "uncritical" role of the lawyer as broker between the revolutionary client and the law. He portrays this role-induced tendency towards compromise as an inherent threat to the revolutionary's interests. But he incorrectly assumes the "the lawyer and the radical have major and pervasive disaffinities of mind and attitude" which are unique to the situation involving radical litigants. As our study of Indian litigants and lawyers has shown, the clash between the actual brokerage role and the promoted image of expert champion in a fight to the finish produces tensions of the same sort between non-radical clients and lawyers.

The literature on radical lawyers contains numerous references to these kinds of tension. Sometimes direct reference to client reactions is made, as when Wexler, after describing "delaying . . . refusing to stipulate, . . . (and) a hundred other techniques that take extensive secretarial and xerographic facilities, (which allow) the lawyers for the other side (to) frustrate the poverty lawyer and tax his limited office budget to the breaking point,'' goes on immediately to say:

> ''All of this is very hard to take; moreover, the poor people are not always delighted with their lawyer. A great many of the problems in poverty law can be tolerated if the lawyer can make it with his clients: but there are important problems of style, differences in income and education, *frustrations and anger about failures* . . . The lawyer who wants to help and wants to be accepted, and *cannot help and is not accepted will be frustrated and often he will leave.''* (Italics added). (Wexler, 1971, 213)

Wexler attributes much of the problem to differences in class as a source of cultural incompatibility. But our argument here is that the ''frustrations and anger'' produced by the gap between the client's expectations and the lawyer's limited ability to produce is much more important in creating friction. It is a gap between the hope created by the expertise image and the ''hundred other techniques'' which a determined opponent can use to divert the law's clearcut mobilization.

Fitzgerald presents a more specific example of this in his study of Chicago's Contract Buyer's League. (Fitzgerald, 1975). He reports in vivid detail the transformation of the buyers from passive, awestruck believers in the promise of expertise generously granted into aggressive, argumentative discontents who reject their lawyers' caution and press for ever more radical actions designed to elevate the pressure on the sellers. Fitzgerald quotes the leading lawyer in the case:

> Repeatedly in this case, lawyers have been forced to improvise and to push beyond the frontiers, so to speak. Not because of their own ingenuity, or anything they started, but rather in spite of themselves, and over their objections that it couldn't be done. This is because the people said: ''Well, screw it, we're going to do it anyhow.'' The lawyers were then forced to do some original thinking to find some avenue of relief for what the people had already decided to do. There is no question about that. (1975, 189)

Elsewhere, Fitzgerald describes the rising irritation of the buyers with their lawyers, and buyer elation when a group of ''untutored'' law students entered the case and valiently (though futilely) vented their senses of outrage at the judge in defense of the clients. Though these shows of unbridled defiance made no difference in the judge's decisions, they brought joy to the frustrated clients and served as a prod to the regular laywers whose faltering efforts were highlighted by the rhetoric. (Fitzgerald, 1972.)

Lefcourt, in describing "The First Law Commune," speaks of the intent of the commune to transform the lawyer-client relationship "by turning legal jargon into everyday language and by encouraging mutual decision-making" (1971, 313) so that the mystique of specialized knowledge and training could be dispelled. This is the same rejection of deference patterns and lawyers' mystique which can be found throughout the literature on radical practice.[13] And yet, Lefcourt laments that "A dramatic change in the lawyer-client communication and relationship has not been achieved." (1971, 313). He points out the paradox we have been discussing by claiming that clients, both political and nonpolitical, expect the lawyer to make all the decisions for them, even though this relationship breeds "a certain amount of mistrust still . . . between lawyer and client, with the client still suspecting that the attorney wants to make all the decisions because 'he knows best' " (1971, 313). Thus, radical lawyers end up with the same problems of mistrust and contradictory expectations as "traditional lawyers (who) presume a trust which actually breeds mistrust" (1971, 312).

It is clear that much of the debate over the issue of whether one should show deference to the court or not (e.g., by wearing a suit instead of jeans) revolves around the relative effectiveness of projecting an expertise image vs. a "champion of the masses" image. When Kunstler worries that bluejeans hurt a client's case, he is referring to the impression created in the minds of the judges, juries, and other lawyers. But the evidence indicates that such actions generate doubts among the clients as well.

Among the aspects of legal practise which predictably produce client mistrust is the fact that turning a lawsuit into a bargaining relationship undercuts both the lawyer's image as expert and his claim of partisan dedication to the client. The client's confidence is subject to considerable erosion simply in the process of seeing his commonsense claim translated into a legal terminology and set of legal theories which pragmatically create strategic room for alternative definitions of reality. A radical client might find this unacceptable on ideological grounds because it obscures the issues. A poor client might object to it because it

[13] For example, see Axelrod (1971, 73) and Wexler, (1971, 217).

removes the case so far from his or her understanding of "the facts" and does not clearly delineate the rights assumed to exist. But even if such clients endorse what they consider to be a deceptive procedure, the lawyer's use of these positions as bargaining chips in a brokerage process involving reliance on inside contacts, inside information, and a balance of favors among legal system actors erodes the client's assumption that the lawyer's value in the case resides in an expertise dedicated to the client's interests. Instead, he may begin to view the legal system as a mire of social obligations tearing away at his rights through the compromises made by his lawyer. For the lawyer to stand firm and pure on those rights is to behave "unprofessionally," because to do so is to violate the accomodative assumptions and relationships of the other professionals, and to risk making a martyr of one's client. But to be accomodative means risking the expenditure of "social credits" within the bargaining network on a client who may well hold the lawyer culpable as a co-conspirator in a con game.

Thus, to the extent that radical laywers continue to serve the traditional brokerage role of the profession, their protestations of devotion to the cause, their efforts to innovate legal niches for their clients, and their claims to be *different* from conventional lawyers will be persistently subjected to contradiction and the suspicion of failure, and will therefore continue to earn them the hostility and ambivalence of many of their clients. The pervasive pressure to negotiate within the "confines" of a formally adjudicative system will continue to gnaw away at both the radical lawyer's claim to expertise as his contribution to the "movement" and the purity of his image as fully committed to the cause.

CONCLUSION

We have reviewed the variety of styles of lawyering "for the people" which have emerged during the last decade, and have analyzed characteristics of both the lawyer's role in general and the different modes of "pro bono" work in particular which make it difficult to identify clearly the boundary between radical lawyers and all others. This difficulty is related to the intimate linkages between the role constraints facing a lawyer and techniques afforded to him by the law.

The problem of bringing a professional's services "to the people" is more than a simple economic question of the distribution of a scarce service, at least when that service concerns law. In other professions, the primary problems *may* be logistical and monetary, there being an effective, routinized paradigm of expertise whose distribution can be measured and evaluated. In such cases, the main professional-client tensions would probably be over cultural misunderstandings, class-related differences in personal style. But in the distribution of legal services, the more fundamental problem concerns the "hidden dimension" of the service being distributed, that of bargaining which so regularly alienates the client from the lawyer. Poor clients and radical clients may differ in personal style from their lawyers, but the lawyer's attempts to minimize such differences by eliminating the trappings of the lawyers' subculture cannot be expected to wipe out the more fundmental sources of the client's alienation.

These kinds of pressures may be tolerable for many as long as there is a sense of "movement," of growing solidarity in a winning cause. But the effects of prolonged stalemate, or even widespread deradicalization, which may be an accurate description of the state of American society in the 1970's, may be devastating in the face of the routine structured pressures we have detailed here. Routinization of a movement into some kind of holding operation would have the effect of eliminating the last basis on which the radical lawyer can claim uniqueness of contribution to the movement (i.e., the innovation of ploys for temporary protection from the "establishment"). During such a phase, then, we might expect that, among the "professions for the people," the law may be one of the hardest hit by defections and the cessation of radical professional activity "for the people."

REFERENCES

Axelrod, Beverly. "The Radical Lawyer" in Black, J. (ed.). *Radical Lawyers* (New York: Avon Books, 1971.

Bazelon, David. "Portrait of a Business Generalist," *Commentary*, 21 (1960). Reprinted in Schwartz, R.D. and Skolnick, J.H. (eds.). *Society and the Legal Order,* New York: Basic Books, 1970, 270-280.

Biderman, Paul. "The Birth of Communal Law Firms" in Black, J. (ed.) *Radical Lawyers,* New York: Avon Books, 1971, 280-288.

Carlin, Jerome. *Lawyers Ethics,* New York: Russell Sage Foundation, 1966.

———. *Lawyers On Their Own,* New Brunswick, N.J.; Rutgers Univ. Press, 1962.

Coulter, Tim. "The Lawyers in the G.I. Movement" in Black, J. (ed.) *Radical Lawyers,* New York: Avon Books, 1971, 167-175.

Fitzgerald, Jeffrey. "Poverty Litigation: The Case Study of the Contract Buyers League and the Courts" *Law and Society Review* 9, 2, (Winter, 1975), 165-195

Gouldner, Alvin. "Cosmopolitans and Locals: Toward an Analysis of Latent Social Roles" Parts I and II, *Administrative Science Quarterly,* 1957, 1958, 281-306, 444-480.

Gustin, B.H. "Charisma, Recognition, and the Motivation of Scientists", *American Journal of Sociology,* 78, 5, Mar. 1973, 1119-1134.

Hale, William Henri. "The Career Development of the Negro Lawyer in Chicago" in Schwartz, R.D. and Skolnick, J.H. (eds.), *Society and the Legal Order,* New York: Basic Books, 1970.

James, Marlise *The People's Lawyers,* New York: Holt, Rinehart and Winston, 1973.

Kidder, Robert L. "Courts and Conflict in an Indian City: A Study in Legal Impact", *Journal of Commonwealth Political Studies,* 11, 2, 1973, 121-139.

———. "Lawyers and Litigation: Understanding Litigation Through Its Effects on the Legal Profession," *Law and Society Review* 9, 1, (Fall, 1974), 11-37.

Kuhn, Thomas. *The Structure of Scientific Revolutions,* Chicago: Univ. of Chicago Press, 1962.

Kunstler, William. "An Interview with William Kunstler" in Black, J. (ed.), *Radical Lawyers,* New York: Avon Books, 1971, 301-306.

Lefcourt, Robert. "Lawyers for the Poor Can't Win" (1971), 123-139. "The First Law Commune" (1971a), 310-326, in Lefcourt, R. (ed.). *Law Against the People,* New York: Vintage Books, 1971.

Marks, F. Raymond (with Leswing, K. and Fortinsky, B.A.). *The Lawyer, The Public, and Professional Responsibility,* Chicago: American Bar Foundation, 1972.

Rueschemeyer, Dietrich. *Lawyers and Their Society,* Cambridge: Harvard Univ. Press, 1973.

Simons, Rita J.; Koziol, Frank; and Joslyn, Nancy. "Have There Been Significant Changes in the Career Aspirations and Occupational Choices of Law School Graduates in the 1960's?" *Law and Society Review,* 8, 1, Fall, 1973, 95-108.

Smigel, Erwin O. *Wall Street Lawyer: Professional Organization Man?* Bloomington, Ind., Indiana Univ. Press, 1969.

Sunday Philadelphia Bulletin, August 8, 1971, Section 2, pg. 2.

Wasserstrom, Richard. "Lawyers and Revolution" in Black, J. (ed.) *Radical Lawyers,* New York: Avon Books, 1971, 74-83.

Wexler, Stephen. "The Poverty Lawyer as Radical" in Black, J. (ed.), *Radical Lawyers,* New York: Avon Books, 1971, 209-230.

THE EMERGING PHYSICIAN:
FROM POLITICAL ACTIVIST
TO PROFESSIONAL VANGUARD

James L. Resnick

During the 1960's, the public witnessed student conflicts that sometimes erupted into violence. One phenomenon obscured by this conflict
was the medical student movement. Unlike other forms of activism, this
movement seldom resulted in demonstrations. But, this was not all that
differentiated this movement from other student movements. The medical movement was a collective action among professional students and,
therefore, must be seen as interwoven with the professional development of students and with the study of the professions.

An article by Bucher and Strauss, "Professions in Process" (1961),
gives us a rationale for seeing medical student activism and other medical activism as a movement. The authors conceive of groupings within
the professions as forming movements because professions, in the process model, consist of segments. Segments are "groupings which
emerge within a profession" (p. 10). They develop common characteristics, such as common missions and sense of identity. The Bucher and
Strauss view contrasts with Goode's view (1957) which sees a profession as having unified values and a single mission.

The authors have conceptualized medical specialties as forming
movements, but the profession may be stratified into movements according to other factors besides specialty. Two of these factors are
work-place and stage of career. Work-place differentiates young doctors into either house staff or ambulatory care staff. By contrast, stage of
career differentiates between those attending medical school and
graduates from medical school.

Strauss (1968) has conceptualized the process of status-passage, that
is, passage between various statuses. It seems fruitful to blend the
analysis of segments and of status-passage by viewing segments as
formed, in part, when people pass through various statuses in the
socialization process.

We will follow the approach of the following table in this paper:

TABLE 1

STATUSES AND SEGMENTS OF MEDICAL ACTIVISTS

A) *Status:* Medical student
Segments: 1. Medical school 2. Student Health
curriculum committees   organization chapters
   Status-passage: Graduation from medical school
B) *Status:* Young physician
Segments: 3. House staff 4. Employees in neighborhood health
   organizations   centers and free clinics
   Status-passage: Completion of internship and/or residency
C) *Status available in the future:* Positions in a national
health insurance system

Whereas some observers would say that medical activism is a single phenomenon, this table shows it is differentiated into at least four segments, partly derived from two statuses. Furthermore, this activism does not operate in a haphazard but in an orderly manner.

Each of the four segments noted above will be analyzed in this paper. Throughout the discussion, we will consider the ideology of the segments, which is largely in opposition to the professional ideology of conventional physicians. A theoretical explanation for the segments and their ideology will be offered at the conclusion of the paper.

In order to clarify our terms, let us note that a "social movement" is usually regarded as a form of collective behavior consisting of people organized or alerted to take action on social change. Following Bucher and Strauss's view of professions as containing movements, the use of the term 'movement' here will refer to the entire collection of segments seeking change in the medical profession. An "activist" is an individual in the movement; it is a term the medical people use about themselves.

The sociology of medical education has tended to gloss over altruism or idealism, which, we will suggest is a basic element in the movement. Howard S. Becker (1961) admits that, in interviewing medical students, he failed to elicit idealistic attitudes because he was predisposed to the cynical attitudes which predominated in the groups he was studying. He says that he altered his approach, but this writer feels that the resulting research gives little indication that idealism was a motivator. Instead, the work portrays the cynicism of a group uniformly committed to the end of getting their work done. This emphasis has tended to make the reader feel that idealism or altruism has little significance for the individual medical student whereas, in fact, it may be if not manifest, certainly a latent factor. In contrast to Becker, this paper treats idealism as still problematic.

The Background and Nature of the Student Health Organization

The impetus for the movement came from dissatisfactions with medical school education and from conditions in society — the Vietnam war, the civil rights movement, and the counter-culture. In regard to dissatisfactions with medical school education, the following three orienting goals were part of the Philadelphia Student Health Project of 1968, according to student Jerry Lozner:

1. to develop a new model of health science education with a high degree of student administrative leadership, and new ties with community groups;

2. to demonstrate an active interest in community medicine and change in health science education to recognize failures of curricula to come to grips with bio-social issues of the day;

3. to help develop a new breed of health professionals prepared to adopt new priorities in their professional lives (Philadelphia Student Health Program, 1968). The first two of these ideals show a concern for improving medical education so it takes cognizance of the community. The third ideal suggests an awareness of an ultimate mission of the movement — for medical education to create a different sort of physician.

As for conditions external to the medical school, no one can underestimate the impact of the Viet Nam War on the consciousness of many who were students at the time. To medical students, in particular, the indiscriminate suffering and death must have seemed particularly wasteful. As Mullan (1970) points out, the prospect of being drafted at the conclusion of medical school was a source of despair, anxiety, and rage for many medical students.

The medical student was also conscious of the civil rights movement. Some medical students were supporters of SNCC (McNamara, 1972).

Older members of the profession created the Medical Committee for Human Rights (MCHR) to oversee the need for medical attention at civil rights demonstrations.

The counter-culture emerged in response to the youth of the times. Dr. Michael Halberstam (1971) has summarized some of the counter-culture values. These values are individuality, local control, and an anti-bureaucratic fervor. According to Halberstam, the radical or counter-culture critique of medical practice is a better explanation for the alienatin people feel from medical care organization than is the liberal viewpoint. The liberal viewpoint bolds, instead, that greater rationalization of services will provide the kind of service people want and need. We will see the counter-culture values institutionalized in the medical movement. Besides the war, according to Lucas (1969), medical students were also affected by the persistence of curable diseases and by people going to bed hungry. These were not times, he says, for business as usual.

Student Health Organization (SHO)

The Student Health Organization (SHO) arose from this ferment. More specifically, in 1964, a group of medical students at the University of Southern California initiated a Student Medical Forum, at which experts like Drs. Alan Guttmacher and Victor Sidel discussed problems of health-care delivery. At one of these sessions, the students discussed the Association of Internes and Medical Students, which had existed from the 1930's to about 1950, as a prototype for a student medical organization. The students decided to start their own projects and, after these were federally funded, the SHO was born (McGarvey, 1968; Bottone, 1971).

For the ensuing several years, projects grew and were federally funded at medical schools all over the country. Although membership was defined as attendance at meetings or participation in projects, it may be estimated that 1,000 health science students (which included nursing and dental students) were participating, as of 1969 (Michaelson, 1969). By the summer of 1968, Washington was supplying $1.25 million nationally for projects in nine areas of the country (Michaelson, 1969).

Students were limited by the tasks which non-licensed physicians could perform. When the SHO first started to evolve in 1964, the students were involved in a number of projects: audio-visual screening of Head Start children, staffing a new family-planning clinic in an East Los Angeles Mexican-American neighborhood, and working with the Medical Committee for Human Rights in Mississippi.

The Philadelphia Student Health Project of 1968 placed 74 health science students in 34 community institutions throughout the city. The students received a $900 stipend for the nine to ten weeks during the summer. They were supervised by professionals in the community. The students' primary reasons for participating was their desire to learn about community needs and urban slum conditions. Other reasons were to bring about social change and to help the poor (The Philadelphia Student Health Project, 1968).

Thus, many members were deeply committed to improving social conditions. They shared similar backgrounds with other activists — upper-middle class homes with professional fathers. The difference was that these Philadelphia medical students had majored in the natural sciences, instead of the humanities or social sciences as had many others throughout the country who were not to go into medicine.

The goals of the Philadelphia project and of the entire SHO showed the same anti-bureaucratic fervor which Halberstam attributed to the New Left. The philosophy of the staff was to allow each student to experience problems of health and urban poor on an individualistic level, through a decentralized organizational structure. They hoped that students would create and initiate reforms from their experience. The project's goals were ". . . . what each individual participant defined as his goal on a personal basis." (Here, too we see an emphasis on the individuality which Halberstam ascribed to the New Left.)

The SHO held national assemblies which were in the form of mass gatherings. The first assembly was held in autumn, 1965. A second was held a year later in the Bronx. Thirty states were represented, and there were 350 delegates from 50 medical schools and 20 nursing schools. A third assembly was held in February, 1968 (McGarvey, 1968). When not united by conventions, the SHO functioned as a loose coalition of local groups.

Before the last assembly, plans had been circulated for an SHO national office. But, the idea was met with some opposition because of the fear of being dominated by a strong, centralized, national organization. So far as this writer knows, no national headquarters for SHO was ever set up.

Four interpretations may be offered as to why the SHO remained on a decentralized level:

1) to maintain its anti-bureaucratic position. According to Dr. Frasier (1969), the form of the organization was based on the students' conception that medical education and health care were authoritarian. This accounted for the loose definition of membership, and the "Let the people decide" approach. There was a conflict between the need for structure, felt by some participants, and the participatory democracy approach which dominated. We will see shortly that this anti-bureaucratic ethos was expressed in an anti-expertise ideology on the part of some students, probably because of the same opposition to authority.

2) to avoid attack from other organizations and people. A precursor to SHO, the Association of Internes and Medical Students, had been investigated by the American Medical Association in 1948 for supposed communist sympathies because it had supported national health insurance. The AMA had retaliated by founding the Student American Medical Association in 1950. Someone could distort and misrepresent the programs of the SHO more successfully if it were a visible and developed organization.

3) to avoid cooptation by other organizations (that is, absorption into their ranks). If the SHO were a national organization, actual cooptation of the group's leaders could occur by their being offered better positions in other organizations. Or cooptation of SHO's ideas could take place. Already, in 1968, some foundations were expressing an interest in funding the SHO which could have resulted in loss of independence. Moreover, William Bronston, the originator of SHO, had decried curriculum reform as a coopting mechanism. He said it is, "a coopting move — a way of absorbing potentially radical energies and sentiments into cooperation with the system in the domination of the masses in the country" (Michaelson, 1969, p. 54). In other words, he feared absorption of the SHO into the medical school structure.

4) to allow for personalized development of participants. Decentralization also provided the greatest opportunity for each participant to involve himself in some aspect of community life without direction from above. The movement believed in personal development of its members, just as it believed in personalized service to patients.

Without changing its decentralized focus which was so in keeping with the times, the SHO met its end about 1970. According to one informant, the SHO disappeared because it lost its funds from the federal agencies. Some of the students had become disenchanted with the way in which the medical schools had controlled the SHO projects, and they did not apply for funds as grantees (John and Barbara Ehrenreich, 1969). Despite the decentralized form of SHO, the organization had been coopted by the Student American Medical Association. SAMA had taken over SHO's summer project idea with a plan of its own, called the Medical Education-Community Orientation Project. This placed interested medical students in preceptorships with practicing physicians in small towns. The goal was to expose students to the workings of medicine in the community. The purposes of the SAMA and SHO programs were similar.

SAMA has continued to become more liberal. It has endorsed national health insurance and pre-paid group practice to some extent. It has frequently disagreed with its parent-body, the AMA. It should finally be noted that SAMA, while it approached some of SHO's values, maintained an organization that was vastly different from SHO's. SAMA had an organized system of delegates from each medical school where there was a chapter which then formed a house of delegates, patterned after the AMA. SAMA, thus, has a difference of style from the SHO. We will see the impact of SAMA and SHO on some other activist organizations later on. For the moment, let us turn to another issue, the ideology of the movement.

The Ideology of the Movement

While the behavior of the medical students might be dismissed as chaotic militancy, closer examination shows that it is inspired by a pattern of professional values. This is one of the factors that makes this a professional movement.

This ideology or pattern of professional values has been developed and extolled by both medical students and young practicing physicians. The ideology is spread by two socializing agents: 1) contact between students and the interns and residents who serve as teachers to the students, and between students and practicing physicians; and 2) the underground press. This press helps to account for similar ideological phenomena in different parts of the country: the ideology is not created by one central body. The role of the underground press may be shown by the fact that the main sources that Dr. Geiger uses, in the discussion of the movement's ideology below, are newspapers called "The Radical Therapist" and "The Body Politic."

A model by Barber (1963) helps us see patterns in the professional values. Barber distinguishes four basic norms that a professional upholds: (1) specialization, as measured by high levels of training; (2) autonomy and control over one's work; (3) ethical standards to guide the practice of the profession; and (4) a concern for community interest. We will substitute knowledge for community interest because the former norm distinguishes professions from occupations better than does the latter norm.

This is a model of an orthodox professional, against which can be assessed the likes and dislikes of the movement. The dislikes are the subjects of professional ideological statements more often than are the likes because they are what the movement must combat, but the likes are also useful in discerning the movement's views. Below are the norms which correspond to particular likes and dislikes.

TABLE 2

Likes and Dislikes of the Medical Movement
and the Norms to which They Correspond

Norm	Likes	Dislikes
1) Knowledge and expertise	Team-work and demystification of the doctor	Elitism
2) Specialization	Generalism; personal care	Specialism
3) Autonomy	Community control	Elitism; traditional doctor-patient relationahip
4) Ethics	Humanitarianism and equality; political morality	Professional morality

Now, let us describe each of these likes and dislikes of the movement.

1. Movement's Preference: Team Work and a Demystification of the Doctor

Much of society accepts the division of labor as a consequence of the way society is organized. But, this is not true of the movement. The movement believes two kinds of elites are created by the doctor's use of his status: one is based on the doctor's status over other health personnel in the hierarchy; the other is based on the doctor's use of technical and specialized knowledge to put a barrier between himself and his patients. As to the first type of elitism, the movement believes that reliance on the physician even for the tasks that he is uniquely qualified for — diagnosis and consultation — creates an artificial elitism that separates him from the nurse, clerk, and others.

This position is taken by the Lincoln Collective in the Bronx. This group was spearheaded by a group of former SHO activists who had congregated in New York. It takes its name from Lincoln Hospital, where the group decided to work. It negotiated with the hospital to start a community internship and residency program in pediatrics which began in July, 1970 (Blum, 1970).

This is an innovative type of pediatrics house staff arrangement. It provides experience in managing problems in the community; for example, lead intoxication, tuberculosis, and malnutrition. Ambulatory pediatrics is emphasized. Every house staff member is assigned to the General Pediatrics Clinic several days per week so that clinic patients who come in can have their own doctor.

Based on its philosophy, the pediatrics department is trying to reorganize, ignoring professional and hierarchical considerations. The goal is to get:

> An atmosphere where work will be divided intelligently, not delegated arbitrarily — where ideas will be exchanged freely and valued for their validity rather than for their sources (McNamara, 1972, p. 172).

Several approaches have been used to effect these goals. Elitism is combatted by a situation in which residents help interns overburdened with admissions. Full-fledged pediatricians register patients if clerks are too busy or take temperatures if nurses are too busy. Another approach has been for all those employees not in supervisory roles to get together to spend time together making mutual decisions on their work.

When it comes to implementing the attempt to break down the doctor's elitism, the movement is not always able to succeed. Free clinics, which are a movement institution, try to have staff perform minor tasks, so that maximum consultation time is available between doctor and patient. But, this attempt to make the doctor more efficient counteracts clinic attempts to demystify the doctor (*Health-Pac Bulletin,* Oct., 1971).

As to the second type of elitism, the problem surrounding this is raised by Dr. H. Jack Geiger, a professor of community medicine in the journal, *Social Policy*. He reviews criticisms of psychiatry in the underground press, and says that "they (the radicals) fail to distinguish between technical knowledge or expertise, itself quite neutral, and its misuse for status and elitist purposes" (1971, p. 26). A retort is made to this position in the same journal by Dr. Howard Levy, the dermatologist and Health-Polich Advisory Center staff member who was court-marshaled for refusing to teach his specialty to Green Berets. Levy denies that radical doctors oppose scientifically derived criteria of technical excellence. He says that no consensus exists in mental health, so that it is reasonable that the radicals, like others, should question the viewpoints of people in psychiatry. Levy's approach is cogent in view of the fact that minimal consensus among its members is a keystone of a profession. But the fact that the radicals question mental health does not mean that they denigrate expertise in fields where they think it is more objectively shown, such as in surgery or in internal medicine.

Another example of the way in which the movement responds to elitism is shown in the report of the Philadelphia Student Health Project in 1968. Two students, in a section on "Professional Values and their Consequences on Serving Clients," give the example of the West Philadelphia Mental Health Consortium, which, they say, was preoccupied with the roles of its members as white professionals. The students say that another student had requested a psychiatric evaluation of an alcoholic by a consortium psychiatrist. According to the student, "The psychiatrist's response was a mixture of apathy, indignation, and a professional-training-bred belief that his profound insights could only be meaningful to a fellow member of the guild. He was not willing to share the fruits of his training with 'Mr. Temple Student.' " The students, thus, attributed the psychiatrist's response to an elitist belief in the superiority of a doctor.

Rayack (1967), an economist, has an analysis of credentials and expertise that is compatible with the movement's views. He says that the principle of certifying specialists, which the American Medical Association upholds, helps to guarantee quality, but it is also a policy for restricting the numbers of physicians in a particular specialty and for relegating those outside the specialty to lower status. The AMA is, thus, accused of contributing to what the movement calls an elitist position. In a similar vein, Freidson (1970) attributes to doctors a "professional dominance'' which they impose on other people. This, then, is the movement's view: the doctor makes himself an elite, above other people — patients and non-doctor colleagues.

2. Movement's Preference: Generalism

The movement favors generalism and disparages specialism. We will discuss this theme in two ways in this section: First, by presenting the movement's critique of specialism as highlighted in the Geiger-Levy controversy. Second, by presenting the movement's goals for generalism, and their convergence with the goals of a new branch of family medical practice.

Before we begin these tasks, let us briefly relate specialism to elitism. Elitism, as we have seen, is that practice which separates specialists from general practitioners. Specialism helps insure elitism, according to the movement. Levy says that specialists receive power and privileges out of proportion to their skill. Presumably, he refers to the increased likelihood a specialist has of getting a hospital appointment over a general practitioner. In his view, generalists should receive more prestige and power than do specialists. The specialist should be regarded as a technician who seves the generalist. Specialists should be used in concert with generalists for both rich and poor, one should not relegate the poor to the generalist.

Geiger had made a number of comments praising specialization, fully aware that the movement derogated it. He said that specialized knowledge had a value in itself. Specialization developed because of limitations on the extent of knowledge any one person could have. Furthermore, ''Whatever its consequences in monopoly control, specialization developed out of a concern for technical quality'' (1971, p. 27).

Geiger is also aware that the movement disparages certification. But, Geiger says, when he rides a jet airplane, he wants someone to pilot it who has been trained in flying jets — even certified as a specialist. He does not regard that as elitist. What Geiger ignores, however, is that a pilot with his experience in propjets has some of the same experience as a jet pilot. By the same token, a doctor who is a generalist has *extensive* training that may qualify him to do some of the jobs of a specialist, even though his training is not so *intensive*.

Now that we have seen how the movement responds to specialism, let us turn to the positive factors that the movement would like to encourage by way of generalism. Maxmen (1971 a) implies that the activists define a good doctor in line with the generalist ethos: besides having a basic knowledge of disease, he should have the ability to care for the whole patient in the context of his social environment.

This statement bears a close resemblance to the position of family practice. "Family practice" is the new name for general practice, and it dates from 1969 when the American Board of Family Physicians was set up to certify physicians as being competent in family practice (J. Michaelson, 1972). Yet, family physicians, as Stevens (1972) points out, do not have, at the moment, any clearly defined function as primary care specialists, as such physicians have in Britain. There, also, specialists only see patients on referral generalists.

Family practice has not received clear criticism from the movement: although Levy does not address himself to family medicine, it is not likely that he would endorse family practice because of its being like all specialties, for elitist purposes. On the other hand, he could regard family practice as not particularly elitist because it is the newest addition to the specialties.

To return to our previous point, the activist emphasis on the "whole patient" is echoed by a family practice emphasis on personalized care. Personal care is defined by the American Academy of General Practice as "care of the whole person and not just of his disease" (1968, p. 1). In addition, both the activist and the family practitioner espouse preventive and comprehensive care. Preventive care comprises such concerns as immunization and accident prevention. Comprehensive care requires competence in a wide range of specialties so as to cover all or most of the patient's needs.

Besides being opponents of specialization, both the movement and family practice are opponents of privilege in the hospital. Menke (1971) points out how essential the hospital is to the doctor's identity. But, both the general practitioner and the practicing activist in his role as community health center doctor had been sometimes denied the privilege of attending their patients while they were in the hospital. In addition, both have a preference for what Krause (1971, pp. 128-134) calls the decentralized model of health care, except that there is some difference in preferred forms of financing and preferred forms of organization — solo or group. Furthermore, both see the need for a doctor to act as a patient-advocate for his patient to guide him through the choice of and referral from other doctors (Bryan, 1968).

How can we account for these convergences in philosophy between the movement and family practice? Perhaps the answer is that they both suffer from status-inconsistency and status-deprivation; neither has an income that matches his social standing nor that which compares with that of the specialist. Moreover, both practice in offices or clinics, rather than primarily in hospitals, and this fact conditions their ideology or philosophy.

One might predict that family medicine and the movement will converge organizationally in the future. The coordinator of one family practice residency program thinks it likely that his specialty will attract activists. Geiger (1971) says that activists regard family medicine as a good model. Finally, residents in family practice turned out beyond expected numbers to attend the activist Second National House Staff Conference in 1972 (Mumford, 1972, p. 8). Even if, as Halberstam (1971) says, the liberals have ignored the radical-activists, perhaps the "conservative" family practitioners will not ignore the radical activists with whom they share so much organizationally and ideologically.

5. Movement's Preference: Community-control

The traditional doctor takes his individual patient as the client; the movement doctor takes the community as his client. In other words, he has a multiple client. Moreover, while the conventional doctor asserts his control over the patient, the movement doctor affirms the control of the community over himself.

McNamara (1972) provides the following definition of community control. It exists when:

> . . . . important planning, policy and operational responsibilities are given to broadly representative neighborhood health boards with locally responsible neighborhood health administrators.

Community control has been a watchword of the movement since 1966, when the government founded neighborhood health centers under government auspices and as part of the War on Poverty. The actual extent of control by community boards has varied from institution to institution, with the grantees, who were usually medical schools and hospitals, being reluctant to share their power. The overall problem of community participation has been documented by Moynihan (1965). More specifically, Parker (1972) says that professionals have viewed the entry of the community into primary care facilities with trepidation.

Levy (1971) says that professional control rather than community control was the watchword of the neighborhood health center programs.

One might wonder about the connotative difference between the cry for community control and for consumer control. A health consumer is someone who uses health facilities. For one thing, the difference between the two terms is one of ideology; liberals tend to refer to consumer control and McCleery (1971) has argued the case for this type of control. Radical activists, in turn, tend to refer to community control. But, the difference is one of substance as well as of rhetoric.

The OEO and other agencies require consumer control (i.e., boards of consumers) in order to receive funds. But, if community people, like businessmen and political leaders who are not consumers are placed on the boards, the boards will not comply with government regulation (Parker, pp. 136-138). Thus, the optimum situation is community people who are also consumers.

The issue of community control, as opposed to consumer control, arose at Lincoln Hospital in New York.

The call for community control arose out of the death of a Puerto Rican woman from a therapeutic abortion in the obstetrics ward. The woman already had two children. A psychiatric resident who had known the patient looked at her chart and discovered that the abortion had taken place in spite of a history of rheumatic heart disease. Other doctors, studying the chart, found that medication given during the abortion had precipitated heart failure.

The resident decided to turn over his findings to the Think-Lincoln Committee, which had been founded by the Young Lords. Think-Lincoln and other community residents confronted the hospital administration with a number of demands. They asked that the hospital pay damages to the woman's family, that they name the abortion clinic after her, and that the obstetrics department head be asked to resign. As Geiger (1971) points out, another demand was most crucial for community control. This was that the hospital set up a watchdog committee of community residents and hospital workers to monitor the abortion program.

Although this demand seemed more geared to preventing another death that were the other demands, it left a number of questions unanswered. If there were to be monitoring, monitoring for what? How? In what relation to community-worker control? If, indeed, this type of control meant the right of non-professionals to discipline professionals, then it is easy to see why many of the house staff were "uptight" about it.

It is somewhat difficult to determine what the implication of the dead woman's situation was to be for other women. But, it is inferred that she did not receive any birth control information because of the doctor's "professionalism." That is, he was not willing to discuss birth control matters with her because his time was too precious. Consequently, she had to rely on abortion as a last resort.

With this supposition in mind, let us review the controversy between Drs. Geiger and Levy on the way in which accountability of physicians can and should be obtained to prevent needless deaths like this one. Geiger notes first that the patient and the community are not guaranteed quality care more by a community group than they are by a physician's group, that both solutions are elitist.

Furthermore, he adds that the community group would lack the technical knowledge to *judge* a doctor's explanations, although they might have the ability to *understand* the explanations. One solution he gives to the role of the community is to suggest that doctors be subject both to peer review — i.e. by their fellow doctors, and, also, by consumers or the community. Relating this to the idea of elitism, Geiger says that expertise does not automatically create elitism, and therefore, that doctors' control does not automatically lead to abuses.

Levy responds to Geiger on accountability by making a number of points: He says community people may make mistakes, but they will not make as serious mistakes as the professionals. Furthermore, the community will care about decent medical care for its members, and the professionals do not have that goal. In a similar vein, Levy says that professionals derive their legitimacy and powers from their credentials; whereas, community groups derive theirs by being responsive to the community. The professionals, he says, are not responsive to the community.

Levy says that community people would only intervene in broad discretionary matters. In respect to birth control, Levy wants women to have the chance to make decisions about their own birth control procedures, rather than be told by the doctor. He says that the need for women taking some of the initiative themselves is caused by the reluctance of the doctors to give thorough explanations.

To some extent, Geiger and Levy appear to be talking past each other. Geiger (1971, p. 33) does say that the potential for elitism among doctors exists, but Levy does not observe this point.

Each sees too much virtue in one or the other parts to the dispute. While Levy puts too much reliance on the community, Geiger puts too much on the profession. Levy does not substantiate some of his points very well: he does not say why he assumes the community will make few mistakes if it is given broad-scale discretion. On the other hand, there is a certain vitality to Levy's emphasis on the community.

The movement's emphasis on the community rather than on the traditional individual patient, is susceptible to some problems. McNamara (1972) admits that it is difficult to create a sense of community among people who have no sense of community living as they do in a debilitated urban setting such as the area surrounding Lincoln Hospital. Taking the position we have attributed to the movement, M. Michaelson (1969) is quoted as saying that the "traditional notion of a patient-centered rather than a community-centered physician is obsolete." In response, Michael Halberstam (1970) contends that the community cannot be taken as the client rather than the individual. The community is divided and it may have aberrations of its own, e.g., Alabama physicians may refuse to treat civil rights workers because they do not correspond with the physicians' notion of a deserving community. Moreover, Halberstam says, "community" is too tenuous in this country to be substituted for patient concern. Although the "community" is not likely to supersede the individual client as the focus of the doctor's concern, it is clear that the movement believes that more control over the treatment of individuals should be vested in the community.

4. Preference: Humanitarianism and a Political Morality

The movement has extolled humanitarianism and a political morality, rather than what is regarded as a doctor's professional morality. According to Maxmen's (1971 b) interviews of SHO activists, medicine was not an end in itself but a means to express a humanitarian ethic. The activists said they saw no difference between organizing a peace demonstration and treating the ill, since both were expressions of the same ideal. Humanitarianism was also shown as rating high among the Philadelphia Student Health Project activists during the summer of 1968. They scored high in favorable attitudes toward the poor, and in their favorable attitude toward integration.

One situation in which the activists believed that political morality superseded professional morality was in the draft board physical examination. The Medical Committee for Human Rights and other groups used clinics and other efforts to find a basis for getting exemptions for a number of young men. Geiger (1971) says that the activists were wrong in their use and defense of this technique. He says that there is no distinction between the MCHR physician and a white Alabama physician who certifies every black for induction, while ignoring the whites.

Geiger criticizes Levy's attempts to reconcile his political and professional goals as sophistry. Levy had said "I oppose the political use of medicine, but I favor the medical use of politics" (Geiger, 1971, p. 30). Perhaps this statement and Geiger's response to it is what resulted in their controversy.

In response to Geiger's criticism of the doctors' approach to physicals, Levy says that they are merely practicing preventative medicine, and this is justification for what they do. Levy observes that Geiger did not believe the war was immoral, and that is why he did not uphold a political morality. Geiger had said that he would uphold a political morality if he were a doctor in a concentration camp asked to experiment on people, and that this was a clear case where pure traditional medicine would not be justified.

In conclusion, two general criticisms may be made. Geiger does not stipulate under what circumstances a person can objectively know that a political morality is justifiable, aside from his example of the concentration camp doctor. For his part, Levy seems to underestimate the extent to which a professional morality includes service and equality injunctions. Perhaps, there is not so great a gap between the two moralities as he thinks.

Now that we have reviewed the preferences of the activist physician, let us consider the following question:

What is the significance of these preferences or norms of the movement, when they are considered as a whole? The two central aspects of its overall ideology are altruism and that health care is a right. These two considerations appear to be mutually dependent, such that the existence of one supposes the existence of the other. Let us examine each of these separately.

The idea of altruism as an umbrella word to convey the total professional ideology of the movement is suggested by Loftus (1971). He identifies altruism as one of the subcategories of responsibility based on a sample that included physician, medical school faculty, and medical students. These categories of responsibility, in addition to altruism, are dependability, initiative, sociability, independence, and conformity. But, altruism is the highest ranking conception of responsibility among medical students. This is the way Loftus defines altruism for his respondents:

> The agent sacrifices himself for the benefit of another (applies especially when that sacrifice goes beyond what is expected by the other). He performs beyond the normal contract in trying to do good for the other. He is concerned with the broader aspects of his position, and with the ramifications as well as the immediate consequences of policies he may make or uphold.

From what we have seen of the movement ideology, the concept of altruism would seem to apply. The movement believes in going beyond the normal patient-physician contract in a number of ways: by upholding humanitarianism; by asserting community-control rather than physician-control of health service; and by asserting the importance of a personalized, family practice style of care.

If the movement doctor is altruistic, then how can we describe the conventional physician? Let us suggest that he is self-directed or autonomous rather than being amenable to the control of others (as is the movement-physician). If the conventional doctor permits anyone else to impinge on his autonomy, it is usually a fellow physician through the mechanism of peer review. In other words, where the conventional physician is supervised by his peers, the activist physician allows supervision by his patients through the mechanism of community control. The principle of autonomy may preclude the conventional physician from seeking anyone's report as to performance, let alone the community's.

Besides altruism, the belief in health care as a right serves to summarize the movement's position. One of the occasions on which the movement expounded the concept of medical care as a right occurred at the 1967 American Medical Association Convention. It was in response to the new AMA President, Milford Rouse, who had spoken of the unsurpassed quality of care in the United States. He had also questioned the need for Medicare and Medicaid legislation. Finally, he had called on the members to protect capitalism in the United States as a way of promoting medicine.

The movement members at the meeting issued a statement against Rouse. It was issued by the black-led National Medical Association, the

Medical Committee for Human Rights, and the Physicians' Forum. (However, they had been prompted to issue it by a SHO activist.) These groups drew attention to what they regarded as Rouse's reactionary comments and announced health care as a right:

> It is time for those whose conscience is horrified by such AMA policies in the field of social medicine to reaffirm that health care is a right which ought to be guaranteed to all by our society, and not a privilege obtainable only through personal affluence (Langer, 1967, p. 286).

Professional services are not to be bought; they are to be made available to all. In this way, the concept of medicine as a right alters the relationship of medicine to the market.

Let us note in passing that the view that medical care is a right suggests that the movement would avow some forms of national health insurance. The Physician's Forum, for example, has endorsed the Kennedy bill for national health care. But the student movement has not vocally espoused health insurance. This is paradoxical in view of the fact that a national health system would provide job opportunities for people with its inclinations and the system would be consistent with the movement's ideology.

The prospect of national health insurance, as we will see in the conclusion, has implications for the role which could be played by the vanguard of doctors who currently occupy roles in neighborhood health centers and free clinics. For the moment, however, let us turn to assessing the impact of the medical student movement on medical education. We have reason to suspect that, because of movement dynamics and ideology, it could have had some effect on medical education.

The Impact of the Movement on Changes in Medical Education

In light of its ideology, what is the student medical movement to do? It could demonstrate against the specialty boards with the hope that they would stop certifying specialists, but the speciality boards have no reason to heed its warning. It could demonstrate against the American Medical Association, the traditional bulwark of medicine, but the AMA has little reason to heed students who are not members and may never be. Instead of these options, and aside from some demonstrations at pharmaceutical companies, most student dissent has been focused on the medical schools. The medical schools stand to lose satisfied graduates and, perhaps, effectiveness by failing to accede to student demands. This is why the medical schools have been vulnerable to the altruistic ideology. The students have seen the medical schools as the enemy, and it is useful to determine what effectiveness or impact they have had.

Before we review the changes in medical education and consider the impact of the movement on them, let us briefly mention the curriculum as it has stood for most of this century. The basic curriculum was heralded by the Flexner report, which was published in 1910. This curriculum began with studies related to the structure of the body, such as anatomy; proceeded to studies of function, such as physiology and biochemistry; and then went on to other subjects. This scientific curriculum usually lasted two years. The importance of the scientific element was summed up this way in the Carnegie Commission of Higher Education Report of 1970:

> The primary thrust of the post-Flexner development in medicine was the recognition of a scientific base in the natural sciences as a *sine qua non* for rational diagnosis and therapy (p. 25).

Only after the first two years of scientific subjects did students move into the clinical curriculum — that is, observation and treatment of patients in hospital or ambulatory settings. During this period, students worked with patients under the guidance of teachers, and learned how to obtain comprehensive, meaningful, and accurate histories of illnesses, how to conduct physical examinations, and how to use laboratory diagnostic aids.

In short, the post-Flexner curriculum had these features: The basic sciences were communicated by emphasis on the departmentally-based science disciplines such as anatomy. There was a sharp distinction between the scientific and the clinical periods in the curriculum. Finally, there were few if any electives.

A gradual change has taken place in this curriculum in the late 1960's and in the 1970's. One of the foremost changes, according to Sheps and Seipp (1972), has been the introduction of interdisciplinary courses on the basic organ systems of the body to replace, somewhat, the traditional departmental science courses mentioned above. At Temple University, this trend is illustrated by interdisciplinary courses in such body systems as the cardiovascular, the endocrine metabolic and the gastrointestinal systems (*Bulletin*, 1971-1973, School of Medicine). The purpose of such courses is supposedly to present information more systematically than it has been given in the past. Besides these, some medical schools have also started interdisciplinary courses in human growth and development, health care delivery, and in clinical medicine — usually during the first year.

From the point of view of Dr. Cooper, the president of the Association of American Medical Colleges (1973), the greatest change in the curriculum is in making it more flexible through electives. At Hahnemann Medical College, part of the third year and the entire fourth year of the curriculum are spent in multiple tracks, which consist of electives, plus science and clinical work, in a student's areas of interest.

Although these changes are important, perhaps the most far-reaching change will prove to be in respect to the clinical part of the curriculum. As we will see, change in the clinical area is highly consistent with the student movement's ideology. We have noted that one of the hallmarks of the classical post-Flexner curriculum was the sharp break between the scientific and the clinical courses. The new curriculums provide clinical courses sooner, more of them, and greater interpenetration with the basic sciences. Most of the schools in the Philadelphia area provide a first year course in clinical medicine. One medical school bulletin says that the school illustrates the fundamentals of history-taking and physical examinations through practice experience in the community, in clinics, and at bedsides.

Why should one expect that the students could have had an impact on the curriculum reforms in general and on the clinical changes in particular? First, let us consider the reforms taken altogether. Several points indicate the great interest that was had in curriculum reform. The cry for relevance in clinical work, basic science work, and electives was heard at many schools. Moreoever, many SHO members became interested in change within the schools. Rather than trying to make the community safe for the medical school, the students began working in 1969-1970 to "make the medical school safe for the community" (Ehrenreichs, 1970). In addition, 39 percent of the participants in the Philadelphia Student Health Project said they planned to attempt curriculum reform in their schools during the academic year following the summer of 1968 (Philadelphia Health Student Project Report, 1968). Some of the students clearly felt that they have had an impact. One third-year student at

Thomas Jefferson Medical College told this writer that he believed that the first-year clinical course at his institution came from student pressure.

Second, we have mentioned the strong value placed on general practice by the activists. They might have believed that this could be best nurtured and developed through clinical experience. Therefore, one would expect the students who supported general practices to militate for reforms that would allow them to see patients as early as possible in their schooling.

However, the students were not the only ones interested in curriculum reforms. Evidence from interviews of medical school students and deans suggests that the medical school faculties were also interested in reforms. Most of the schools deny any direct impact of students on the curriculum. The deans of these schools said they had students on their curriculum committees, and that the students participated in an interchange of ideas. A dean of one school indicated that students had had an effect on instituting changes in the comprehensive and primary care courses whereas another dean at the same institution attributed changes in these courses to the prodding of the federal government. This was an isolated example of possible direct impact. But, the overall picture that emerges is of a complex process of student, faculty, and administration interaction where impact from one source is hard to assess.

The deans at several institutions claimed that student impact had to be minimal because plans for curriculum reform were begun five or six years before students actually became committee members. Students had become members in or around 1968.

In 1970, after some of the educational reforms were already underway, the Carnegie Commission on Higher Education issued a report which called for, among other things, the change in the balance between science and clinical instruction. The Report asked for improving the curriculum by tying more closely together basic science and clinical instruction; they now too often stand as unrelated worlds (1970, p. 9). The Student American Medical Association also got in the act by publishing *A Handbook for Change* (Graham and Royer, 1972). The book calls for changes in teaching methods and in curriculum. Thus, others besides medical schools and their immediate students were involved in curriculum reforms.

How are we to account for the reforms that took place? One answer is to attribute them to the activist students, who called for such reforms in areas such as clinical medicine and, in some cases, who vowed to carry out these reforms. But, a more plausible explanation is to attribute the reforms to the medical schools.

If we attribute the reforms to the medical schools, two possibilities exist: One is that the medical schools actually wanted the reforms. The other is that the schools just went along with the students, in an attempt to mollify the students' program without truly embracing it. This latter explanation suggests that cooptation took place.

No clear-cut answer is possible. The students who were active are no longer in medical school, and those who are accessible have incomplete views of the events. Some of the deans are also inaccessible. Moreover, each group is liable to some distortion. The medical schools' claim that they originated the reforms may be a face-saving fabrication. Similarly, the students' claim that they were coopted may be an instance of excessive pride. The truth lies somewhere in the middle.

Perhaps we may conclude that the students were a catalyst to the curriculum reform developments. These reforms could be viewed as a gradual evolutionary process. One dean took the catalyst perspective when he said that he did not know what would have occurred if the students had not become involved. That is, the curriculum reform would have had a different complexion if the students had not been involved. Now that we have assessed the role of the medical students, let us consider another segment in the movement, the house staff.

Activism and Altruism among the House Staff

Like the 38,000 medical students, the 50,000 house staff in this country are a segment of the medical profession, as defined by Bucher and Strauss (1961), and is one which has been active in recent years. But, perhaps because the house staff is closer to practicing medicine than are the medical students, the activist house staff is a better indicator of the applicability of the altruistic ideology to medical practice than are the students.

The house staff did not embark on any national collective action during the 1960's. Then, in 1971 and 1972, two national conferences of house staff were held. The reports of these conferences provide the source for much of our information.

The material indicates that the house staff attending the conferences is altruistic and that a cadre of former Student Health Organization (SHO) members are even more altruistic. Based partly on the existence of this

SHO cadre, we will suggest that the movement, while it consists of a number of segments, is drawn mainly from a single generation.

Before we consider house staff on the national scene, first let us mention the collective bargaining problems of house staff on the local scene. House staff must get themselves accepted as collective bargaining agents with their hospitals. They face at least two major problems in this attempt: first, a state labor relations board must recognize them as employees with the right to bargain, rather than as students without this right; and second, the house staff must decide what kind of leverage they wish to exert over the hospitals. One alternative is to strike, but this imperils people's lives. Another alternative, which has been followed in Boston and Los Angeles, has been to stage a heal-in. In a heal-in, every patient seeking care, regardless of medical condition, was admitted to the hospital, as a way of dramatizing the house staff's plight.

The house staff present at the 1972 conference believed that unionization had great benefits for them. In response to a statement, "Unionization poses a threat to the M.D.'s autonomy," 21 percent agreed, but 50 percent disagreed. The reason for this fear is that under unionization as some doctors contemplate it, the doctors in a given area would alter their fees so that they would be approximately equal to each other. But, the house staff apparently believed that unionization did not pose this threat.

The salaries of house staff are such that one might expect all altruistic activity and sentiment to be very limited. In 1962, the average salary of the intern was $2800 (Bottone, 1971, p. 27). To improve this salary level, a task force of the First National House Staff Conference in 1971 recommended a median figure of $10,000 for interns and residents. Average salaries had increased somewhat since the 1962 level, but they had not reached the $10,000 level as of 1971.

However, despite their personal financial conditions, the house staff is altruistic. One of the best keys to the altruism of the 215 participants in the 1972 conference are the answers that were given to open-ended questions distributed by Mumford (1972). The questions asked about the problems which the house staff felt were facing the medical profession. Forty-seven percent wrote comments relating to the delivery of services and to social issues concerned with such delivery. An example of a major problem was "extending patient care to *all* people." Another 30 percent wrote in other comments consistent with the altruistic ideology such as the need for more general practitioners. One group expressed the need for broad-based changes in medicine, but 11 percent said that the problems facing medicine are the threat of government interference or actual interference. This criticism of the public role in medicine was contrary to the altruistic ideology, with its emphasis on an open and publicly-accountable medicine. The majority of the responses were, however, consistent with the ideology.

Another indication of the role of altruism is the statements of conference participants as to what they wanted to accomplish at the conference. Thirty-three percent said "methods to improve delivery" (of health care), whereas only 17 percent said "ideas for improving the education of doctors" and 11 percent said "bettering the condition of house staff" (Mumford, 1972, p. 24).

Some observers have suggested that the income levels of altruistic physicians will be less than those of other physicians. Consequently, it is interesting to note that the relationship between house staff's views of problems facing the profession and their income expectations were statistically significant. Of those who said the greatest problem facing the profession was delivery of services, 50 percent expected to make between $30,000-$50,000 at the height of their careers. Of those who said that the greatest problem was the need for change, 60 percent expected $30,000-$50,000. But, of those who said the greatest problem was socialized medicine or government intervention, only 13 percent said $30,000-$50,000 and 44 percent said $90,000 (Mumford, 1972, p. 16).

Thus, there is a relationship between types of problems recognized and the level of income expected. In other words, apparently people who are altruistic in their medical commitments believe that they will probably earn less than will other physicians. This expectation is probably realistic because, as we shall see in the next section, people who take altruistic positions in neighborhood health centers do earn less than other physicians.

Although the entire conference can be seen as liberal, Mumford isolated 32 out of the 215 conferees who appear even more liberal than the conference as a whole, probably because they were former SHO members. They espoused a position which had the following planks: desire to join non-physicians in collective action, change in the delivery system, house staff responsibility for this change, and acceptance of government action.

Mumford found that the differences between the former SHO people and the rest of the participants were statistically significant in a number of areas. Even the proportions of participants from the different specialties were based on significant relationships. Specifically, the numbers of former SHO members in pediatrics and in psychiatry were statistically significant. This can be explained by observing that these two specialties both treat the "whole patient," and thus have an approach which is consistent with the ideology of the SHO.

Since one of the goals of the activist ideology is that of instituting national health insurance, it is not surprising that the percentages of SHO people endorsing health care as a right and national health insurance as a desirable means are statistically significant. In response to the statement, "it is the responsibility for the entire society through the government to provide everyone with the best available medical care whether or not he can affort it," 94 percent of SHO people said "yes" in comparison with 67 percent of all the others.

Fifty-nine percent of the SHO respondents compared with 29 percent of the others disagreed with the statement: "Further government intervention in medicine will reduce the quality of medical care." The author interprets the SHO posture as desiring greater government activity in the area of national health insurance.

Finally, there is some indication of an anti-elitist attitude on the part of the SHO members, comparable to the anti-elist plank in the altruist ideology. On the subject of whether there should be an upper limit to physicians' salaries, 50 percent of SHO respondents said "yes," whereas only 23 percent of the others said "yes."

What larger significance does this information on the former SHO members have for our understanding of the movement? It implies that the movement is drawn from a single generation, and that the house staff carry on the ideology of other segments of the movement. As if to support this position, Mumford (1972, p. 10) reports that as many as half of the respondents had previously been active on committees in medical school, 15 percent had been SHO members and 45 percent had been members of the Student American Medical Association. We have seen that particularly the SHO members and medical school committee members have been very active. That they would be active as house staff seems plausible.

One important continuity between the segments of the movement is in their political style. Specifically, the house staff members had the same reluctance to form a centralized organization as did the SHO. The First National House Staff Conference in 1971 set up a coordinating committee to plan the next year's activities, but not before a great amount of reflection on political style had taken place. Delegates were divided in their preference for either a local or a national organization, and a coordinating committee was the resulting compromise.

This committee was charged with a number of tasks: (1) to create a national communications network among house staff; (2) to facilitate discussion about creation of a national organization; (3) to plan for another conference; and (4) to publicize any harrassment occurring to an individual that results from actions taken in this conference. The eventual charging of these tasks to the coordinating committee seemed to go counter to the sentiment in the following statement:

> Perhaps it would be best to capitalize on their (house staff organizations') strength be establishing a loose *confederation of associations.* If it had no policy-making powers, no spokesmen and addressed itself only to providing pathways of communication amongst house staffs it could not be subverted (Proceedings of the First National House Staff Conference, 1971, p. 139).

In other words, there was some of the same fear of cooptation that characterized the SHO groups. The fact that a central coordinating committee was set up at the 1971 conference shows this fear had dissipated somewhat. The fact that the house staff central committee survived is shown by the fact that it organized a 1972 convention. However, it organized no 1973 conference, and the reason for this is not clear. The decision not to do so may have been a conscious strategy, or it may have been as a result of cooptation that already had taken place. Consequently, the desire for a local form of organization, in line with SHO tradition, may have been more reasonable than the option that was actually taken.

In short, altruism appears to exert a powerful pull on the nationally organized house staff, and it resembles the altruism of an earlier time. Some of the house staff, particularly the former SHO people, see the social policy of the house staff as being consistent with the interest in higher salaries. Fitzhugh Mullan, a former SHO officer, is quoted as saying that house staff would be better able to concern themselves with altruistic actions if they had higher wages (Hayton, 1971).

The altruism of the house staff activists is less strident than that of the SHO people in the 1960's, but its message is much the same. This is not surprising, because the activist house staff member of today is in great measure the activist of yesterday. As McNamara says:

> . . . The revolutionary college student of the early 1960's became the revolutionary medical student of the late 1960's and is now the revolutionary house staffer of the 1970's (1972, p. 171).

Some Ways in which Activists in Neighborhood Health Centers and Free Clinics Threaten Conventional Physicians

Whereas the house staff are located in hospitals, another segment of the movement practices medicine in ambulatory settings such as neighborhood health centers and free clinics.

There are about 140 neighborhood health centers and 200 free clinics in this country. Neighborhood health centers were created by the federal government while free clinics were created either by movement physicians, neighborhood groups, or political parties. Neighborhood health centers offer comprehensive care, but free clinics are more limited in focus. They offer pregnancy tests, venereal disease tests, and treatment of colds and minor infections. Some offer sickle cell and tuberculosis testing. Despite their differences, both neighborhood health centers and free clinics bear the imprint of the activist physician and his ideology.

It is felt that the activist physicians in these settings are important because they are a threat to more conventional segments of the profession. They constitute a threat for a number of reasons: their commitment to service, the institutional distinctiveness of NHC's (neighborhood health centers) and free clinics, and the doctors' ideal-typical characteristics. Let us consider each of these threats in turn.

As for the first one, the conventional physician espouses care for the poor, but the NHC physician dispenses such care more fully. According to Odin Anderson (1963. p. 286):

> The provision of free care by the medical profession was a natural continuation of the traditional expectation of the profession as providing a service clothed with the public interest.

Thus, the provision of clinic care is seen as a traditional obligation of the physician. In this sense, there is nothing so radical about the behavior of physicians in NHC's until one examines the degree of commitment of these physicians in comparison to conventional ones.

For the conventional physician, it is estimated that he spends four percent of his time working in a clinic (Evans, 1972). At a particular university medical school outpatient clinic in Philadelphia, this time has been estimated as amounting to one morning a week. Furthermore, this service is generally required in return for the hospital privileges the doctor has at the hospital which runs the clinic. In contrast, a physician at a NHC usually works full-time; consequently, his commitment is greater than the person who is part-time. In this sense, the NHC physician is a threat to the conventional physician because he conforms to the norm of service more fully than does the conventional physician.

A second threat to the conventional physician is the institutional form of the NHC's and of the free clinics. Both of these settings are a threat, more specifically, because of their arrangements for the review of a doctor's work and their financing arrangements.

Review of a doctor's work in NHC's is carried out by peers and by the community. Because of the multi-specialty nature of the NHC, peer review offers the physician the spectre of supervision by someone who is not in his field. It is unnerving to the conventional physician to see NHC's permit this type of review because he fears that this might be instituted, in some way, in private practice.

The free clinics have gone a step further than the NHC's with the patient-advocate. According to the *Health-PAC Bulletin* (October, 1971), the patient-advocate had three functions: (1) to help the patient understand the procedures; (2) to challenge the professionalism of the rest of the staff; and (3) to raise the political consciousness of patients and staff. He is potentially a person to deprofessionalize the doctor. In practice, the advocate sometimes just helps to expedite patients, so that the doctor will not be frightened away by undue interference in his activities. But, the advocate is also a threat for the conventional physician because the ombudsman, as the advocate is called in Europe, has been proposed in this country for medicine and for other service professions.

The financing of these two kinds of practice-settings are also a threat to the conventional physician. NHCs used to be financed by outright government grants. Now, these grants are being phased out, and NHCs are expected to be self-supporting. Financing is to come from Medicaid or from patient-payments on a sliding scale related to income. For their part, free clinics usually are either free or require a nominal fee, not exceeding a couple of dollars. The conventional physician sees this form of financing as being destructive of the fee-for-service arrangement and as a prologue to health insurance on a national basis for those besides the poor and the aged. Consequently, the financing arrangement of the NHCs and free clinics are a threat to the conventional physician.

One indicator that they are perceived as a threat is the conclusion to an article called "Challenging Fee-for-service — The Free Clinic Movement," which appeared in the journal *Medical Economics* (October 9, 1972). It says:

> The free clinics clearly offer no competitive threat to private practice. But they are a growing challenge to the conscience and imagination of every doctor (p. 130).

The writer of this paper thinks that free care, contrary to the quotation, is a threat to private practice because it questions the entire legitimacy of fee-for-service practice. The quotation is too quick to deny the importance of a type of care which the article admits serves two million people; but the quotation is correct in noting that free clinics are a model for some doctors. It is precisely in their dual rule as a threat and as a model that free clinics have an impact on the profession. We will return to the idea of the activist as a model in the conclusion to this section.

Besides the service-commitments and the institutional arrangements, the conventional physician is threatened also by the personal characteristics of the activist.

Broadly defined, the NHC physician shows the following characteristics:

Demographic characteristics

1. Race: predominantly white, but an important minority are black
2. Sex: predominantly male
3. Age: under 35 years

Socio-economic Status Characteristics

4. Social class: tending to be upper-middle class
5. Training: tending to be board-eligible or board-certified
6. Income: ranges between $15,000-$30,000
7. Source of income: salary, rather than fees

Professional commitments

8. Area of practice: in a specialty concerned with primary care; thus, a

family practitioner, internist, pediatrician or gynecologist.
9. Professional associations: tending to belong to groups such as the Medical Committee for Human Rights, Physicians' Forum, or National Medical Association. Not a member of the American Medical Association.

What are the implications of this ideal-type personified by the NHC physician? A number of themes may be extracted from these components. First, it seems that the conventional physician feels threatened to a large extent by characteristics that are similar to his own. The NHC physician has approximately the same social class position as the conventional physician, and they share a high level of training. It is more likely for one to be uneasy about someone like himself who has a different ideology than it is to be uneasy about someone who is different from oneself with a different ideology. The NHC physician is, on the one hand, close to the conventional physician in status characteristics — and may even be his son — but, on the other, the ideology places them further apart than if the NHC physician were of a lower-class.

Second, age is a divisive factor between the two groups of physicians. We have already noted that the movement has been the product of a single generation. This generation has been drawn together in its activities in SHO, medical committees, and house staff. But, the same ideology that makes for intra-generational cohesiveness also makes for inter-generational hostility. The older doctors feel attacked by the younger generation of NHC physicians because the altruist ideology threatens the privileges that the older generation has worked so hard to attain.

Third, the fact that NHC physicians are salaried also threatens the conventional doctor; that doctors can succeed without competing for patients must be a source of chagrin to the conventional doctor. He begins to wonder if the entrepreneurial career is worth it all when he has before him the model of the NHC physician who can earn a reasonable income while working regular hours.

In sum, the conventional physician is threatened in at least three ways by the activist physician: by his service commitments, by the institutions he works in, and by his ideal-typical traits.

Despite the fact that they are a threat, the NHC and free clinic physicians must be tolerated. They serve the lower class, and thus perform the tasks which conventional physicians would otherwise need to perform. They must be tolerated and allowed to persist and because their ideology and practice is attractive, it is possible that they will attract sympathizers for and converts to their style of practice. One indication that this has occurred may be noted. Fredericks et al. (1971) found that a pool of 12,000 physicians exists who are potentially interested in poverty work if a position were offered them, and one would speculate that they have been influenced by the model of the NHC physician.

Consequently, one may say that the activist physician is in a position to influence the kinds of commitments doctors make. He is, thus, not only a threat to the conventional physician, but a model for some who are dissatisfied with their present commitments. In these considerations, lie the importance of the activist physician in novel work settings.

The Future of the Movement:
The Prospect of National Health Insurance

How could national health insurance modify the movement? National health insurance would make the careers of its doctors much more staifsying than has been the case with, for example, NHC doctors. Daugudis (1970) claimed that doctors have difficulty visualizing the full "trajectory" of their careers in NHCs; that is, they do not consider NHCs as places to spend their careers. In a similar vein, Wise (1970) says that recruitment has been difficult — at least at his NHC — because NHCs are a loosely structured innovation. National health insurance would presumably solve these problems.

Stevens (1971) forecasts national health insurance by 1980, and it may be noted that some of the forms which it might take have been advocated by the movement. Specifically, neighborhood health centers might be used. This could be an extension of what officials in the government say — that NHCs are already being turned into institutions that cater to the middle-class, as well as to the lower-class.

Another delivery form would be to use primary care units. These would be set up if people were required to register with one physician, as is the case in England. If, as Stevens thinks, primary care were separated from specialty care, this might have the effect of doing what the movement wants — establishing family practice as more basic and more essential to health than is specialty care. Other solutions to the delivery problem would be more consistent with the liberals than with the movement — such as pre-paid multi-specialist groups and expansion of the hospitals.

Regardless of the precise way in which it is implemented, national health insurance would put into effect many of the ideological planks of the movement. This would implement the belief in health care as a right, since it would be extended to all people and, as in the Kennedy bill, on the basis of federal tax revenues. The goal of equality would be served because everyone would have access to a doctor. As has been said, there could be an emphasis on general practice and some degree of community or consumer control. Finally, the health insurance system would also deprofessionalize the doctor by putting him in the company of a health team.

Thus, to answer the question posed at the beginning of this section, national health insurance would make the movement's ideology into an accepted mainstream value-system. It would increase the number of people sympathetic to the movement because doctors would need to be recruited who agreed with the health insurance system.

Many of the changes could occur even if national health care does not materialize in the near future. In Ginzberg's view (1973), many of the trends represented by the activist physician will be more likely: Salaried physicians will be more common; family practice will increase because the specialties are overcrowded; control by the public will be intensified because of a better-educated public; finally, the process of demystification of the doctor will go on.

From the point of view expressed above, the doctors in house staff organizations or free clinics or NHCs are not merely political activists, but they are the professional vanguard. They are at the front lines because of their forms of practice or their ideology. National health insurance would bring the rest of the profession in close pursuit.

A Note on the Future of
Clinical Education and Activism

We had referred to the rapid change in the medical schools from a strict separation between pre-clinical and clinical work to a state of interpenetration of the two types of education. What makes the clinical changes so noteworthy is from a viewpoint based on professional socialization. Specifically, these changes in the clinical content have intermeshed the clinical or apprenticeship period of training with the didactic or basic science period of training. Moreover, as Sherlock and Morris (1967) point out, the usual pattern in the professions is for didactic training to be completely finished before apprenticeship begins. Based on interviews, let us suggest that the past activists have been those who sought clinical training before their didactic training was complete; in other words, the activists were people who proceeded through their status of medical student in an irregular fashion. This applies, once again, to the concept of status-passage which has been developed by Strauss (1968).

Clinical practice is conducive to activism. This is so because a medical student sees what he regards as the inequities of the health system sooner than he would otherwise, and he decides to do something about it. If he waits to experience these inequities as an intern or resident, he is already too professionalized to stray far from the fold.

As Mullan (1970) says, the intern is made to feel very proud of his new-found professional status, and he is unwilling to "rock the boat." But, when the aspiring physician is still a medical student, we would expect that exposure to these inequities would stimulate the activist ideology. One may develop a belief in the need for equal treatment by observing unequal treatment.

The question which we wish to pose may be phrased as follows: Will students become activists if they are exposed earlier to clinical work? Or, will they become conventional physicians because this earlier clinical work has now been institutionalized? Rather than either of these alternatives, it seems more likely that the ideological baggage of the medical student will be permanently altered so that he is a combination of the activist and the conventional. But only time will tell.

Explanations for the Development of the Segments and for their Ideology

We have now considered four segments — two related to the status of medical student; namely, the SHO, and medical school curriculum committees. The other two are related to the status of young practicing physician; namely, the house staff organization members and the participants in a neighborhood health centers (see Table 1, p. 2).

The development of the segments is best explained by Dahrendorf's (1959) distinction between quasi-groups and interest-groups. The problem he is dealing with is the problem of group-formation. Quasi-groups are "aggregates of incumbents of positions with identical role interests" (Dahrendorf, 1959, p. 180), whereas interest-groups are the full-fledged groups which develop from quasi-groups under the influence of leaders, goals, and a conducive social environment.

From this point of view, the segments are quasi-groups which are in the process of becoming interest groups. The segments in activist medicine develop from quasi-groups associated with the statuses of medical student and doctor. These statuses may be thought of as recruiting fields, from which certain leaders, such as the SHO leaders, recruited members.

The opposing quasi-groups are leaders of hospitals who, it was claimed, maintained outmoded methods of practice and the leaders of medical schools who delayed exposure to clinical practice and had curricula that appeared inflexible. In other words, these people provided the constraints that helped to develop activism.

As fledgling formal organizations, these segments support Thompson's (1967) principle that the main problem of organizations is to combat uncertainty. More specifically, the segments emphasize local or decentralized action because, as Thompson says, dependence introduces constraints and contingencies. For example, the house-staff organization segment wants to avoid dependence on medical schools, hospitals, other doctors' associations, the government, and private foundations and, thus, has not, to this writer's knowledge, developed a national organization. The greater the permanence of the segment, the less it must fear cooptation by other organizations.

The Dahrendorf theory also provides an explanation for the development of the activist ideology. But, two other explanations, which we will consider first, might be called 1) the experiential one; and 2) the structuralist one.

The experiential explanation stresses that ideology develops as people interpret their experiences in the course of work or educational activities. Thus, one might argue that the ideology of generalism develops in the minds of young neighborhood health center physicians who have had difficulty in treating their patients in hospitals because they did not yet have any specialty training and did not have the privileges accorded specialists. This explanation does not suppose that they are antagonistic to the heads of hospitals as an opposing quasi-group, as does Dahrendorf's theory, but merely that they are interpreting their experience during socialization.

The structuralist explanation for ideology has some support in this paper because, as we have seen in the instance of neighborhood health centers and free clinics, the financing technique would be conducive to health care as a right and doctor-supervision would be conducive to team work and the demystification of the doctor.

The argument is that, if these structures did not exist, the participants in these clinics would not develop the ideology. This is a kind of structural determinism that has been in vogue in the past in sociology in the great debate on the causal primacy of structure as opposed to ideology.

However, the explanation based on Dahrendorf seems must fruitful. As a quasi-group becomes an interest group, it develops an ideology so as to best do battle with the opposing groups and to reach such goals as that of acquiring new members. Dahrendorf (1959, p. 186) cites the role of Weber's Calvinism for early English capitalists as a sociological prototype for this process.

Contrary to the experiential explanation, Dahrendorf shows that experience does not occur in a social vacuum, but it occurs in potential conflict-situations. Thus, the student-house staff ideology that develops, such as "generalism," results from conflict-experience with the specialists who form the other quasi-group.

Furthermore, the Dahrendorf explanation subsumes the structuralist one because it suggests that ideology would not develop if the groups involved did not occupy positions of differing authority in the hospitals and medical schools. Thus, the Dahrendorf explanation is more effective than either of the other competing ones. The origin and dynamics of the segments is now clearer than before.

A progression from political activism by the Student Health Organization to vanguard professional behavior by young physicians has taken place within a single generation. Indeed, Mumford (1972) suggests that the members of the house staff organizations are some of the same people who were SHO activists at an earlier date. But, this writer thinks that vanguard behavior is best illustrated by the SHO activists and others who have become physicians in neighborhood health centers and free clinics.

But, how would the clinic doctors operate as a vanguard? If these doctors act consistently with their ideology and if they win converts, the medical profession will ultimately develop a complexion different from that which is given it by medical school physicians or conventional doctors. There is a growing disaffection with the American Medical Association, as indicated by the decreasing proportion of doctors who are members (Culliton, 1972). Perhaps some of these doctors will join ranks with the vanguard on particular issues. Regardless of what happens, one conclusion is clear: new physicians have emerged from the medical profession.

BIBLIOGRAPHY

American Academy of General Practice 1968 *Organization and Management of Family Practice*, advisory manual for family physicians. Kansas City, Missouri: The American Academy of General Practice.

Anderson, O.·1963 "Health-Service Systems in the United States and Other Countries: Critical Comparisons." In E. Gartly Jaco (Ed.), *Patients, Physicians and Illness*, second edition. New York: The Free Press, 1972.

Barber, B. 1963 "Some Problems in the Sociology of the Professions." *Daedalus* 92, no. 4 (fall): 669-688.

Becker, H. S. 1961 "Interviewing Medical Students," *American Journal of Sociology* 62: 199-201.

Blum, R. 1970 "The Lincoln Collective." *The New Physician* (October).

Bottone, A. 1971 "The Sorcerer's Apprentice — The History of the Activism Movement among young Health Professionals." In *First National House Staff Conference*, Proceedings and Recommendations. S. G. McCloy (Ed.) Dept. of Health, Education and Welfare, Public No. (HSC) 72-9: 26-37.

Bryan, J. E. 1968 *The Role of the Family Physician in America's Developing Medical Care Program*. St. Louis: Warren H. Green.

Bucher, R. and A. Strauss 1961 "Professions in Process." *American Journal of Sociology* 66 (January): 325-34. Reprinted in A. Strauss *Professions, Work and Careers*. San Francisco: The Sociology Press, 1971: 9-23.

Carnegie Commission on the Future of Higher Education 1970 *Higher Education and the Nation's Health*. New York: McGraw-Hill.

"Challenging Fee-For-Service — The Free Clinic Movement" 1972 *Medical Economics* (October 9).

Cooper, J. A. D. 1973 "Medical Schools, in responding to social need, are reforming themselves." (Editorial) *Journal of Medical Education* 48 (March): 291.

Culliton, B. J. 1972 "AMA: Graduate Medical Plan OK'd, Other Issues Confronted." *Science* 177 (July 7).

Dahrendorf, R. 1959 *Class and Class Conflict in Industrial Society*. Stanford: Stanford University Press.

Daugudis, J. 1970 "Doctors of the people, by the people, for the people." *The New Physician* (November): 909.

Ehrenreich, J. and B. 1971 *The American Health Empire*. New York: Vintage Books, Random House.

Evans, L. R. 1972 "Medicine." In R. F. Odgers and B. G. Wenberg (Eds.), *Introduction to Health Professions*. St. Louis: C. V. Mosby.

First National House Staff Conference 1971 (March) *Proceedings and Recommendations*. S. G. McCloy (Ed.). Dept. of Health, Education and Welfare Publication No. (HSC) 72-9.

Frasier, S. D. 1969 "The Medical Student as Activist." *The Pharos*. 32, no. 4 (October).

Fredericks, M. Et al. 1971 "Physicians and Poverty Programs." *Hospital Progress* 52 (March): 57-61.

Freidson, E. 1970 *Professional Dominance*. New York: Atherton Press.

Geiger, H. J. 1971 "Hidden Professional Roles: The Physician as Reactionary, Reformer, Revolutionary." *Social Policy* 1, no. 6, (March-April).

Ginzberg, E. 1973 "The Young Physician — Living with Uncertainty." *The Pharos* 36, no. 1: (January).

Glasgow, J. N. 1972 "A Comparison of Six Major Proposals for National Health Insurance." *Connecticut Medicine* 36, no. 2 (February).

Goode, W. J. 1957 "Community within a Community: The Professions." *American Sociological Review*. 20: 194-200.

Graham, R. and J. Royer (Eds.) 1972 *A Handbook for Change*. Rolling Meadows, Illinois: Student American Medical Association.

Halberstam, M. J. 1971 Replies to Michaelson's "Failures of American Medicine." *American Scholar* 39 (spring).

Halberstam, M. J. 1971 "Liberal Though, Radical Theory, and Medical Practice." *The New England Journal of Medicine*. 284, no. 21 (May 27).

Hayton, B. 1971 "Medicine's young activists push for a new era," *Physician's Management* 11 (August): 37-45.

Health-PAC 1971 "Free Clinics." no. 34 (October). New York: Health Policy Advisory Center.

Krause, E. 1971 *The Sociology of Occupations*. Boston: Little, Brown.

Langer, E. 1967 "AMA: Some Doctors are in revolt, but revolution is not in sight." *Science* 157 (July 21): 285.

Loftus, G. 1971 "Differential Conceptions of Physician Responsibility among Medical Subgroups." *Journal of Medical Education*. 46 (April): 290-298.

Lucas, C. C. 1969 "Medical Students view change." *The Pharos* 32, no. 4 (October).

McCleery, R. 1971 *One life – One physician*. Washington, D. C.: Public Affairs Press.

McGarvey, M. et al. 1968 "A Study in Medical Action — The Student Health Organization." *New England Journal of Medicine*. 279, no. 2 (July 11): 74ff.

McNamara, J. 1972 "The Revolutionary Physician — Change Agent or Social Theorist." *The New England Journal of Medicine* 287, no. 4 (July 27): 171 ff.

Maxmen, J. 1971 "Medical Student Radicals: Conflict and Resolutions." *American Journal of Psychiatry*. 27, no. 9 (March): 131 ff.

Maxmen, J. 1971b "Medical Student Radicals: Conflict and Resolutions." *American Journal of Psychiatry*, 27, no. 9 (March): 131 ff.

Maxmen, J. 1971a "Activism in Medical school — an experiential study." *Journal of Medical Education*, 46 (January): 58-63.

Michaelson, J. 1972 "Achieving Primary Care." In *Proceedings* of the Second National House Staff Conference. (March) Washington: Institute for the Study of Health and Society.

Michaelson, M. 1969 "Medical Students: Healers become Activists." *Saturday Review* 52 (August 16): 41-43.

Moynihan, D. P. 1969 *Maximum Feasible Misunderstanding*. New York: The Free Press.

Mullan, F. 1970 "A House officer looks at medical student activism." *American Journal of Psychiatry* 126, no. 7 (January): 1010.

Mumford, E. 1972 "Final Evauation Report." In *Proceedings* of the Second National House Staff Conference (March). Washington, D. C.: Institute for the Study of Health and Society.

Parker, A. 1972 "Consumer Participation in Health Programs." In *Proceedings* of the Second National House Staff Conference (March). Washington, D. C.: Institute for the Study of Health and Society.

Philadelphia Student Health Program 1968 U. S. Department of Health, Education and Welfare, Public Health Service, Health Services and Mental Health Administration, Division of Regional Need Programs.

Rayack, E. 1967 *Professional Power and American Medicine:* The Economics of the American Medical Association. New York: The World Publishing Co.

Sheps, C. and C. Seipp 1972 "The medical school, its products and its problems." *Annals* of the American Academy of Political and Social Science 399 (January).

Sherlock, B. J. and R. T. Morris 1967 "The Evolution of the Professional: A Paradigm." *Sociological Inquiry*. 37 (Winter): 27-46.

Stevens, R. 1971 *American Medicine and the Public Interest*. New Haven: Yale University Press.

Strauss, A. 1968 "Some Neglected Properties of Status Passage." In H. S. Becker et al. (Eds.), *Institutions and the Person*. Chicago: Aldine.

Temple University 1971-1973. *Bulletin*. School of Medicine.

Thompson, J. D. 1967 *Organizations in Action*. New York: McGraw-Hill.

Wise, H. 1970 "Physicians in Health Centers." *Postgraduate Medicine*. (June): 133 ff.

IN THE SERVICE OF MAN: RADICAL MOVEMENTS IN THE PROFESSIONS*

Robert Perrucci

*Reprinted from: *Sociological Review Monograph* No. 20 (Dec. 1973)

The decade of the 1960's witnessed major upheavals in every American institution. Following closely on the heels of the anti-war movement came a revolt against the symbols of authority in the universities, the courts, the schools, the churches, and the professions. While the noisier and more public attacks on institutions were being made by those *outside* of them, there were also small pockets of organized criticism and discontent being mobilized *within* major institutions for the purpose of seeking radical change. This paper is about the "radical caucuses" or separatist movements within the major professions. We shall try to describe the conditions under which they emerge, the composition of their membership, and the specific nature of their goals and strategies. We shall also attempt to analyze the special dilemmas facing radical movements, and the specific conditions necessary for their continuity and effectiveness.

Professionals and the Culture of Waste

Although the growth and visibility of radical movements in the professions seemed to coincide with the emergence of movement-related organizations concerned with civil rights and the American war in Vietnam, it is likely that such organized discontent can be traced more accurately to the nature of work in advanced capitalist society.

The occupational structure has changed very dramatically since the turn of the century, and with a speed that has altered the character of work within a single generation of workers. In 1900, approximately 17 percent of the labor force was employed in white collar occupations, 45 percent in manual and service work, and 38 percent in agriculture. Some seventy years later white collar occupations account for 42 percent of the labor force, manual and service occupations rose slightly to 48 percent, and agriculture declined sharply to less than 10 percent of the labor force. Within the general trend, the greatest growth has been in the higher skill-education categories such as professional and technical occupations.

The ranks of the well-established and newer professions including medicine, law, engineering, science, and social work are being joined by an ever increasing number of occupational groups who are seeking to find their place in the sun; to share the increased power, prestige, and income that accompanies professional status. Claims to the status of professional are made by salesmen, real estate agents, advertising men, public relations experts, insurance men, industrial managers, and funeral directors. The claims of the new aspirants seem to have little to do with the service which they provide and, indeed, show little recognition of what is meant by the "service ethic" of dealing with man's needs without a consideration of self-interest. Rather, these groups seem more inclined to believe that achieving recognition as a profession is primarily a matter of publicity and public relations; if you say a thing often enough to enough people you are bound to convince someone.

It is felt that the activities of these aspiring occupational groups, in the work they do and their claims to professional status, reveal a number of significant problems of the work of professionals specifically, and about work in general:

(1) The work performed in occupations which have earned recognition as professions has usually been of a special nature in that it embodies a relativels rare body of specialized knowledge that is used for the benefit of man. Moreover, the services rendered to man have, in theory, been designed largely with his interests in mind, rather than (or at least in addition to) the interests of the professional or the profession. The work activities of the newest occupations to claim professional status have reintroduced a certain skepticism in the public mind about whether any of the professions is as altruistic as it claims to be.

(2) The activities of both the established and aspiring professions have raised new doubts about the particular needs that are being served by these occupations, how these needs are being defined, and by whom. The traditional sense of serving the needs of man has meant dealing with particular crisis situations which could not be handled by the person afflicted. Since the crises situation was one in which the afflicted person was very vulnerable, complete trust had to be placed in the professional. In combination with that trust, special rewards are conferred upon the

professional by those whom he serves. One would now be hard put to find either a sense of dealing with critical human needs or a relationship of mutual trust in connection with many of the services performed by established professions, and for most of the services performed by the aspiring professions.

(3) The coincidence of the increasing power and pecuniary reward attained by professionals, and the increasing number of human problems that are unmet by these same professions, raises serious questions about the amount of concern about serving human welfare. Established professionals are increasingly suspected of having rather pronounced motivations of self-interest which can hardly be distinguished from the more obvious self-interest of the real estate agent or public relations expert. How are we to morally distinguish the indifference of physicians to the millions of Americans who lack medical care from the prejudice of realtors who will not sell houses to blacks; or the unscrupulousness of advertising men who labor to increase the sale of harmful and useless products; or the dishonesty of public relations men who knowingly convey false and misleading images? The one element that links these activities is money. Physicians do not bother about the health care of those who can't pay, and realtors, advertising agents, or public relations men serve only those "needs" which do pay.

(4) The existence of increasing personal gain by professionals combined with a failure to serve real human needs has created discontent among younger professionals over the manner in which their professions operate and their repeated failure to deal with yet unsolved problems in health care, legal aid, pollution, housing, and the like. There appears to be growing discontent among doctors, lawyers, clergymen, professors, and scientists regarding the way they have been wasting their talents. Doctors have formed committees on the medical and health needs of the poor, the consequences of nuclear explosions, the effects of air pollution, water pollution and noise, and they have served as medical personnel in support of anti-war demonstrations. Lawyers have become increasingly involved in providing legal assistance to low-income residents who face exploitative landlords and finance companies. Clergymen have become closely involved in assisting draft resistors, anti-war protests, migrant workers, minority group members and the poor. Their efforts have gone far beyond the traditional role of the clergy in dealing with spiritual needs, and they have extended to

active protest itself. University professors are showing increased awareness of and activism about the question of the university's role in society, the kind of educational experience provided for students at college, and the university's responsibilities to the needs of the noncollege community. Scientists in growing numbers are thinking about refusing, and actually refusing, to work on military projects, and are instead planning redirection of energies and resources to meet major social needs.

The radical activities of these professionals, although representative of only a small segment of the respective occupational groups, indicate a kind and degree of discontent with their work which may be more important than it appears. These activities represent not only job discontent and a search for redirection of personal lives and talents, but also dissatisfaction with the professions as a whole. The activities engaged in are unpopular both in the society and in the respective professional associations. That the protests cannot be stopped indicates, moreover, that their support in the professions may extend beyond the activists. That the protests are not more widespread relates, of course, to matters of power and politics in the professional associations. Most of the protesting professionals are among the younger members who do not hold positions of influence and power in their associations. Yet, the fact that discontent is expressed among the youngest suggests that the full impact of dissatisfaction among professionals is yet to be felt.

The actual work done by many members of the established, newer, and aspiring professions is carried out within the framework of a culture of waste. This culture justifies and even requires an incredible waste of the talents of professionals by underutilizing their training, encouraging the emergence of specializations that serve the highly developed needs of the wealthy and powerful, and by failing to act as a profession and attempt to meet the persistent needs of people who lack the means or the knowledge to use their services.

Engineers by the tens of thousands, for example, are involved in work that rarely uses their talents; this situation is undoubtedly responsible for their high levels of job discontent (Ritti, 1971; Wilensky, 1966). The exploitation of engineers' considerable talents for the production of weapon systems, space exploration, or products that feed a mindless consumerism continues in the face of alternative needs to deal with housing, urban transportation, air and water pollution, and regional development.

Physicians are being educated in numbers far below estimates to meet national needs, and those that are being trained are recruited increasingly to the more exotic and lucrative practices dealing exclusively with high status diseases. The fee-for-service system, so ardently supported by the medical profession, encourages a maldistribution of physicians by region, population density, income, and race. People without access to medical care, to say nothing of their ability to pay for it, seem to concern medical professionals less than a staunch defense of their own market value.

Members of still other professions have experienced similar misgivings about the way in which their talents are channeled and utilized. Most of those who work in public bureaucracies, such as teachers and social workers, seem to devote much of their time to maintaining a symbiotic relationship between the profession and the organization. Unfortunately, the client often becomes incidental in these efforts to preserve the prerogatives of the respective institutions. An excellent description of this process is provided by Blumberg (1967) in an analysis of the relationship between the lawyer, client, and court. What he finds is a legal version of a confidence game, with the lawyer choosing legal strategies that will lead to a speedy conclusion, but only after taking steps that will assure his fee. The client is caught between two bureaucratic structures — the legal profession and the courts — each of which has an interest in preserving the other and ensuring that they will be able to work together again in the future.

While individual professionals have recognized the problems posed by their failure to adequately serve their clients, the professional societies have chosen to remain aloof from all matters that fall outside a narrow professionalism. Miller (1972) indicated how professional societies have chosen to define their positions on controversial matters as "objective" or "uninvolved". Often, however, this position is little more than a safe way of supporting existing institutional arrangements. As Miller puts it: ". . . in almost every instance I have found, when a scientific society has elected to remain aloof from taking a stand on such a question, it has, in fact, taken an influential position on that question. In other words, so far as I can tell, whatever a scientific society may think it is doing or not doing in relation to public policy in the current state of affairs, the end result is a *de facto* position, and likely to be one of considerable importance." (p. 247).

The Radical Movement: Composition and Critique

The existence of internal dissension and conflict within a profession is neither new nor surprising. Despite a view whereby professions are characterized by a high degree of homogeneity, shared values and commitment stemming from professional socialization (Goode, 1957) there is also evidence of the high degree of conflict and diversity within the collegial body (Bucher and Strauss, 1961; Bucher, 1962; Ladinsky and Grossman, 1966; Perrucci and Gerstl, 1969).

The existence of political activism within the professions also is neither new nor surprising. In a thorough examination of interest groups in science, Nichols (n.d.) describes the activism of such moderate political organizations of scientists as the Federation of American Scientists and the Council for a Livable World, both concerned with influencing American policy on armaments with traditional lobbying methods. Less political groups such as Scientists Institute for Public Information, Society for Social Responsibility in Science, and Physicians for Social Responsibility were concerned with making scientific and technical information available to the public, thereby creating an informed public opinion.

What does distinguish the new radicalism from earlier expressions of discontent with professions, and from earlier forms of political activism are (1) the large number of radical movements in existence in a variety of professions; (2) the composition of their membership and leadership; (3) the nature of their critique of American society and their profession; and (4) their programs of action.

A search for radical movement organizations composed of members of a profession was not especially easy. While there are reasonably extensive lists of movement organizations that are goal or issue specific to be found in such publications as *People's Yellow Pages* published by Vocations for Social Change, the names of such organizations in specific professions had to be obtained from reading movement literature. We were able to identify eighteen organizations representing medicine, science and engineering, law, psychology, social work, sociology, economics, political science, geography, history, and university teaching. Excluded from our lists are organizations that are composed of mixed occupational membership, or the many anti-war organizations that exist in specific professions. While it is possible that many anti-war organizations (e.g. Fellowship for Reconciliation; Catholic Peace Fellowship) presently have, or may in the future have, concern for changing their professions, according to literature available to us at present, their primary interest is in the war in Vietnam.

After isolating these eighteen radical movement organizations, we still did not have available an abundance of primary or secondary literature about each organization. Understandably, our most extensive source materials deal with the largest of the radical organizations, which often have a newsletter or periodical to express their views.

On the question of membership characteristics of radical organizations, one thing seems very clear. These organizations are made up mainly of very young professionals, or of students completing their professional training (Farnsworth, 1970; Ehrenreich and Ehrenreich, 1970; Lefcourt, 1971; Nichols, n.d.; Bloomfield, 1972; Miller, n.d.). In contrast, members of older activist organizations in the professions were mainly of middle-age, were established members of their professions, and some were prominent figures.

Exact or even approximate figures on the number of members in movement organizations are difficult to obtain. Such information is not released by the organizations, and is not available in their literature. There is some evidence, however, that the largest of the existing radical organizations is the Medical Committee for Human Rights (MCHR), with estimates of membership running between 6,000 and 15,000. The next largest is Scientists and Engineers for Social and Political Action (SESPA) with membership estimates of between 2,500 and 5,000 persons.

In any event, use of membership figures as estimates of the relative strength of a movement within a profession would be very misleading. First of all, who is or is not a member of a movement organization is very unclear. For example, the publication of the Sociology Liberation Movement (*The Insurgent Sociologist*) is produced by a very small working commune, but there are about 1,000 subscribers to the periodical. A more important argument against using membership numbers as an index of strength is the fact that large numbers are not necessary for the effective action of such organizations. Older activism in the professions, and even in current moderate political groups, has followed the path of conventional liberal politics whereby the number of members is translated as potential voters or potential contributors. Once action is removed from conventional politics, as is the case in radical movements, the importance of a large number of members declines.

When we examine the basic rationale for the critical analysis put forward by radicals in professions we find important similarities. One aspect of the radical critique reflects an intense dissatisfaction with the failure of a profession to deal with a wide range of human problems. This condition is traced partly to the narrow conception of professionalism which emphasizes detached application of an expertise to the problems of an individual client. This narrow conception of a professional's role, which is often held up by the traditional professional as one of the strengths of professionalism, is reinforced by authoritarian hierarchies in professional societies and work settings which establish limits upon the "proper" role of the professional. The radical critique urges the introduction of explicit normative elements which concern how and for whom and for what ends their expertise will be used. The wish is to move beyond questions of technique and means to questions about the kind of society in which one works. Thus, a narrow professionalism would promote assistance of a welfare client to obtain help for needs specified by existing welfare procedures and regulations. A radical professionalism in contrast would promote organization of welfare clients to challenge these very procedures and regulations.

Very closely tied to the initial element of the radical critique, and perhaps the most distinctive feature of the new radicalism, is the recognition that the maintenance of professions in their present state is due to more than the existence of conservative controlling elites within each profession. That which perpetuates ineffective, status quo professions is the nature of a corporate capitalist society. Corporate power controls the resources that could be made available to change professions so as to make their services available to all citizens.

This particular combination of elements of the radical critique is reflected in the following remarks of a "movement lawyer."

> When I got out of law school I went to work for Edward Bennett Williams in Washington, D. C. Ninety per cent of my practice during the three years I was there was defense work in criminal cases. So I was able to watch how the principles enunciated by the American Bar Association worked in practice.
>
> I would be wrong if I said that I started from a neutral stance. I started from a kind of radical, critical stance. But I thought that the role of the trial lawyer as advocate in the adversary system had some independent vitality. I thought that, merely by taking the position of representing any criminal defendent without fear or favor, one could play a positive role in social change. I thought

that it was not necessary, or even desirable, for a lawyer to go beyond that kind of ethically neutral stance which took for granted that the system was in the long run interested in justice. (Tigar, 1971, p. 28).

This initial experience of a lawyer is followed by a period of disillusionment over the failure of the legal system to work on behalf of the poor and powerless. He also becomes aware of the "concentration of economic power largely unamenable to influence or suasion by those at whom the power is directed." (Tigar, 1971, p. 32). The following kind of analysis begins to emerge from examination of the legal system.

Most of the members of the bar associations — in particular, most of its leading members — are engaged in the systematic defense of privilege. Their clients have money and power, and these lawyers are paid quite handsomely to advise and litigate on behalf of the social concerns associated with money and power. (Tigar, 1971, p. 27).

The writings of a group of young lawyers, all of whom are members of the National Lawyers Guild, also stress how the legal system in general, and "the enforcement of criminal sanctions, is dictated by the necessities of the economic and political system in which the profit motive is central." (Lefcourt, 1971, p. 23).

The critique and analysis provided by radical organizations in the medical profession, such as the Medical Committee for Human Rights, follows a similar pattern. The problems of America's health care system are traced to a medical-industrial complex of medical schools, health product companies, insurance companies, nursing homes, proprietary hospitals, and the fee-for-service independent doctors. A concise statement of movement ideology follows:

. . . health care should not be a commodity to be bought by 'consumers' and sold by 'providers,' but should be free at the point of delivery. (That is, the costs should be borne by the entire society, through an equitable tax system.) That medical empires should be decentralized and be subject to community and worker control. That in all health institutions priority should be put on patient care, with special emphasis on preventive health services. That the health products industry should be nationalized, and run as a nonprofit enterprise. That medical schools should open their doors to black, brown, and white women applicants and working-class youths, and should provide opportunities up to the M.D. level for all health care workers. That doctors everywhere should be salaried employees of community institutions, not private entrepreneurs.

. In short, the health system should be recreated as a democratic enterprise, in which patients are participants (not customers or objects) and health workers, from physicians to aides, are all colleagues in a common undertaking. (Ehrenreich and Ehrenreich, 1970, p. 20).

Similarly, Scientists and Engineers for Social and Political Action (SESPA) identify themselves as workers who must join the ranks of all other workers to radically transform the economic structure of the United States. The views of SESPA are indicated in a statement made by them before the 1970 meetings of the American Association for the Advancement of Science:

In 15 minutes Philip Handler (NOTE: He is president of the National Academy of Sciences) is going to talk to you for an hour and a half about how procedures and practices in the Pentagon can be made more rational, and how the scientific community can help prop up the ruling class' corporate profit by distributing scarcity more effectively. We're here in the interests of the people upon whom the power of the ruling class is exercised, and the people who are not interested in rationalizing their role, but destroying it. . . . As you go scrambling after grants and support from institutions like NSF, NIH, DOD, ONR, FART, etc., etc., it is, of course more pleasant to imagine a government trying to help the poor and such, and corporations funding billion-dollar foundations in order to improve the quality of people's lives. . . . But we don't have two governments, one which malevolently kills in the ghetto, in Latin America and in Southeast Asia. Nor do we have two corporate structures, manipulating for profit on the one hand, while desiring social equity and justice on the other. Rather there is a single government-corporate axis which supports research with the intention of acquiring powerful tools, of both the hard and soft ware varieties, for the pursuit of exploitative and imperial goals. (*Science for the People*, 1971, p. 6).

Finally, we include a quote from the constitution of the New University Conference (NUC) which parallels the critiques described above.

The New University Conference (NUC) is a national organization of radicals who work in, around, and in spite of institutions of higher education. Formed in a time of imperialist war and domestic repression, the NUC is part of the struggle for the liberation of all peoples. It must therefore oppose imperialism, racism, economic exploitation and male supremacy.

We believe that institutions derive legitimacy and have the right to exist only to the extent that they serve the people. We see campuses not as havens, but as the immediate, though not exclusive settings for most of our activities.

We join all those committed to struggle politically to create a new, American form of socialism and to replace an educational and social system that is an instrument of class, sexual, and racial oppression with one that belongs to the people. (NUC Newsletter, August 15, 1969, p. 2).

These criticisms of the professions, and of the economic and political structure of society reveal a need for fundamental and far-reaching change if the problems identified are to be remedied. The nature of these changes, and the strategies for change are the subject of the next section.

Dilemmas and Prospects of Radical Change

The ultimate test of the effectiveness of radical movements in transforming the professions and in serving human welfare is the extent to which their action programs further their organization's goals, sustain their present membership, and attract new adherents to the movement. In the earlier sections of this paper we presented our views about the general conditions giving rise to radical movements, and we described radical professionals' critiques of their profession and of American society. Our concern now is to examine the specific programs of action put forward by radical movement organizations in the professions. We shall discuss these programs within the framework of four basic dilemmas facing radical professionals.

First is the apparent disjunction between the critical analysis of movement organizations and their specific action programs. The critical analysis is broad in scope, involving a general institutional analysis. The inadequacies and failures of the professions are traced to the nature of a capitalist state dominated by institutional elites who seek to maintain a system of national priorities consistent with their own interests. This seems to call for change strategies that seek to influence institutional elites, undertake lobbying efforts, and alter the institutional structure through political change. However, most of the actions undertaken by radical organizations are local in nature and scope, are developed to deal with local problems, and draw upon available local resources.

Although the emphasis on local action fails to deal with the problems caused by corporate elites and capitalism, it is, nonetheless, quite consistent with other aspects of movement ideology. The rejection of the political process as a means for producing change leads radical movements away from lobbying coalition politics, and toward the making of local issues and actions the basis for organizing. In addition, the rejection of authoritarian hierarchies with their own elites makes radical movement members suspicious of any attempts to create national radical organizations which establish policy and set strategy from within a centralized authority structure.

Many of the local actions taken by radical professionals are designed to get professionals to confront the issues and questions which concern the way in which their work is used by corporate elites and means by which they could develop a movement which would use their talents for constructive social change. SESPA members have been involved in work stoppages, protests at meetings of professional societies, workshops designed to explain and demystify science for nonscientists, and contributions of scientific services to aid the development of revolutionary regimes in Cuba and Vietnam (*Science for the People*, 1971, p. 18). Many issues of *Science for the People* contain reports from local SESPA groups. These reports reveal a great variety of actions suited to local issues such as the firing of a scientist or engineer for political activities, the organization of consciousness-raising seminars, picketing of local weapons laboratories, and simply describing the successes and failures of local groups along with inclusion of advice to others about pitfalls and useful actions.

Local actions by the MCHR have focussed almost entirely on the development and operation of free community clinics. Estimates of the number of operating free clinics in 1971 range between 125 (Nichols, n.d., p. 66) and 200 (Bloomfield and Levy, 1972). Most free clinics are not established by MCHR, but by local community groups ranging from Black Panthers and Young Lords to conventional civic and business groups. MCHR groups provide free services, money, and advice to clinics. Free clinics are designed to be very different from hospitals. Some engage in a voluntary system of job rotation, with the exception of doctors' tasks, but with inclusion of doctors in participation in menial tasks of the clinic. Patients are assigned "advocates" who become very familiar with the patient's history, and are responsible for the patient being fully aware of the clinic's services, and the clinic of the patient's needs. Attempts are also made to provide comprehensive service to a community, including preventive work, but this is often impossible because of limited resources.

While it is clear that the structure and policies of free clinics are designed to avoid the most dehumanizing features of America's health care system, it is also clear that these local actions are not very likely to affect the medical-industrial complex that is at the heart of the problem. Much the same can be said for radical lawyers who defend the poor and the politically opressed, since their actions deal with specific rather than institutional injustices.

The second dilemma is created by the radical professionals' basic optimism that the problems which they identify are solvable. More importantly, they are viewed as solvable by the application of technology and expertise which is guided by a more humane set of values. In contrast to radical organizations which have a "counter culture" and anti-technology emphasis, radical professionals do not see technology itself as the moving force which shapes the entire institutional structure of society. This also contrasts with the views of those social analysts who trace the centralization of economic and political power to the complexity of technology in advanced industrial societies (Galbraith, 1968).

The rather naive view of technology as a benign force which can be redirected by an alternative value system is analogous to the view of establishment scientists that technology itself is nothing more than "organized knowledge for practical purposes." (Mesthene, 1972). McDermott (1969) has criticized the definition whereby technology is flexible and pure, simply requiring wisdom and informed planning to insure that positive benefits outweigh negative consequences. He argues instead that technology is an institutional system with an ideology, elites, and supportive links with other social institutions.

Thus, radical professionals seem committed to using their trained expertise, and the technology on which it is based, to solve societal problems, despite their own analysis that technology is an integral part of the economic and political power responsible for the problems in the first place.

The third dilemma, which is related to the second, is based on the recognition by radical professionals that it may be not be possible for them to do their work without in some way aiding the establishment powers which they oppose. The early protest of scientists against military research resulted in their refusal to participate in such programs as Operation Spicerack at the University of Pennsylvania, the Institute for Defense Analysis at Columbia University, the Stanford Research Institute, and M.I.T.'s Instrumentation Laboratory (Nelkin, 1972). But as many radical scientists have recognized, this is simply not enough.

Questioning the 'humanity' of individual scientific projects is not enough. Scientific workers themselves are seriously wrong in assuming that personal prostitution to the rich and powerful can be avoided simply by refusing to participate in only that work which is narrowly useful to those in power. . . . It is not surprising to find the ruling class funding applied research which is narrowly beneficial to them. . . . But this same ruling class also supports almost all our basic or, to use the euphemism, 'pure' research. . . . Theoretical and experimental physicists provided the knowledge out of which hydrogen bombs were made. Mathematicians, geophysicists, metallurgists, astro-physicists, and others wittingly or unwittingly made the discoveries necessary to construct ballistic missiles. Physicists working in the areas of optics and infrared spectroscopy enabled government and corporate engineers to build detection and surveillance devices currently in use in Vietnam. Anthropologists studying social systems of mountain tribes in Southeast Asia did work for the Central Intelligence Agency, even if unwittingly. The basic research of molecular biologists, biochemists, cellular physiologists, neuropsychologists, and physicians was essential for the creation of chemical and biological weapons, defoliants, herbicides, DDT, and gaseious crowd control devices. Findings in the social psychology of attitude change have helped the advertising industry to manipulate public taste and buying habits for the benefit of the corporate profit-makers. Methodology developed in the area of psychometric testing and evaluation enabled the Selective Service System to pick, channel, and train men for war. The work of sociologists and anthropologists on the Third World has been used by the U.S. government to help maintain ruling elites in powers (*Science for the People,* 1971, p. 15).

There is only one conclusion possible from such an analysis: to stop doing *any* research, or to stop doing one's professional work. How radical professionals would then decide to use their knowledge for the people remains the central unanswered question.

The fourth and final dilemma is concerned with whether or not movement professionals can maintain their radical vision and life style in the face of competing professional roles which are change-oriented but less radical in nature. Most professions appear to have a more conventional version of the radical professional; a version which allows a critical stance, an intense interest in social change, and the enjoyment of all the rewards that are available to a professional who remains within the profession. This is not to say that the conventional version of the radical role is unimportant for dealing with changing the professions and solving

social problems, but simply that it is less concerned with making fundamental changes in our economic and political institutions.

The ambivalence of radical professionals toward the activities of
"conventional radicals" is seen in the following response by Michael
Tigar, a movement lawyer, to a question about the importance of poverty lawyers in the California Rural Legal Assistance program who
undertake class-action suits on behalf of the poor.

> I don't put it down. It is certainly necessary. Lawyers have made some dents
> in the system on behalf of the poor. But one is left with lingering doubts. The
> first has to do with what Kenneth Davis calls "discretionary justice." I spent
> some years litigating with the Selective Service System. I am still doing it.
> The fact is that the Selective Service bureaucracy of more than four thousand
> local draft boards across the country, like every other bureaucracy, is largely
> immune from the impact of court decisions, even court decisions affecting
> that agency. Power is wielded on a discretionary basis on the local scene
> away from the place where central responsibility is lodged. So, an important
> precedent stemming from a court decision, even though it is supposed to
> apply to the actions of a large number of people, simply doesn't. . . . the
> structure of legal rules does not permit you to get at the real centers of power,
> the centers of economic power. California Rural Legal Assistance has done
> nothing to break the back of the economic power that dominates life in the
> central valley of California, and makes the plight of the farm workers and
> their families so miserable (Tigar, 1971, p. 29).

These four dilemmas which face radical professionals create special
problems for the continuity of radical organizations. Young professionals attracted to the radical vision will find it difficult to deal with these
dilemmas and avoid becoming disillusioned or coopted. Amid all these
difficulties, there does seem to be one pattern of radical professional
activity which is viable. This is the pattern of a law commune described
by Lefcourt (1971). The law commune is a working group of four lawyers
and four nonlawyers who work for and support a broad range of political
struggles. As Lefcourt puts it: ". . . the Law Commune distinguishes
itself from most law firms by its challenge not only to the legal profession, but to the ideology of the judicial superstructure and the existing
economic and political system" (p. 310).

What is important about the structure of the law commune is that it
contains all of the resources necessary to sustain its members. It provides financial resources, colleague support, legitimacy, and relative

independence from hostile organizations or employers. Moreover, it protects radical professionals from the dilemmas described above. The central question, however, is how applicable the law commune model is for other professions. If radical professionals can develop independent working organizations, they will have the basis for continuity, and will develop a model of a radical life style that other young radicals can use. If they cannot, they will remain caught between their dependence upon employing organizations and their opposition to the practices of their profession, never able to rise above their professional class to become a truly revolutionary group.